Proceedings, 2019, XoveTIC 2019

Proceedings, 2019, XoveTIC 2019

The 2nd XoveTIC Conference (XoveTIC 2019)
A Coruña, Spain, 5–6 September 2019

Volume Editors

Alberto Alvarellos González
José Joaquim de Moura Ramos
Beatriz Botana Barreiro
Javier Pereira Loureiro
Manuel F. González Penedo

MDPI • Basel • Beijing • Wuhan • Barcelona • Belgrade

Volume Editors

Alberto Alvarellos González
University of A Coruña
Spain

José Joaquim de Moura Ramos
University of A Coruña
Spain

Beatriz Botana Barreiro
University of A Coruña
Spain

Javier Pereira Loureiro
University of A Coruña
Spain

Manuel F. González Penedo
University of A Coruña
Spain

Editorial Office
MDPI
St. Alban-Anlage 66
4052 Basel, Switzerland

This is a reprint of articles published online by the open access publisher MDPI in 2019 (available at: https://www.mdpi.com/2504-3900/21/1). The responsibility for the book's title and preface lies with Alberto Alvarellos González, who compiled this selection.

For citation purposes, cite each article independently as indicated on the article page online and as indicated below:

LastName, A.A.; LastName, B.B.; LastName, C.C. Article Title. *Journal Name* **Year**, *Article Number*, Page Range.

ISBN 978-3-03921-443-3 (Pbk)
ISBN 978-3-03921-444-0 (PDF)

Cover image courtesy of CITIC—Research Center of Information and Communication Technologies, University of A Coruña, Spain (Rights acquired from istockphoto.com).

Contents

Acknowledgments

Financial support from Consellería de Educación, Universidade e Formación Profesional of the Xunta de Galicia (Convenio I+D+i and Centro singular de investigación de Galicia accreditation 2016–2019) and the European Union (European Regional Development Fund- ERDF) is gratefully acknowledged.

Proceedings

Development of an Artificial Vision System for Underwater Vehicles †

Cristian Méndez Sanmartín * and Moisés Bautista Briceño

Integrated Group for Engineering Research (GII), University of A Coruña, Campus de Esteiro, 15403 Ferrol, Spain
* Correspondence: cristian.mendez@udc.es; Tel.: +34-881-013-866
† Presented at the 2nd XoveTIC Conference, A Coruña, Spain, 5–6 September 2019.

Published: 22 July 2019

Abstract: Beyond certain depth there is no light, supposing the main obstacle in the use of optical systems beneath the water. Therefore, the underwater vision system developed is composed of a set of underwater lights which allow the system to work properly and the cameras. These are integrated with the navigation system through the Robot Operating System (ROS) framework, which handles the acquisition and processing of information to be used as support for the navigation and which is also essential for its use in reconnaissance missions.

Keywords: Autonomous Underwater Vehicle (AUV); autonomous navigation; artificial vision; Robot Operating System (ROS)

1. Introduction

Marine activities have experienced a considerable increment in the last few years due to the increasing energy demand in renewable energy resources, with offshore wind farms leading, and it is expected to keep growing. Therefore, the number of offshore structures is rising, and they are moving further from shore. The goal of these power plants is to get to the more constant offshore winds leading to improvements in efficiency and the reduction of the impact in land [1] (pp. 47–48).

Nevertheless, this power plants must operate in harsh environments with very adverse weather conditions so, regular inspection, maintenance and repair tasks (IMR) are required and they become difficult, expensive and risky, and, above all, they are traditionally executed by professional divers. Much research in the marine field is devoted to reducing the costs and minimizing the risks for the workers in their tasks, in addition to overcoming certain physical limitations that preclude specific human operations. However, the tendency is to go deeper in the ocean and some areas become inaccessible for a diver. At the same time, underwater activities carried out by human require much time due to the large extensions of seabed that that must be covered. In these scenarios, the efforts are focused on reducing the costs and minimizing the risks for the workers on their tasks [2].

The logical path to follow in this field resides in the evolution from Remotely Operated Vehicles (ROV) towards Autonomous Underwater Vehicles (AUV). However, there are still some technical challenges related to this conversion, such as underwater communications, power supply, autonomy, autonomous navigation and localization, among others. Related to this field, the Integrated Group for Engineering Research (GII) is taking steps towards constructing an AUV by carrying out modifications over its own ROV. The current state of work includes tasks such as the integration of the acoustic communications system and the robotic arm, the development of the data acquisition and security system, the programming of the intelligence onboard and the development of the artificial vision system, which is the theme addressed in this paper.

2. System Development

Due to the submarine does not have much space in its containers and in underwater environments we have power limitations due to the battery capacity, the developing system must be compact, low-power, accurate and accessible to be installed. Currently, this system is composed of a Raspberry Pi 3, with an installed image of Ubuntu 16.04 (Xenial) Mate for ARM with ROS Kinetic Kame, and a Low-Light HD USB Camera from Blue Robotics.

The mentioned Raspberry Pi assumes the role of being the data acquisition node and through the ROS OpenCV camera driver [3] and using the cv_bridge package, we are able to deal with the camera information and the images taken in OpenCV format in order to publish them in a topic with the ROS image message format as it is seen at the Figure 1. This proceeding helps us to retrieve the image from the ROS image message format and convert it to OpenCV format with any other device used as subscriber, as long as it is being connected to the ROS network [4].

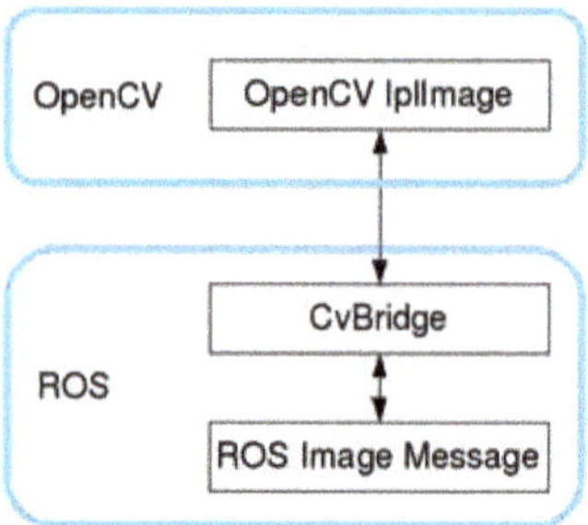

Figure 1. Cv_bridge package operation scheme for image information transfer.

The results obtained with the current hardware lead us to a publication rate of 15 messages per second, which is enough due to underwater systems are quite slow, but it must be revised for future implementations. The results of the vision system can be seen below in the Figure 2.

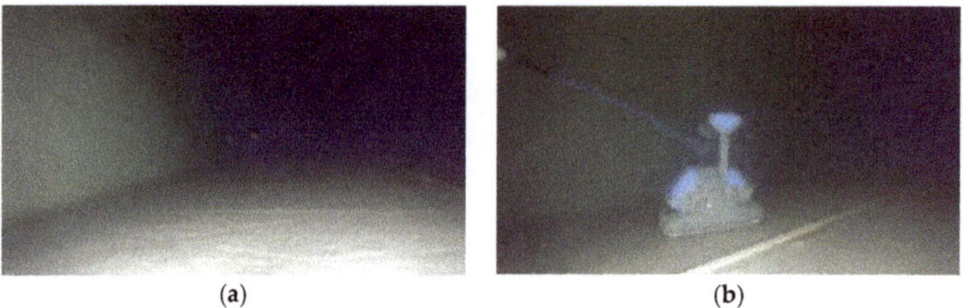

(a)
(b)

Figure 2. Images taken with the vision system of the Kai submarine in the hydrodynamic test channel: (a) Bottom of the ship model basin; (b) Process of cleaning up the ship model basin.

3. Challenges and Future Work

There is still much work in progress needed to be addressed. For instance, the first point we must work on is the hardware replacement challenge. We need to use more powerful hardware to manage dynamically more than one camera with better framerate and where we could run stereo vision algorithms.

The second challenge and the most difficult is the development and implementation of a data fusion algorithm with which we could combine the image obtained from the cameras and the image provided through an image sonar.

Finally, we need to run more tests in order to use this merged image to improve navigation in order to be a little step closer towards an AUV and implement other functionalities such as artificial recognition.

Funding: This research received no external funding.

Conflicts of Interest: The authors declare no conflict of interest.

References

1. OECD. *The Ocean Economy in 2030*; OECD: Paris, France, 2016; pp. 17–48; doi:10.1787/9789264251724-en.
2. López, F.; Ramos, H. A hybrid ROV/AUV vehicle for underwater inspection and maintenance of offshore structures, in Maritime Transportation and Harvesting of Sea Resources. In the Proceedings of the 17th International Congress of the Maritime Association of the Mediterranean (IMAM 2017), Lisbon, Portugal, 9–11 October 2017.
3. Cv_camera. Available online: http://wiki.ros.org/cv_camera (accessed on 12 September 2019).
4. ROS. Available online: https://www.ros.org/ (accessed on 12 September 2019).

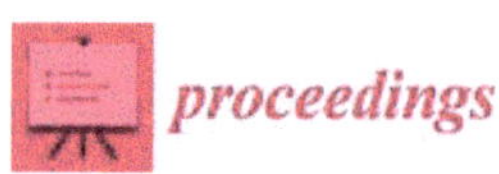 *proceedings*

Proceedings

Studying How Innate Motivations Can Drive Skill Acquisition in Cognitive Robots [†]

Alejandro Romero [1,*], Francisco Bellas [2], Jose A. Becerra [2] and Richard J. Duro [2]

[1] Integrated Group for Engineering Research, Universidade da Coruña, 15403 Ferrol, Spain
[2] CITIC Research Center, Universidade da Coruña, 15071 A Coruña, Spain
* Correspondence: alejandro.romero.montero@udc.es
† Presented at the 2nd XoveTIC Conference, A Coruña, Spain, 5–6 September 2019.

Published: 22 July 2019

Abstract: In this paper, we address the problem of how to bootstrap a cognitive architecture to opportunistically start learning skills in domains where multiple skills can be learned at the same time. To this end, taking inspiration from a series of computational models of the use of motivations in infants, we propose an approach that leverages two types of cognitive motivations: exploratory and proficiency based, the latter modulated by the concept of interestingness as an implementation of attentional mechanisms. This approach is tested in an illustrative experiment with a real robot.

Keywords: Cognitive Developmental Robotics; open-ended learning; motivational system; skill learning

1. Introduction

With the aim of designing robots with a higher degree of autonomy, the field of Cognitive Developmental Robotics (CDR) takes inspiration from models of cognitive human development. Robots are endowed with cognitive architectures which, starting from basic innate knowledge provided by the designer, are able to generate new knowledge, mainly models and skills, in a fully autonomous way throughout their "lives". Being able to learn in such an open-ended manner implies dealing with an unlimited sequence of a priori unknown tasks in unknown domains [1].

Consequently, the problem is not that of providing a robot with competences to perform particular tasks in known environments, but to provide the robot with mechanisms that allow it to figure out what tasks to carry out, and how, to achieve its objectives in the situations it faces. In other words, it needs to self-discover and self-select goals. It is important to emphasize here that a goal determines a task the robot must carry out (to reach the goal) and, consequently, a skill it must learn in order to be able to achieve it.

On the other hand, the robot also needs to determine how valuable any goal is (what is its utility) and, by extension, what may the expected utility of any point in state space be with regards to that goal. The mechanisms in charge of this are generally called motivational mechanisms or value systems. This work is framed within the problem of creating adequate motivational systems for autonomous robots, specifically, within the MDB cognitive architecture [2], to efficiently learn and purposefully behave in open-ended settings, and focusing on the initial stages of skill learning.

2. Unrewarded Skill Acquisition and Interestingness

At initial stages of interaction with an unknown world, the robot can only rely on what it has been innately endowed with by the designer, and it must use it to progressively acquire new skills that will allow it to become more proficient. Consequently, designing an appropriate set of innate drives is key to the adequate performance of the robot.

In the approach chosen within the motivational engine of the MDB [3], inspired by the observations of child cognitive development, we propose that two types of drives constitute the minimum set of cognitive drives required for this process. On the one hand, the robot needs to explore its state space in order to find utility. This exploration must be efficient and, consequently, some type of cognitive drive related to exploration must be included. In particular, in the experiments we present in the next section, we have made use of a drive related to novelty. However, to learn a skill, it is also necessary to train and become proficient at it. That is, the robot needs to be motivated to concentrate its interaction with the environment on cases that can lead to learning the skill. That is, to establish a virtual goal in that point and learn its utility model. We will call this a Proficiency based type of motivation. In particular, as skills are usually learned in order to be able to produce some effect on the environment, we will make use of an effectance based motivation in the experiments.

To induce training, we incorporate the concept of interestingness within the related Proficiency based motivation as a virtual utility value that can change in time as the robot becomes more proficient at achieving the corresponding goal. Thus, when an effect is produced by chance for the first time, the point in state space where that occurred becomes interesting (its interestingness level increases). This is reflected within the motivational engine as a virtual utility value when the goal is achieved and within the attention mechanism of the robot by increasing the saliency of the state-space point in the process of choosing where to go next. However, interestingness is also modulated by the proficiency in achieving the goal: the more proficient the robot is, the less interesting the virtual goal becomes. Once the robot is very proficient, the skill for achieving the goal will have been acquired and it can be sent to Long Term Memory (LTM) for storage and future recall.

3. Real Robot Experiment

The Baxter robot is placed in front of a white table with three different objects it can detect: a brown box, a red ball and a small plastic jar which lights up when it is grabbed. The robot can detect the distance to the objects by using their color and shape.

The execution of the experiment, illustrated in the images of Figure 1, can be described as follows: the robot started its operation without any explicit goal nor skill apart from the two innate motivations mentioned above. Consequently, it started moving its right arm guided by the novelty motivation. Eventually, this novelty seeking motivation leads it to hitting and pushing an object, in this case the ball (see Figure 1 (a)), thus generating a change in the perceptions of the robot that it will interpret as an effect of its actions on the environment. This increases the interestingness value of the point in state space where the change occurred and establishes it as a virtual goal to be achieved. As the robot becomes more proficient, the robot loses interest in moving the ball and goes back to seeking novelty. At this point the value function (VF) obtained for the push-ball skill, shown in Figure 2 (a), is stored in the LTM of the MDB for future use.

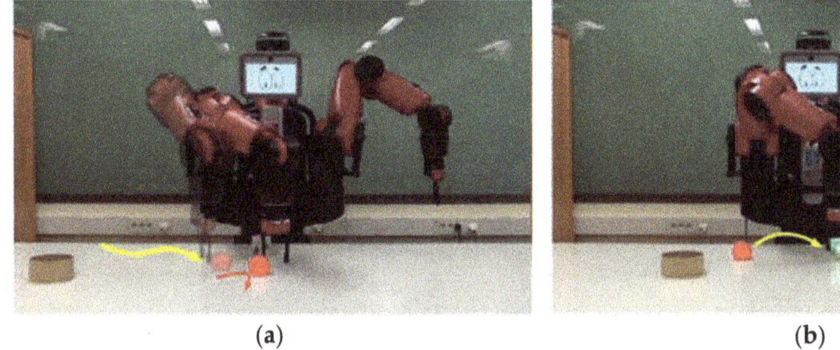

(a)   (b)

Figure 1. Experimental setup with the Baxter robot. (**a**) Pushing skill; (**b**) Grasping skill.

As the robot continues to explore, some object may end up between its gripper pads triggering the close gripper reflex action. This action really does not cause any effect in any of the objects except for the jar. When it is the jar the one the gripper closes on, it lights up. This obviously is an effect and, as in the previous case, an interestingness value is assigned (see Figure 1b). Again, the proficiency based motivation starts guiding the robot response and a second VF learning process is launched. As the grasping skill associated to this VF improves, the interestingness value decreases until the corresponding VF (Figure 2b) has been correctly learnt and is stored in the LTM. The process continues with a new exploratory stage and, if pertinent, new activations of the effectance drive that will allow learning new skills.

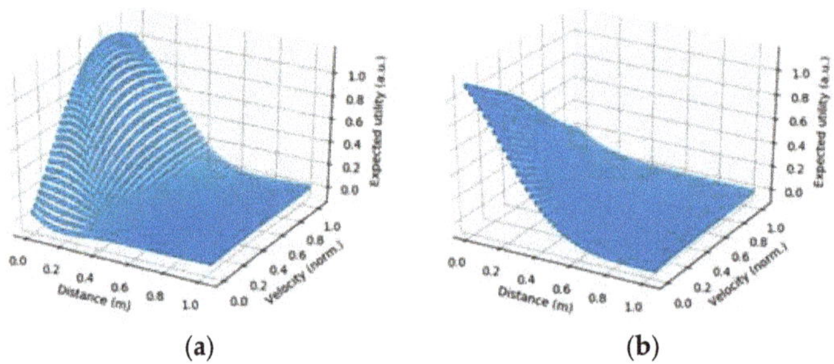

(a)   (b)

Figure 2. 3D representation of the skills learned in terms of distance and speed of the gripper. (**a**) VF associated to the push-object skill; (**b**) VF associated with the grabbing skill.

Author Contributions: Conceptualization, R.J.D. and A.R.; Methodology, A.R., F.B. and R.J.D.; Software, A.R. and J.A.B.; Validation, A.R., F.B. and R.J.D.; Writing—original draft preparation, A.R.; Writing—review and editing, A.R., F.B. and R.J.D; Visualization, A.R.; Supervision, R.J.D and F.B.

Funding: This work has been funded by the EU's H2020 research programme (grant No. 640891 DREAM), MINECO/FEDER (grant TIN2015-63646-C5-1-R), Xunta de Galicia/FEDER (grant ED431C 2017/12), and Spanish Ministry of Education, Culture and Sports for the FPU grant of A. Romero.

Conflicts of Interest: The authors declare no conflict of interest.

References

1. Doncieux, S.; Filliat, D.; Diaz-Rodriguez, N.; Hospedales, T.; Duro, R.; Coninx, A.; Roijers, D.; Girard, B.; Perrin, N.; Sigaud, O. Open-ended learning: a conceptual framework based on representational redescription. *Front. Neurorobot.* **2018**, *12*, 59.
2. Bellas, F.; Duro, R.J.; Faina, A.; Souto, D. Multilevel Darwinist Brain (MDB): Artificial Evolution in a Cognitive Architecture for Real Robots. *IEEE Trans. Auton. Ment. Dev.* **2010**, *4*, 340–354.
3. Romero, A., Prieto, A., Bellas, F., Duro, R.J. Simplifying the creation and management of utility models in continuous domains for cognitive robotics, *Neurocomputing* **2019**, *353*, 106–118.

Proceedings

The Influence of Immersive Environments on the Empathy Construct about Schizophrenia [†]

Paulo Veloso Gomes [1],*, António Marques [1], Javier Pereira [2] and João Donga [1,3]

[1] LabRP, Laboratório de Reabilitação Psicossocial, Escola Superior de Saúde do Politécnico do Porto, 4200-072 Porto, Portugal
[2] CITIC-Research Center of Information and Communication Technologies, University of A Coruña, 15071 A Coruña, Spain
[3] Escola Superior de Media Artes e Design do Politécnico do Porto, 4480-876 Vila do Conde, Portugal
* Correspondence: pvg@ess.ipp.pt; Tel.: +351-222-061-000
[†] Presented at the 2nd XoveTIC Conference, A Coruña, Spain, 5–6 September 2019.

Published: 22 July 2019

Abstract: This work explores the potential of the use of interactive and immersive technologies to create impactful experiences that generate emotions, contributing to the process of activation or somatic excitation that triggers links that strengthen cognitive functions. It is intended to demonstrate to what extent the use of immersive environments, by generating a strong emotional load, contribute in a more effective way to the empathy construct about Schizophrenia.

Keywords: Mental Health and Welfare Literacy; schizophrenia; empathy; immersive environments; virtual reality; augmented reality; 360 Video

---

1. Introduction

Mental illness has an associated stigma from which there are serious consequences. This stigma, besides being a factor of social exclusion, can also negatively influence the provision of health care through inhibition of the search for medical care, the lack of motivation to adhere to the treatments applied and making difficult the information acquisition process essential for the promotion of health literacy. Consequently, stigma leads to increased associated mortality through factors such as treatment abandonment or suicide [1].

Literacy in Mental Health is essential to improve understanding and consequently acceptance of mental illness, contributing to overcoming prejudices and combating the stigma that leads to social exclusion [2].

Factual knowledge alone is not enough for there to be an effective understanding capable of generating empathy and attitudes. Emotions trigger the attention functions that are essential for the cognitive functions of perceptual, symbolic, and logical processing, help to memorize, facilitate, and clarify the perception of things, and empower executive functions for problem solving [3].

This paper describes the process of designing, developing and testing the multidimensional artifact "e-EMotion-Capsule" that exploits immersiveness to generate emotions through the creation of impacting environments.

The physical or emotional sensations felt by the individual generate emotions in order to create empathy and trigger feelings that promote actions.

2. Objectives

The objective of this work is to develop an innovative intervention methodology that, through the generation of impactful experiences, allows the use of emotion as a catalyst in the transmission of applied knowledge to the promotion of Literacy in Mental Health and Welfare.

1. Design a model for the construction of a technological artefact that uses interactive and immersive technologies to generate impactful experiences.
2. Compare the impact caused by experiences that resort to different immersive concepts, virtual reality, 360 video and mixed environment (real scenarios and augmented reality).

3. Materials and Methods

A comparative study was designed to analyze and compare the impact of three immersive environments that reproduce episodes of the life of a person with schizophrenia. The study will be applied to a group of students who will be future health professionals and who may in future integrate mental health teams. The first immersive environment uses virtual reality scenarios (AIrv), the second uses a 360 video (AI360) and the third uses a mixed environment (AIrm) using real scenarios and augmented reality (Figure 1).

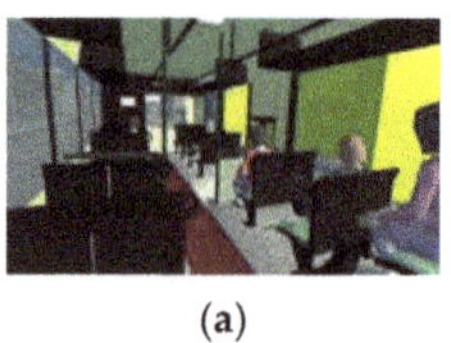
(a)
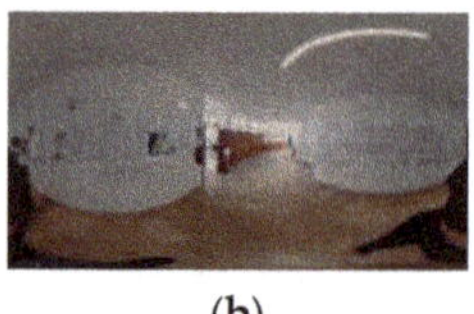
(b)
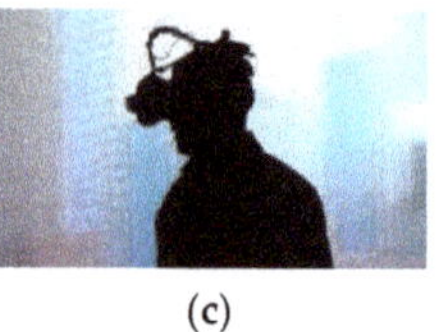
(c)

Figure 1. Representation of immersive environments: (**a**) AIrv—virtual reality; (**b**) AI360—360 vídeo; (**c**) AIrm—real scenarios/augmented reality.

After the observer is exposed to the target, the respective intrapersonal consequences are measured through the responses that occur in the observer by exposure. This measurement considers three dimensions, cognitive (interpretation), affective (empathy) and motivational (attitudes) that guide the behavioral responses.

In order to carry out the measurement, self-report evaluation instruments and psychophysiological measures are applied to analyze impact. The immersive environments differ in several factors that influence the lived experience, the type of interactivity possible to experience, the type of narrative and the scenarios used.

In the first phase, the work uses the Research-Action Methodology to design a model for the construction of the technological artefact, prepare the construction of the prototype and the tests to be implemented, identify the relevant indicators and prepare its application.

The second phase applies the developed model to specific cases, using specific Focus Groups.

The third phase focuses on evaluation of the impact of intervention and results discussion.

The physical or emotional sensations felt by the individual generate emotions, and the emotions trigger feelings that promote actions [4].

Since empathy is an important factor for positive human interaction, exposure to immersive environments awakens sensory experiences that are determinant for cognitive transmission.

4. Discussion/Conclusions

The learning process implies the interdependence of cognitive, emotional and behavioral responses involved in a social context [5].

It is intended to determine how the exposure to each of the three immersive environments contributes to increase the degree of empathy, knowledge and attitudes towards a person with schizophrenia.

The three environments under study are compared considering two dimensions, the environmental dimension and the impact dimension (Table 1).

The dimension "environment" focuses on the intrinsic characteristics of each of the immersive environments, considering the interactivity, immersiveness and realism of each environment. The "impact" dimension compares the result created by the exposure, considering the cognitive aspects, the empathy generated and the propensity to take attitudes.

Table 1. Comparison of study dimensions.

Dimension/Scale	AIrv	AI360	AIrm
ENVIRONMENT			
Interactivity	-/+ [1]	-/+ [1]	-/+ [1]
Immersion	-/+ [1]	-/+ [1]	-/+ [1]
Realism	-/+ [1]	-/+ [1]	-/+ [1]
Narrative type	-/+ [1]	-/+ [1]	-/+ [1]
IMPACT			
Cognitiveness	-/+ [1]	-/+ [1]	-/+ [1]
Empathy	-/+ [1]	-/+ [1]	-/+ [1]
Attitudes	-/+ [1]	-/+ [1]	-/+ [1]

[1] The scale will be defined according to the characteristics of the dimension under study.

It is important to determine the influence that each type of immersivity exerts on the observer in each of the considered dimensions, affective cognitive and motivational. Analyze if one of the environments stands out in one or more dimensions, so that it can determine which is the most appropriate for each specific type of intervention.

Author Contributions: Conceptualization, P.V.G.; methodology, P.V.G. and A.M.; validation, P.V.G. and J.D.; investigation, P.V.G.; writing—original draft preparation, P.V.G.; writing—review and editing, P.V.G.; visualization, P.V.G. and J.D.; supervision, A.M. and J.P.; project administration, P.V.G.

Funding: This research received no external funding.

Acknowledgments: This research was carried out and used the equipment of the Psychosocial Rehabilitation Laboratory (LabRp) of the Research Center in Rehabilitation of the School of Allied Health Technologies, Polytechnic Institute of Porto.

Conflicts of Interest: The authors declare no conflict of interest.

References

1. Vigo, D.; Thornicroft, G.; Atun, R. Estimating the true global burden of mental illness. *Lancet Psychiatry* **2016**, *3*, 171–178.
2. Capacitar as Pessoas e as comunidades para agir. Available online: http://fundacaovale.org/Paginas/News-Capacitar-pessoas-e-alavancar-negocios-nas-comunidades-tambem-e-inovar.aspx (accessed on 2 June 2029).
3. da Fonseca, V. Importância das emoções na aprendizagem: uma abordagem neuropsicopedagógica. *Rev. Psicopedag.* **2016**, *33*, 365–384.
4. Virtual Reality Perspective-Taking Increases Cognitive Empathy for Specific Others. Available online: https://doi.org/10.1371/journal.pone.0202442 (accessed on 2 June 2029).
5. Feist, J.; Feist, G.J. *Teorias da personalidade*, 6th ed. São Paulo, 2008; ISBN: 978-85-7726-019-5.

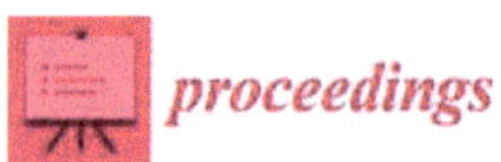 *proceedings*

Proceedings

Anomaly Detection in IoT: Methods, Techniques and Tools †

Laura Victoria Vigoya Morales *, Manuel López-Vizcaíno, Diego Fernández Iglesias and Víctor Manuel Carneiro Díaz

Department of Computer Science, University of A Coruña, 15071 A Coruña, Spain
* Correspondence: l.v.vigoya@udc.es
† Presented at the 2nd XoveTIC Conference, A Coruña, Spain, 5–6 September 2019.

Published: 22 July 2019

Abstract: Nowadays, the Internet of things (IoT) network, as system of interrelated computing devices with the ability to transfer data over a network, is present in many scenarios of everyday life. Understanding how traffic behaves can be done more easily if the real environment is replicated to a virtualized environment. In this paper, we propose a methodology to develop a systematic approach to dataset analysis for detecting traffic anomalies in an IoT network. The reader will become familiar with the specific techniques and tools that are used. The methodology will have five stages: definition of the scenario, injection of anomalous packages, dataset analysis, implementation of classification algorithms for anomaly detection and conclusions.

Keywords: Intrusion Detection Systems; analysis; metric; algorithm design; computer network management

---

1. Introduction

The anomalies in a network cannot always be categorized as an attack, but they give important insights into the traffic behavior they may have. Although they are not always harmful elements, they can help identify important and critical information in various applications [1]. In the detection of anomalies, the scarcity of data with the appropriate characteristics makes it necessary to carry out systematic analysis that allows parameterizing the data to avoid problems in the accuracy of the results. To analyze such data and find a relationship or predict known or unknown data, data mining techniques are used. In these we find, clustering, classification, and techniques based on machine learning. The purpose of this work is to present the methodology developed to detect traffic anomalies, based on a real IoT system, and after its application determines the efficiency and effectiveness of the proposed methodology, using specific techniques and tools. The methodology will have five stages: set the scenario, inject of anomalous packages, dataset analysis, implement of classification algorithms for anomalies detection and develop the conclusions, recommendations, and implications.

2. Network Distribution and Dataset Generation

The first phase of the methodology consists in generating a labeled dataset that allows injecting selected characteristics in classification and prediction algorithms. To develop our scenario, we rely on the installed system of the CPD, located in the CITIC. The data was obtained after performing the mathematical modeling of a real IoT system. This consists of a network of 16 temperature sensors, 4 InRows with two devices responsible for sensing the temperature of the airflow and two for the coolant fluid of the unit, one for input and one for output, respectively. The data from the sensors were sent to the monitoring system every 5 min for a week. During the data analysis, we found that the data complied with seasonality conditions. This assertion allowed us to use time series and forecasting for analysis and prediction of series behavior [2].

For the simulation and generation of the labeled dataset, a virtualized system was implemented. The pilot comprises five virtual machines, where four of these nodes represent the controllers of the sensors of each of the simulated InRows and the fifth machine consists in the MQTT broker that allows to publish and subscribe to topics. Every node (ubuntu 18.04) has an NTP client that allows controlling the temporal synchrony between all the nodes and the broker, while the broker contains an MQTT v3.1 mosquitto server [3] that can handle requests in port 1883 MQIsdp (MQSeries SCADA protocol). Once the traffic has been captured it is possible to modify most of the fields of the different TCP/IP protocols: Ethernet, IP, TCP or MQTT, with python-scapy 2.3.3-3 library [4]. This allows not only to modify any field of the captured packets but also to reinsert these modified packets into the network, simulating anomalous situations such as interception, duplication or removal of packages. The dataset finally contains a seven days network activity labeled with attacks distributed over this period with diverse intrusion scenarios.

3. Dataset Analysis

The purpose of the dataset analysis is to determine the most relevant characteristics that can affect the classification, to be incorporated into the machine learning algorithms. To interpret the data, the traffic is collected using sniffing tools in the broker. For the analysis, we export the pcap to a csv using tshark and study what is involved in the process [5]. In this stage, to generate models that determine the behavior of anomalous traffic in the network, a statistical analysis of conditions such as protocol, source and destination IP addresses, source and destination ports, flags, time, duration, mean bytes, number of packets and weekday was performed. MQTT protocol is an application layer protocol, so it is on top of TCP/IP heap. Therefore, both the client and the broker need to have a TCP/IP stack and the analysis must be done taking this into account [6].

4. Identification of Machine Learning Algorithms and Optimization of Early Detection

Once the marked dataset has been generated and the main characteristics have been determined, machine learning algorithms are used to classify packages. For this task we can make use of logistic regression, LDA, QDA, K-nearest neighbors (KNN) method, Tree-Based methods, Support Vector Machines (SVM), etc.[7]. The results can be evaluated using different metrics: the traditional precision, recall and F1, and Early Risk Detection Error (ERDE) [6].

5. Conclusions

This work presented a methodology to develop a systematic approach to dataset analysis for detecting traffic anomalies in an IoT network. Having a methodology allows to standardize, structure and organize the work and in this way generate efficiency and effectiveness in the realization of the project.

Author Contributions: All authors have equally contributed to this article.

Funding: This research received no external funding.

References

1. Agrawal, S.; Agrawal, J. Survey on Anomaly Detection using Data Mining Techniques. *Procedia Comput. Sci.* **2015**, *60*, 708–713.
2. Forecasting: Principles and Practice. Available online: http://OTexts.com/fpp2 (accessed on 10 July 2019).
3. An Open Source MQTT Broker. Available online: https://mosquitto.org/ (accessed on 10 July 2019).
4. Scapy. Available online: https://libraries.io/pypi/scapy/2.3.3 (accessed on 10 July 2019).
5. Tshark: Terminal-based Wireshark. Available online: https://www.wireshark.org/docs/man-pages/tshark.html (accessed on 10 July 2019).

6. Fernandez, D.; Vigoya, L.; Cacheda, F.; Novoa, F.J.; Lopez-Vizcaino, M.F.; Carneiro, V. A Practical Application of a Dataset Analysis in an Intrusion Detection System. In Proceedings of the 2018 IEEE 17th International Symposium on Network Computing and Applications (NCA), Cambridge, MA, USA, 1–3 November 2018.

7. An Introduction to Statistical Learning. Available online: https://doi.org/10.1007/978-1-4614-7138-7 (accessed on 10 July 2019).

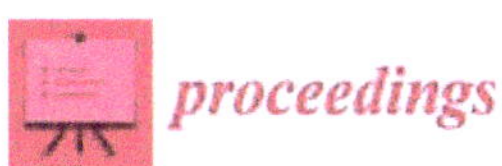 *proceedings*

Proceedings

Exploring the Feasibility of Low Cost Technology in Rainfall Monitoring: The TREBOADA Observing System †

Ignacio Fraga, Alberto Alvarellos and José P. González-Coma *

Centre for Information and Communications Technology Research (CITIC), University of A Coruña, Campus de Elviña, 15071 A Coruña, Spain
* Correspondence: jose.gcoma@udc.es
† Presented at the 2nd XoveTIC Conference, A Coruña, Spain, 5–6 September 2019.

Published: 22 July 2019

Abstract: In order to characterize the spatial and temporal variability of the rainfall, we have developed an observation system to monitor the precipitation over the metropolitan area of A Coruña. The observation system (called TREBOADA) consists of a network of rain gauges, comprising gauges operated by the regional weather agency and rain gauges deployed specifically for TREBOADA. The latter ones are built using low cost technology, which significantly reduces the cost of each gauge. Data from the rain gauges are combined with rain observations from the meteorological radar to produce high resolution rain products.

Keywords: Environmental monitoring; low cost technologies; Arduino

1. Introduction

Urban environments are becoming more vulnerable to flood events due to multiple factors. On the one hand, the changes in the land use and the rapid urbanization have increased the amount of rainfall conveyed to the streams and drainage systems. On the other hand, the climate change has increased rainfall intensities and decreased rain frequency, resulting in higher peak discharges and more likely flash floods. Against this background, increasing the resilience of the cities is the recommended approach [1]. This strategy demands observing and forecasting systems capable of accurately monitoring the rainfall. To explore the feasibility of low cost technologies in this field, we have developed an observing system which combines data gathered using low cost devices with data freely obtained from the regional weather agency (MeteoGalicia).

2. System Description

The TREBOADA observation system computes the spatial and temporal evolution of the rainfall, combining rain data from three sources: low-cost rain gauges specifically developed for this observation system, rain gauges operated by MeteoGalicia and rain data from the meteorological radar also operated by MeteoGalicia.

To combine these data, the krigging with external drift methodology is used [2]. Every 10 min, this interpolation technique is performed to produce a map showing the distribution of the rain intensity over the metropolitan area of A Coruña. This map is made publicly available through a web app [3], which contains a GIS (Geographical Information System)-based viewer and graphs of the rainfall registered by the rain gauges during the last few hours.

The low cost gauges comprise a pluviometer, a processing module and a power supply module (Figure 1). The pluviometer used is an AeroCone tipping bucket gauge, manufactured by Davis. Tipping bucket rain gauges collect the rainfall with a funnel, which conveys water to one of two calibrated buckets, balanced on a pivot. When the bucket fills up its weight tips the pivot, rising the other bucket and locating it beneath the funnel. The movement of the pivot also triggers a reed switch and empties the first bucket.

The processing unit consists of an Arduino MKRFOX 1200 and an external DS3231 real time clock (RTC). The power supply module consists of a 6 W 12 V solar panel (Fadisol C-0154B), connected to a Yuasa 12 V 4 A battery through a solar charge controller (Fadisol C-0189). The output of the battery is connected to the Arduino through a step-down, to power the device with the adequate voltage. The power module was designed to guarantee energy supply during long periods even in case of failure of the solar panel. The Arduino samples the number of pulses of the pluviometer's reed switch and sends the amount of rainfall registered and the corresponding time to a server located in the CITIC (Centre for Information and Communications Technology Research, University of A Coruña) using the Sigfox Communication Network.

Remarkably, the cost of the processing and power supply modules is around 150€, which represents around 15–20% of the cost of the equivalent modules provided by the most frequent manufacturers of meteorological instrumentation.

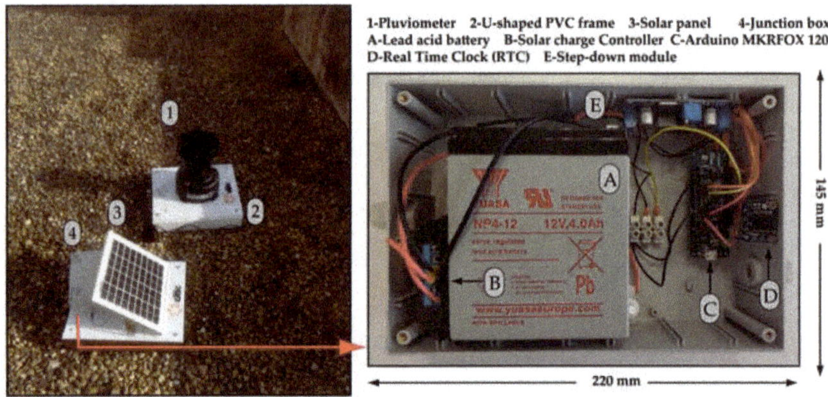

Figure 1. Low-cost rain gauges developed in the TREBOADA observing system.

Author Contributions: All the co-authors have contributed to the conceptualization of the paper and the research presented. I.F. and J.G. contributed to the development of the integration of radar and rain gauge data. A.A designed and developed the low-cost monitoring network.

Funding: The authors received financial support from the Xunta de Galicia (Centro singular de investigación de Galicia accreditation 2016-2019) and the European Union (European Regional Development Fund-ERDF) under grant number ED431G/01. The development of the Treboada observation system was funded by the CITIC.

Conflicts of Interest: The authors declare no conflict of interest.

References

1. Djordjevic, S.; Butler, D.; Gourbesville, P.; Mark, O.; Pasche, E. New policies to deal with climate change and other drivers impacting on resilience to flooding in urban areas: the CORFU approach. *Env. Sci. Pol.* **2011**, *14*, 864–873.

2. Delrieu, G.; Wijbrans, A.; Boudevillain, B.; Faure, D.; Bonnifait, L.; Kirstetter, P.E. Geostatistical radar–raingauge merging: A novel method for the quantification of rain estimation accuracy. *Adv. Water Resour.* **2014**, *71*, 110–124.

3. Treboada website. Available online: http://treboada.citic.udc.es (accessed on 10 July 2019).

 *proceedings*

Proceedings

The Integration of RFID Technology into Business Settings †

María Martínez Pérez *, Carlos Dafonte and Ángel Gómez

CITIC—Department of Computer Science, University of A Coruña, Campus de Elviña s/n, 15071 A Coruña, Spain

* Correspondence: maria.martinez@udc.es; Tel.: +34-981-167-000 (ext. 1264)

† Presented at the 2nd XoveTIC Conference, A Coruña, Spain, 5–6 September 2019.

Published: 22 July 2019

Abstract: At present, the term Internet of Things (IoT) is a key aspect in determining the sustainability, safety, quality and efficiency of the majority of the most important business sectors in society. The capacity to track processes that are undertaken, facilitates the recording of data of the professionals and clients involved. Identification technologies such as RFID (Radio-Frequency Identification) when integrated into sectorial activities, can generate multiple benefits.

Keywords: RFID; traceability; Internet of Things (IoT)

---

1. Introduction and Objectives

Society, is nowadays, surrounded by a multitude of new technologies that can track tasks [1] that we carry out on a daily basis. That is to say register and analyze the most important parameters of whatever process (precise identification, localization in real-time, temperature monitoring, etc.) whether it be in the elaboration or transport of a pharmaceutical, identification of a patient [2], controlling attendance or a study of the routes taken by visitors at a conference or in a museum or amusement park etc.

All of these technologies have given rise to a range of new terms in use today such as (IoT: Internet of Things) which allows for the interconnection of objects allowing for tracking of any element that requires control, providing safety, security, quality and efficiency in our daily activities.

RFID is a state-of-the-art technology that permits radiofrequency communication between a tag and a fixed reader or mobile phone and is another component within the ecosystem of IoT. RFID has different standards and functional frequencies. NFC is part of this technology and provides significant advantages. The key is to assess what RFID can contribute through introducing traceability into a particular area and analyze whether RFID is the most appropriate technology to ensure efficiency and safety in the task to be undertaken. The key parameters for decision-making and design of a successful RFID system for the selected business sector are described below.

2. Results

The results described as follows are based on the experience of the authors in integrating RFID technology especially into the health services area [3–7].

There are multiple configurations for an RFID system, but their way of functioning is the same. RFID technology basically enables communication between a tag and a reader through Radiofrequency. The tag will then send its identification and additional data to a reader which after reception will forward the data to the application responsible for managing it (see Figure 1).

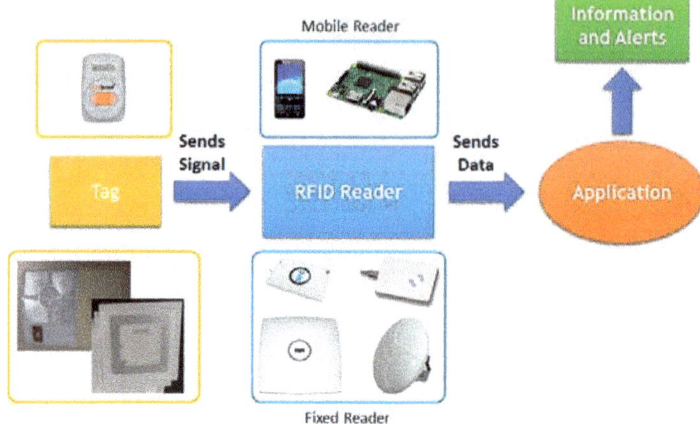

Figure 1. RFID system.

As can be seen in Figure 2, RFID is the appropriate technology to implement into a business sector if it is necessary to precisely identify and/or locate in real-time assets and/or people to be studied.

Figure 2. Principal functions of RFID technology.

The engineers responsible for implementing the RFID system have, at a minimum, to define the key parameters as shown in Figures 3 and 4 in order to obtain the technical architecture of the RFID system that is adequate for the functionalities to develop.

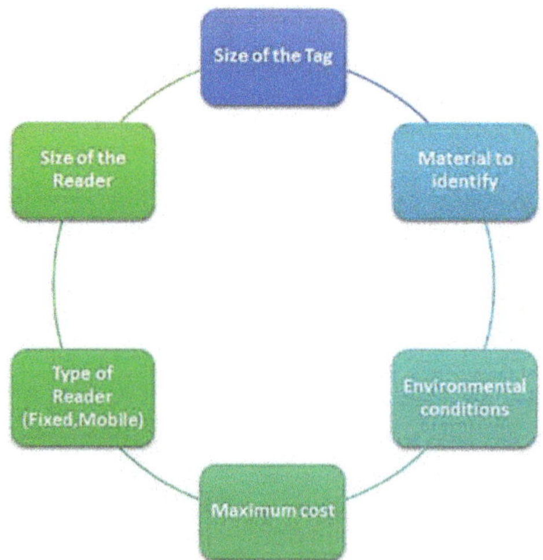

Figure 3. Key parameters in the design of an RFID system.

The surrounding conditions and material are important to identify given that RFID technology can have interferences to its reading because of certain materials so alternatives should be considered to address these problems.

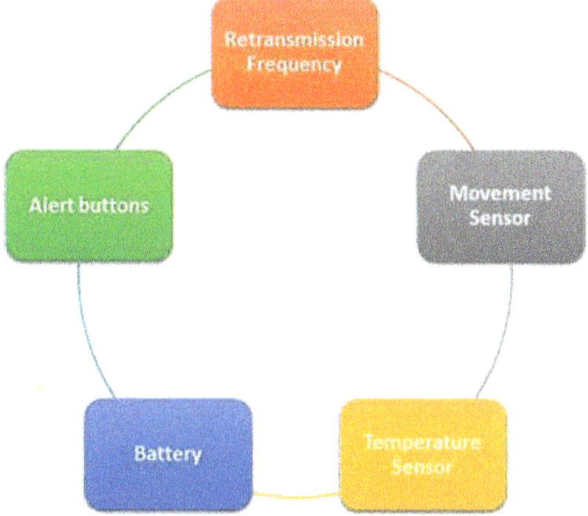

Figure 4. Key parameters in the design of an RFID system.

Most of the key parameters displayed in Figure 4 affect a key component of the RFID system: the tags. This element determines, to a large extent, the other elements so that finding the appropriate tag (in size, shape and material) assures the correct operating protocol in the process into which it is to be integrated.

To conclude, possible RFID systems in a variety of business sectors are listed below, in which the concepts previously described can be applied with the resulting improvements to the activity process:

- Tracking of products (medication, foodstuffs, organs, health products etc.); likewise the identification of transport and containers.
- Tracking of foodstuffs or gourmet products in cultivation or fishing, transport and subsequent sale and delivery (lot nº, expiry date, whereabouts, times, temperature, etc.)
- Tracking of luggage in airports: identification, check-in details, avoidance of theft or recovery of items
- Tracking of animals for identification, control of protected species or domestic animals
- Tracking of documents in any area. For example medical clinical histories
- Tracking of circuits/routes in conferences, car parks, businesses, museums, hospitals, cinemas, amusement parks
- Personalized mailing of information to users about tagged objects to their mobile devices
- Management of access to congresses, car parking sites, businesses, museums, cinemas, amusement parks, etc.
- Management of payments: for example shops and tollgates
- Management of loans and returns of documents, books, and multimedia etc. For example, in libraries
- Management of stocks and expiry dates: automatic inventory in real-time in shops and warehouses

3. Discussion and Conclusions

The possibility of tracking business processes in a company greatly facilitates the recording of the most relevant information pertaining to it. For example, an analysis of this information may reveal potential bottlenecks so that action can be subsequently taken to avoid them or identify successful practice that, clearly, should be followed up.

To assure the successful integration of identification technology within a sector, it is crucial to carry out a technical and economic viability study in which the results may recommend a combination of various technologies or the implementation of one IoT into those processes in which the work protocol and potential rewards justify it. RFID as a state-of- the-art technology has many capacities and applications but it must be preceded by a viability study and a design of the technical architecture of the system in which it is to be integrated.

Author Contributions: M.M.P., C.D. and Á.G. conceived, designed, and performed the experiments and developed all the tools. The paper was written by all of them.

Conflicts of Interest: The authors declare no conflict of interest

References

1. ISO 9000:2015. Sistemas de gestión de la calidad https://www.iso.org/obp/ui/es/#iso:std:iso:9000:ed-4:v1:es (accessed on 25 June 2019)
2. Osborn, S.; Williams, S. Seven steps to patient safety. In *An Overview Guide for NHS Staff*, 2nd ed.; The National Patient Safety Agency: London, UK, 2004.
3. Martínez Pérez, M.; Cabrero-Canosa, M.; Hermida, J.V.; García, L.C.; Gómez, D.L.; González, G.V.; Herranz, I.M. Application of RFID technology in patient tracking and medication traceability in emergency care. *J. Med. Syst.* **2012**, *36*, 3983–3993.
4. Martínez Pérez, M.; Dafonte, C.; Gómez, Á. Traceability in Patient Healthcare through the Integration of RFID Technology in an ICU in a Hospital. *Sensors* **2018**, *18*, 1627.
5. Martínez Pérez, M.; Vázquez González, G.; Dafonte, C. Safety and Traceability in Patient Healthcare through the Integration of RFID Technology for Intravenous Mixtures in the Prescription-Validation-Elaboration-Dispensation-Administration Circuit to Day Hospital Patients. *Sensors* **2016**, *16*, 1188.
6. Martínez Pérez, M.; Vázquez González, G.; Dafonte, C. Evaluation of a Tracking System for Patients and Mixed Intravenous Medication Based on RFID Technology. *Sensors* **2016**, *16*, 2031.
7. Martínez Pérez, M.; Vázquez González, G.; Dafonte, C. The Development of an RFID Solution to Facilitate the Traceability of Patient and Pharmaceutical Data. *Sensors* **2017**, *17*, 2247

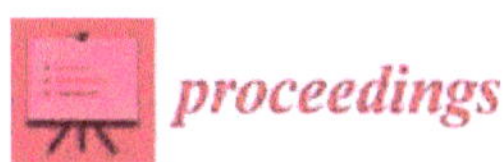

Proceedings

The Sense of Presence through the Humanization Created by Virtual Environments †

João Donga [1,2,*], António Marques [2], Javier Pereira [3] and Paulo Veloso Gomes [2]

[1] ESMAD, Escola Superior de Media Artes e Design do Politécnico do Porto,
   4480-876 Vila do Conde, Portugal
[2] LabRP, Laboratório de Reabilitação Psicossocial, Escola Superior de Saúde do Politécnico do Porto,
   4200-072 Porto, Portugal
[3] CITIC-Research Center of Information and Communication Technologies, University of A Coruña,
   15071 A Coruña, Spain
* Correspondence: jpd@esmad.ipp.pt
† Presented at the 2nd XoveTIC Conference, A Coruña, Spain, 5–6 September 2019.

Published: 23 July 2019

Abstract: This work focus on the study of solutions that using video 360 and virtual reality that allow children's and older people that are away of their family environments for various reasons to be able to feel they are participating at family or school events. The solutions proposed should deliver a strong sense of presence to the users and the interface must be friendly. The validation will be made by user observation and inquiries.

Keywords: video 360; virtual reality; telepresence; embodiment; presence; augmented human; head-mounted display; immersion; user experience

---

1. Introduction

Nowadays, with increasing life expectancy, there are more and more elderly people living alone in their homes or in institutions. Loneliness is one of the main problems affecting this community and there are various means of communication available to communicate with family and friends. This study seeks to create communication mechanisms that allow a high sense of presence.

2. Discussion

The solutions currently used to allow the communication between target users (elderly people) and the outside are based on the use of the mobile phone or the use of videoconferencing mechanisms using laptops or smartphone apps. We intend to study the extent to which these solutions offer a satisfactory sense of presence and create alternative solutions using video 360 to increase this sense of presence to more satisfactory levels (Figure 1).

Presence is the feeling or experience of "being" in the VR environment [1]. Witmer and Singer [2] define presence as "the subjective experience of being in one place or environment, even when one is physically situated in another". Often confused, the terms immersion and presence should not be considered has equivalent terms. Mel Slater defines the terms this way [3]:

- Immersion refers to the objective level of sensory fidelity a VR system provides.
- Presence refers to a user's subjective psychological response to a VR system.

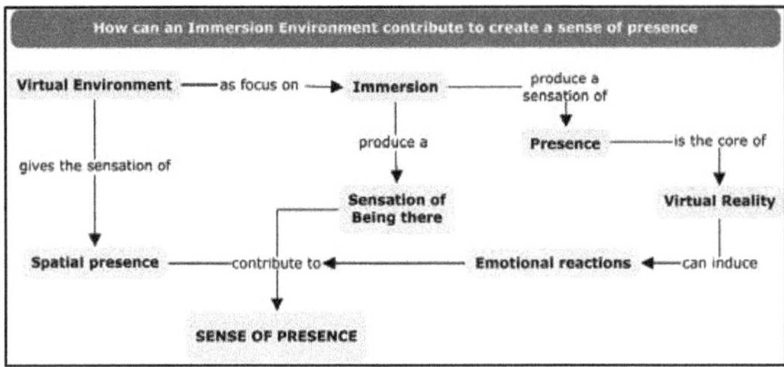

Figure 1. A graphic illustration of the contribution of immersive environments to create a sense of presence.

To create a VR solution with a strong sense of presence we have identified several aspects and we divide them in three main categories: emotion, environment and communication (Figure 2).

- Environmental presence is perception that a virtual environment exists and that the user is present within it [4]. A high degree of environmental presence will increase immersion of virtual experience.
- Communication and interaction with others in virtual reality is very important component for social presence [5].
- Presence has been found to be mediated by human, context, and medium characteristics. Amongst the human factors, a possible relationship between presence and emotions has been noted [6].

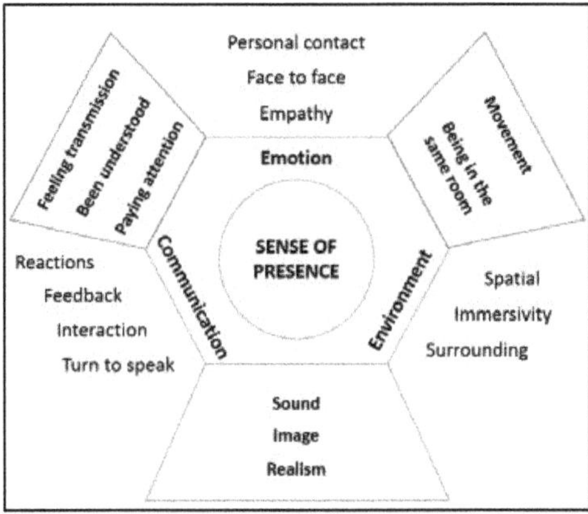

Figure 2. A graphic illustration of the relationship between emotion, communication and environment and their relation with sense of presence.

Cinematic Virtual Reality is argued to hold the potential to provide a more immersive viewing experience, in which the user feels a sense of presence, or a feeling of "being there", similar to traditional computer- generated imagery based VR [7].

Previous research also shows mixed effects about sense of presence in 360° video. MacQuarrie and Steed found that watching 360° videos in a head-mounted display (HMD) created a stronger sense of presence than a surround video display or a regular TV and less concern about missing out on content [8].

In the first phase, the work uses the Research-Action Methodology to design a model for the construction of the technological artefact, prepare the construction of the prototype and the tests to be implemented, identify the relevant indicators and prepare its application.

The second phase applies the developed model to specific cases, using specific Focus Groups. The third phase focuses on evaluation of the impact of intervention and results discussion. This evaluation will be made using questionnaires to measure the sense of presence, usability and user interface.

Author Contributions: Conceptualization, J.D.; methodology, J.D. and A.M.; validation, J.D. and P.V.G.; investigation, J.D.; writing—original draft preparation, J.D.; writing—review and editing, J.D.; visualization, J.D. and P.V.G; supervision, A.M. and J.P.; project administration, J.D.

Funding: This research received no external funding.

Conflicts of Interest: The authors declare no conflict of interest. The funders had no role in the design of the study; in the collection, analyses, or interpretation of data; in the writing of the manuscript, or in the decision to publish the results.

References

1. Wallach, H.S.; Safir, M.P.; Samana, R.; Almog, I.; Horef, R. How Can Presence in Psychotherapy Employing VR Be Increased? Chapter for Inclusion in: Systems in Health Care Using Agents and Virtual Reality. In *Advanced Computational Intelligence Paradigms in Healthcare 6. Virtual Reality in Psychotherapy, Rehabilitation, and Assessment*; Brahnam, S., Jain, L.C., Eds.; Springer: Berlin/Heidelberg, Germany, 2011; Chapter 7, pp. 129–147, doi:10.1007/978-3-642-17824-5_7.
2. Witmer, B.G.; Singer, M.J. Measuring presence in virtual environments: A presence questionnaire. *Presence* **1998**, *7*, 225–240.
3. Slater, M. A note on presence terminology. *Presence Connect* **2003**, *3*, 1–5.
4. A Situated Cognition Perspective on Presence. Available online: https://www.researchgate.net/publication/28764862_A_situated_cognition_perspective_on_presence (accessed on 14 July 2019).
5. Short, J.A.; Williams, E.; Christie, B. *The Social Psychology of Telecommunications*; John Wiley & Sons: New York, NY, USA, 1976.
6. Banos, R.M.; Botella, C.; Liano, V.; Guerrero, B.; Rey, B.; Alcañiz, M. Sense of presence in emotional virtual environments. In Proceedings of the Presence 2004: The 7th Annual Workshop on Presence, Valencia, Spain, 13–15 October 2004; pp. 156–159.
7. Aitamurto, T.; Zhou, S.; Sakshuwong, S.; Saldivar, J.; Sadeghi, Y.; Tran, A. Sense of Presence, Attitude Change, Perspective-Taking and Usability in First-Person Split-Sphere 360° Video. In Proceedings of the 2018 CHI Conference on Human Factors in Computing Systems, Montreal, QC, Canada, 21–26 April 2018; pp. 1–12, doi:10.1145/3173574.3174119
8. MacQuarrie, A.; Steed, A. Cinematic virtual reality: Evaluating the effect of display type on the viewing experience for panoramic video. In Proceedings of the 2017 IEEE Virtual Reality (VR), Los Angeles, CA, USA, 18–22 March 2017. pp. 45–54.

Proceedings

UAV Trajectory Management: Ardupilot Based Trajectory Management System [†]

Javier Losada Pita [1],* and Félix Orjales Saavedra [2]

[1]   Navantia-UDC Joint Research Unit, University of A Coruña, 15403 Ferrol, Spain
[2]   Integrated Group for Engineering Research, University of A Coruña, 15403 Ferrol, Spain
*   Correspondence: javier.losada@udc.es
†   Presented at the 2nd XoveTIC Conference, A Coruña, Spain, 5–6 September 2019.

Published: 23 July 2019

Abstract: In this paper we explain the structure and development of a trajectory management system on board a UAV capable to achieve complex trajectories and versatile to adapt disturbances during flight. This system is built in Python and runs in a companion computer on board the UAV while maintains communication with a ground station over a radio link.

Keywords: UAV; Ardupilot; Python; DroneKit; Mavlink

---

1. Introduction

UAV operations are growing fast the last years due to the versatility they offer [1]. They can perform diverse kind of missions, from aerial photography to long distances deliveries. These missions all can be benefited by a system capable to control a trajectory to maintain an autonomous flight adapting his behavior in real time to variable conditions like wind, obstacles, vehicle failures, No fly zones, etc. These conditions can lead, in the worst scenario, to the loss of the vehicle which would lead to economic losses and a large safety problem when flying over populated areas.

Usually UAV autonomous missions consist of a series of waypoints preprogrammed which the flight controller will try to follow no matter what happens until the mission is complete or the pilot manually cancels the mission. This increases the likelihood that a mission will not perform successfully due to external disturbances [2]. In this paper we develop a trajectory management system capable to adapt to changing flight conditions gathering data from the surroundings with sensors connected to the companion computer (cameras, Lidars, radars, etc.).

2. System Definition

Using a companion computer on board the UAV allow us to receive and send data to the flight controller. In this case the vehicle flight controller uses Ardupilot as firmware, which can communicate with a computer using Mavlink protocol. For this task we send and receive Mavlink messages, with Dronekit API for Python, over a serial port (USB-TTY) connected to the flight controller as can be seen in Figure 1. In this way we have access to all telemetry data and can command the vehicle by modifying attitude attributes as target position or velocity.

In order to maintain control with a ground station we have created an UDP port to send the telemetry data to a mission control software (Mission Planner, QGroundControl, etc.) and a SSH port to have a remote terminal with the companion computer. This ports communicate with the ground station through a radio gateway connected with both computers, UAV and ground, over Ethernet.

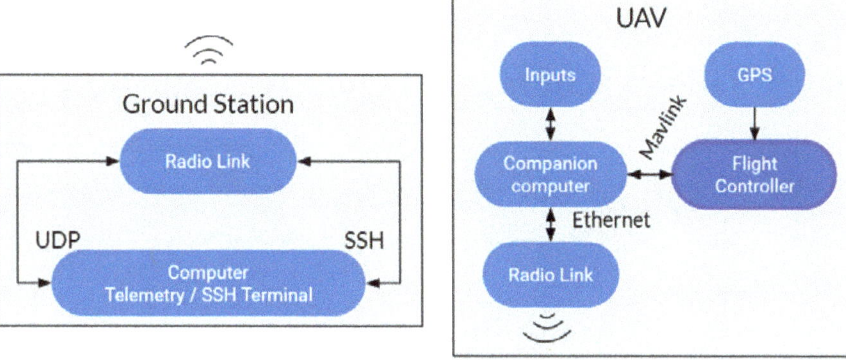

Figure 1. System configuration.

To test the system, we programmed an example trajectory in a constant altitude which was performed in a simulation by modifying vehicle's velocity in real time as shown in Figure 2. The companion computer got control of the vehicle when flying and perform the maneuver until RTL mode was activated (Return To Launch position).

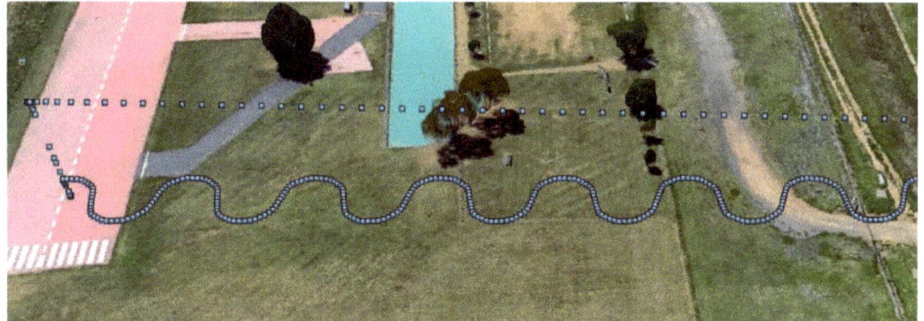

Figure 2. Sinusoidal trajectory performed by the simulated UAV.

The system was designed in a way that allows receiving data from external sensors or the built-in sensors of the flight controller (IMU, barometer, etc.) and modify his behavior in real time so the vehicle can adapt to possible surrounding disruptions. By this way this trajectory management system opens multiple possibilities to design an UAV capable of adapting to the surrounding conditions in real time and be able to add as much sensors as needed for the application it will perform.

References

1. Brief, L. Growth Opportunity in Global uav Market. Available online: https://www.lucintel.com/GrowthOpportunityinGlobalUAVMarket.pdf (accessed on 12 July 2019).
2. Idries, A.; Mohamed, N.; Jawhar, I.; Mohamed, F.; Al-Jaroodi, J. Challenges of developing UAV applications: A project management view. In proceedings of 2015 International Conference on Industrial Engineering and Operations Management, Dubai, UAE, 3–5 March 2015. IEEE: Piscataway, NJ, USA, 2015; pp. 389–398.

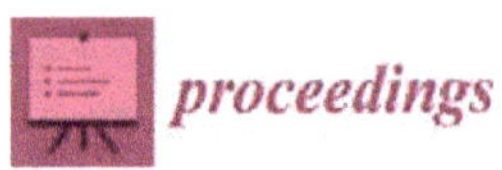 *proceedings*

Proceedings

Analog Video Encoding and Quality Evaluation †

Jose Balsa *, Óscar Fresnedo, José A. García-Naya, Tomás Domínguez-Bolaño and Luis Castedo

CITIC Research Center, Universidade da Coruña (University of A Coruña), 15071 A Coruña, Spain

* Correspondence: j.balsa@udc.es

† Presented at the 2nd XoveTIC Conference, A Coruña, Spain, 5–6 September 2019.

Published: 23 July 2019

Abstract: The most widespread analog video encoding systems in the literature are based on the use of the 2D and 3D DCT. These systems use both transformations indistinctly without assessing their suitability. In this paper, we present procedures to compress video using 2D and 3D-DCT and we evaluate the video quality for different compression levels.

Keywords: analog video encoding; video quality evaluation

1. Introduction

Nowadays, the multimedia use of computers and mobile devices is increasing because of its applications. Within this, the transmission of information quickly and without delay is essential for applications and users. In this environment, video transmission plays a predominant role with a great challenge due to the relationship between transmitting a large amount of data and compressing it by introducing a high computational load.

In recent years, if we talk about video transmission and compression, we are talking about digital processes. These systems are capable of delivering high performance in the vast majority of possible scenarios. Although it is true that these digital systems present some well-known problems. On one hand, video compression techniques look for spatial and temporal correlations and require a high computational load. On the other hand, if data cannot be recovered without errors, retransmissions are needed, which degrades the delay of the communication link.

An alternative approach to digital systems is to use analog transmissions, which provide low delay and low complexity. Most of the existing works regarding analog video encoding and transmission propose hybrid analog-digital schemes, where the analog part consists on the use of the discrete cosine transform (DCT). The idea of using the DCT is that the components at higher frequencies correspond to the most important visual information; hence, some of the coefficients can be discarded without affecting the image quality. Some of the proposed systems use the 2D-DCT [1], whereas others consider the 3D-DCT [2,3]. However, in most of them, the digital part is a key component. In order to compare the image quality after the transmission there exist different metrics: peak signal-to-noise ratio (PSNR) is considered in [1–3], whereas structural similarity (SSIM) and signal-to-distortion ratio (SDR) is employed in [3].

In this context, we compare both transformations, 2D and 3D DCT, in videos with movement and static scenarios. We have to stablish some metrics to evaluate and compare the system evaluation parameters such as the compression ratio, related to the transmitted frequencies, and image quality, measured in terms of PSNR and SSIM.

2. System Description

We propose two analog schemes for video encoding: one using the 2D-DCT and another one employing the 3D-DCT. The 2D-DCT system encodes each individual video frame using the analog scheme proposed in [4] for still images, although in this case the correlation between frames is not considered. In this system, each frame is divided into 8 × 8 blocks and the DCT transformation is applied to each block. The resulting DCT coefficients are stacked onto a vector following a zigzag pattern. Thus, the resulting vector will be sorted from low to high frequencies. The symbols corresponding to the higher frequencies are discarded, thus compressing the image and reducing its visual quality.

Regarding the 3D-DCT system, the entire video is firstly divided into sequences of 8 frames each. Next, each sequence is divided into blocks of 8 × 8 pixels, thus the whole video is split in cubes with dimension 8 × 8 × 8. We now define de concept of *symbol* as the pixel intensity (luminance in our case) expressed as an integer number ranging between 0 and 255. A weight is then assigned to each symbol according to its low or high frequency using the 3D pattern defined in [5] to rearrange the symbols into a sequence from the lower to the higher frequencies. As in the 2D-DCT case, the symbols corresponding to the higher frequencies are discarded, hence compressing the image and reducing its visual quality.

Next, a comparison with the original video sequence is carried out to determinate the video quality related to the compression factor. The metric consists in comparing each original frame with the compressed one and averaging out the result. More specifically, in this paper both the SSIM and PSNR as considered since they are the most used metrics to perform this type of comparisons [1–3].

3. Results

The results presented here are the product of averaging out three different video sequences. We have also taken into account different scenarios to get a fair comparison. We tested resolutions ranging from SD to 1080p, as well as with different static and motion sequences.

Figure 1 shows the results obtained from the system simulations. The results show that the quality of the video is higher for the 3D-DCT than for the 2D-DCT and for both metrics: PSNR and SSIM. Note that in Figure 1a, when the compression factor becomes 1, the PSNR approaches infinite.

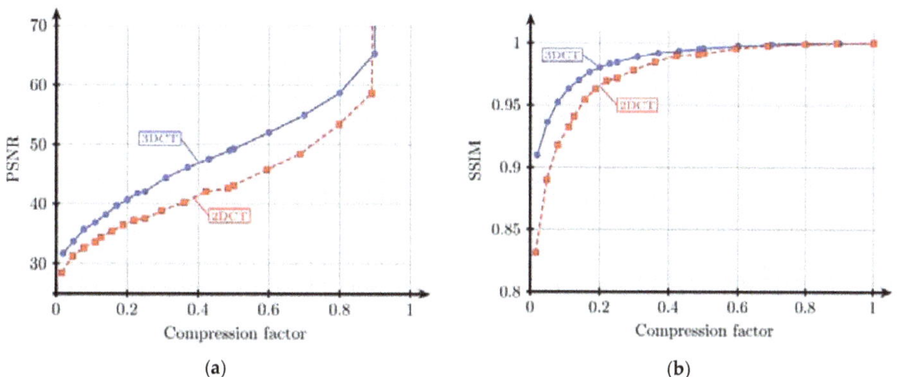

Figure 1. Quality comparison between 2D- and 3D-DCT versus the compression factor for the two considered metrics: (**a**) PSNR in decibels, and (**b**) SSIM.

4. Conclusions

The results show that with the same video quality it is possible to achieve a higher compression level when the 3D-DCT is employed instead of the 2D-DCT. This is because the 3D-DCT considers both spatial and temporal correlation at the same time, hence reducing the amount of redundant information in the three dimensions.

In view of the results, it can be safely concluded that the 3D-DCT can be considered as an improvement with respect to the 2D-DCT for video applications.

Author Contributions: Conceptualization, J.B., T.B., O.F. and J.G.; software, J.B.; investigation, J.B.; writing—original draft preparation, J.B.; writing—review and editing, T.B, O.F. and J.G.; funding acquisition, L.C.

Acknowledgments: This work has been funded by the Xunta de Galicia (ED431C 2016-045, ED431G/01), the Agencia Estatal de Investigación of Spain (TEC2016-75067-C4-1-R) and ERDF funds of the EU (AEI/FEDER, UE).

Conflicts of Interest: The authors declare no conflict of interest.

References

1. Fan, X.; Wu, F.; Zhao, D.; Au, O. C.; Gao, W. Distributed Soft Video Broadcast (DCAST) with Explicit Motion. In Proceedings of the 2012 Data Compression Conference, Snowbird, UT, USA, 10–12 April 2012.
2. Jakubczak, S.; Katabi, D. SoftCast: Clean-slate scalable wireless video. In Proceedings of the 2010 48th Annual Allerton Conference on Communication, Control, and Computing (Allerton), Allerton, IL, USA, 29 September–1 October 2010.
3. Liang, F.; Luo, C.; Xiong, R.; Zeng, W.; Wu, F. Hybrid Digital–Analog Video Delivery With Shannon–Kotel'nikov Mapping. *IEEE Trans. Multimed.* **2018**, *20*, 2138–2152.
4. Balsa, J.; Domínguez-Bolaño, T.; Fresnedo, Ó; García-Naya, J.A.; Castedo, L. Transmission of Still Images Using Low-Complexity Analog Joint Source-Channel Coding. *Sensors* **2019**, *19*, 2932.
5. Chan, R. K. W.; Lee, M. C. 3D-DCT quantization as a compression technique for video sequences, In Proceedings of the International Conference on Virtual Systems and MultiMedia VSMM '97 (Cat. No. 97TB100182), Geneva, Switzerland, 10–12 September 1997.

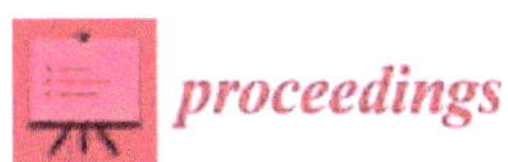 

Proceedings

Pilot Study about a Multifactorial Intervention Programme in Older Adults with Technological Devices Based on GeriaTIC Project †

María del Carmen Miranda-Duro *, Laura Nieto-Riveiro and Thais Pousada García

TALIONIS Group, CITIC, Oza, Universidade da Coruña, 15071 A Coruña, Spain
* Correspondence: carmen.miranda@udc.es
† Presented at the 2nd XoveTIC Conference, A Coruña, Spain, 5–6 September 2019.

Published: 25 July 2019

Abstract: This pilot study was carried out with a sample of six older persons in a residential center in A Coruña. It is a "quasi-experimental" study, directed to assess the effect of an intervention on a given population, performing "pre" and "post" intervention measurements, but without comparison with a control group. The multifactorial intervention had a duration of 3 months, which includes the use of technological devices, like a wristband of physical activity and sleep.

Keywords: aged; participatory health; participatory medicine; quality of life; technological development; wearables

1. Introduction

Worldwide, nowadays, we are present to the population progressive ageing, more strong in Japan and some of European Union countries. Despite of the fact that ageing is not a pathology or illness, it is considered as the higher vital stage when appears a pathology of chronic disease. Agree with the World Organization of Health, it is considered to detect and treat illness on time, with the purpose of reduce the consequences, throw an integral system of primary attention [1–3].

Urinary incontinence, falls and sleep disorders are included into the more frequent geriatric syndromes. This pilot study is focus on falls and sleep disorders.

In the field of health, more technological companies are positioned to develop wearable devices and applications to monitoring daily people, which allows to follow-up the health status of the users and their benefits. The use of these devices, permit quantify movement and body parameters as: pulsation, cardiac rhythm, respiratory rhythm, blood pressure, glucose level, oxygen saturation level, temperature, sweating, etc. Currently exist numerous commercial solutions for monitoring health parameters of the users through technological sensors, capable to transmit collected data to other devices as mobile phone or a computer. There are different solutions as activity trackers quantifying physical activity and/or sleep, scale, glucose quantifier, blood pressure quantifier, pulsation quantifier, etc. [4].

Nowadays, exists different solutions that would be use in this project. However, the geriatric syndromes that are focused the project on, don't have commercial devices to treat it. A significant part of the research labor in this project is to define low-cost fiable sensor devices without wasting efficiency [5].

This project is based on the use of wearable devices employed to the quantification of different biomedical parameters, which use to monitor and analyse aspects as sleep, physical activity and others. In this research, it has been developed a web application where people register some daily life details every week. Both of the use of wearables and the web register are agree with participatory health and participatory medicine. In this way, people become active agents to the own management of health [6].

2. Objectives

The main objective of this study is determine the impact in the quality of life of a multifactorial intervention programme, based on Geria-TIC project, developed to institutionalized older adults with sleep disorders and falls. Specifically, benefit the reduction of the symptoms and signs of these syndromes, analyse the changes produced in older adult's participant's occupations, empower the use of technological devices in the daily life of older adults and the own health management, and promote major responsibility and active participation of the older adult in their own health and ageing process.

3. Material and Methods

This pilot study is a quasi-experimental research developed in A Coruña (Spain) during 3 months. The participants of the study are older than 65 years old, users of a residential home. It includes those people who are at risk of falling due to a previous fall in the last year or fear of falling. On the other hand, the vertical of sleep disturbances includes those people who present a diagnosis of insomnia and/or hypersomnia or, failing that, who present the signs and symptoms during a continuous period.

The technological development of the project began in October 2016, and the changes and adaptations made to date continue. Prior to contact with potential participants, approval was requested by the ethics committee of the protocol designed, obtaining a favorable report from the Autonomous Committee of Research Ethics of A Coruña-Ferrol (2017/106).

The beginning of this pilot study was in March and the end was in July 2019. In this period, there were the initial assessment, the intervention development and the final assessment.

The tools of the assessment that were used were the EuroQol-5D-5L to evaluate the quality of life, the Index of Barthel to assess the degree of independence, and the Mini-Mental Examination Test to assess cognitive impairment.

In the case of sleep disorders, the Oviedo Sleep Questionnaire and the Pittsburgh Sleep Quality Index [7,8] have been administered. In terms of the fall vertical, the Tinetti Scale, the Time Get Up and Go Test and the Falls Efficacy Scale International [9] have also been administered.

A multifactorial intervention programme was developed with a duration of 3 months. This programme includes the use of a bracelet to record physical activity and sleep, and the use of a mobile application on the tablet for the registration of occupations, and the advice on the performance of occupations, physical activity, and relaxation.

Regarding the materials used in the study, it is important to note that an application web was being developed called ClepiTO. This application is a health manager, thus promoting participatory medicine, in which participants will make a daily and fortnightly record of different occupations and/or relevant information on urinary incontinence, sleep disorders and the risk of falling. This application will be linked to ClepIO. This is an online health application aimed at managing the medical history and the personal health record, as well as carrying out the control of the treatments received.

4. Results and Conclusions

For the time being, no results are available to draw definitive conclusions about the impact of this pilot study based on Geria-TIC project. Even so, the observation that is being made during the intervention reflects that the participants show a high level of motivation, interest and involvement towards the activities developed. However, it is necessary to wait for the final collection of data and its subsequent analysis, as well as future tests with larger samples, to determine if the project has a real impact on the quality of life. According to the data obtained through the activity wristbands, there has been a noticeable increase in the steps taken per day, and show great acceptance and incorporation of physical activity in their day to day. It is expected that the data obtained on the quality of life will be maintained or that the score will be increased.

Author Contributions: L.N.-R. and T.P.G. conceived and designed the experiments; L.N.-R. performed the experiments; L.N.-R. and T.P.G. analyzed the data; T.P.G. and M.d.C.M.D. contributed materials and analysis tools; L.N.-R. and M.d.C.M.D. wrote the paper.

Funding: GERIA-TIC project, co-funded by the Galician Innovation Agency (GAIN) through the Connect PEME Program (third edition) (IN852A 2016/10) and EU FEDER funds. Collaborative Genomic Data Integration Project (CICLOGEN), Data mining techniques and molecular docking for analysis of integrative data in colon cancer, funded by the Ministry of Economy, Industry and Competitiveness. Galician Network of Research in Colorectal Cancer (REGICC) ED431D 2017/23; Galician Network of Medicines (REGID) ED431D 2017/16, funded by the Department of Culture Education; and University Planning aids for the consolidation and structuring of competitive research units of the University System of Galicia of the Xunta de Galicia and Singular Centers (ED431G/01), endowed with FEDER funds of the EU. Financial support from the Xunta de Galicia and the European Union (European Social Fund - ESF), is gratefully acknowledged.

Conflicts of Interest: The authors declare no conflict of interest. The founding sponsors had no role in the design of the study; in the collection, analyses, or interpretation of data; in the writing of the manuscript, and in the decision to publish the results.

References

1. Abellán, A.; Aceituno, P.; Pérez, J.; Ramiro, D.; Ayala, A.; Pujol, R. *Un perfil de las Personas Mayores en España 2019. Indicadores Estadísticos Básicos*; Informes Envejecimiento en Red No. 22: Madrid, Spain, 2019. Available online: http://envejecimiento.csic.es/documentos/documentos/enred-indicadoresbasicos2019.pdf (accessed on 1 July 2019).
2. World Health Organization. ¿Qué Repercusiones Tiene el Envejecimiento Mundial en la Salud Pública? Available online: http://www.who.int/features/qa/42/es/ (accessed on 1 July 2019).
3. Scobie, J.; Asfour, L.; Beales, S.; Gillam, S.J.; McGeachie, P.; Mihnovits, A.; Mikkonen-Jeanneret, E.; Nisos, C.; Rushton, F.; Zaidi, A. *Global AgeWatch Index 2015: Insight Report*; HelpAge International: London, UK, 2015. Available online: https://www.helpage.org/global-agewatch/ (accessed on 1 July 2019).
4. Giner, P.; Cetina, C.; Fons, J.; Pelechano, V. Developing mobile workflow support in the internet of things. *IEEE Pervasive Comput.* **2010**, *9*, 18–26.
5. Gershenfeld, N.; Krikorian, R.; Cohen, D. The internet of things. *Sci. Am.* **2004**, *291*, 46–51.
6. Android4all. Analysis Xiaomi MiBand. Available online: http://andro4all.com/2015/01/xiaomi-mi-band-caracteristicas-precio-opiniones (accessed on 1 July 2019).
7. Buysse, D.J.; Reynolds, C.F.; Monk, T.H.; Berman, S.R.; Kupfer, D.J. The Pittsburgh Sleep Quality Index: A new instrument for psychiatric practice and research. *Psychiatry Res.* **1989**, *28*, 193–213.
8. Bobes, J.; González-G-Portilla, M.P.; Sáiz P.A.; Bascarán M.T.; Iglesias, C.; Fernández-Domínguez, J.M. Propiedades psicométricas del cuestionario Oviedo de sueño. *Psicothema* **2000**, *12*, 107–112.
9. Podsiadlo, D.; Richardson, S. The Timed Up and Go: A test of basic functional mobility for frail elderly persons. *J. Am. Geriatr. Soc.* **1991**, *39*, 142–148.

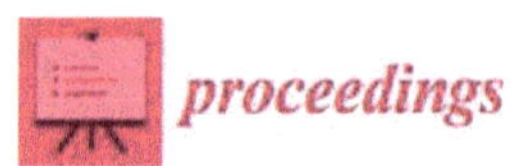 *proceedings* 

Proceedings

Promoting Reminiscences with Virtual Reality: Feasibility Study with People with Dementia [†]

Tiago Coelho *, Cátia Marques, Daniela Moreira, Maria Soares, Paula Portugal and António Marques

School of Health—Polytechnic of Porto, Center for Rehabilitation Research (Psychosocial Rehabilitation Lab), 4200-072 Porto, Portugal
* Correspondence: tfc@ess.ipp.pt; Tel.: +351-222-061-000
† Presented at the 2nd XoveTIC Conference, A Coruña, Spain, 5–6 September 2019.

Published: 26 July 2019

Abstract: This study aimed to examine the feasibility of promoting reminiscences with people with dementia, using 360° videos presented with virtual reality headsets. Four individual sessions were conducted with nine people with dementia. Average duration of the exposure was approximately ten minutes. The experience appeared to be pleasant for most of the participants (with the exception of one of the participants who reported visual limitations). Most participants shared positive memories while viewing the recordings. None of the participants experienced any significant increase in symptoms associated with nausea and disorientation.

Keywords: dementia; reminiscence; virtual reality

1. Introduction

Dementia is a syndrome characterized by cognitive decline (affecting domains such as memory, language, attention and judgment), psychological and behavioural symptoms (such as depression, anxiety, apathy and aggression), and disability in everyday activities [1]. The prevalence of dementia is increasing worldwide, escalating caregiver burden and societal costs with social and health care [1]. Non-pharmacological treatments are essential to improve the well-being of people with dementia and their families. Some of these interventions seek to use preserved remote autobiographical memories to improve the patients' mood, behaviour and overall quality of life [2]. Reminiscence therapy is a well-supported example of these approaches, involving the discussion of past personal experiences, usually with the aid of prompts such as photos or objects [2]. However, there is a lack of evidence regarding the use of more immersive cues, such as permitted by virtual reality (VR). Therefore, this study aimed to assess the feasibility of promoting reminiscences with people with dementia, using 360° videos of locations or activities relevant to each individual (considering their life story), displayed in VR headsets.

2. Materials and Methods

A convenience sample of 9 people with mild or moderate dementia, without severe visual deficits, was recruited. Participants had to have family members or other relevant individuals that could provide information about the participants' life story. Semi-structured interviews were conducted with patients and family members/informants to identify meaningful activities, contexts and events of the participants' past. Researchers analysed the content of the interviews and discussed which positive and pleasant memories could be depicted trough video recordings in 360°. A tailored program of four video recordings was defined for each individual, including settings such as childhood house and workplace locations, as well as leisure and religious venues. Reminiscence intervention consisted of four individual sessions conducted in two weeks. Each session included an initial preparation, exposure to one of the 360° videos with a VR headset (10–15 min) and a final discussion. Questions regarding positive memories (associated with the video) were made during the exposure to promote their recollection and discussion. To assess the feasibility of this approach, the Simulator Sickness Questionnaire [3] was used, and an observation scale was prepared to register the participants' behaviour during the exposure.

3. Results

A preliminary analysis of the data showed that the average duration of the exposure was approximately 10 min. The experience appeared to be pleasant for most of the participants, as they freely explored the 360º environment. Participants, when encouraged or spontaneously, described what they were seeing or recalling during the exposure. Shared memories were mostly positive. Only one participant did not appear to enjoy the experience, showing some signs of agitation and asking to remove the headset after 5–6 min. This participant reported difficulty in seeing and understanding the environments and refused to participate in one of the sessions. Regarding simulator sickness, none of the participants experienced any significant increase in symptoms associated with nausea and disorientation. Mild eyestrain and blurred vision were reported in some cases.

4. Discussion

As no significant detriment to the well-being of the participants was observed, these findings demonstrate the feasibility of these kind of approaches. Future studies should focus on measuring the medium and long-term effects of promoting reminiscences with VR headsets, particularly on the psychological and behavioural symptoms of people with dementia.

Author Contributions: Conceptualization—T.C.; methodology—T.C., P.P.; formal analysis—T.C., C.M., D.M., M.S.; investigation—T.C., C.M., D.M., M.S.; resources—A.M.; preparing the original draft—T.C.; review and editing—T.C., P.P., A.M.; visualization—T.C.; project administration—T.C., P.P., A.M.

Funding: This research received no external funding.

Acknowledgments: The authors would like to thank the collaborating institutions that ensured the transportation of the participants and provided a location to perform part of the tasks of the research.

Conflicts of Interest: The authors declare no conflict of interest.

References

1. World Health Organization. *Dementia: A Public Health Priority Geneva*; World Health Organization: Geneva, Switzerland, 2012.
2. Woods, B.; O'Philbin, L.; Farrell, E.M.; Spector, A.E.; Orrell, M. Reminiscence therapy for dementia. *Cochrane Database Syst. Rev.* **2018**, *3*, Cd001120.
3. Kennedy, R.S.; Lane, N.E.; Berbaum, K.S.; Lilienthal, M.G. Simulator Sickness Questionnaire: An Enhanced Method for Quantifying Simulator Sickness. *Int. J. Aviat. Psychol.* **1993**, *3*, 203–220.

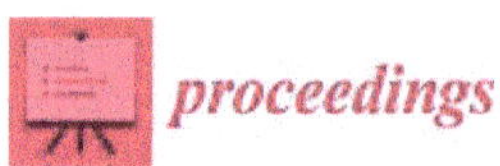 *proceedings*

Proceedings

Sleep Disturbances in Nursing Home Residents: Links to Quality of Life and Daily Functioning

Patricia Concheiro-Moscoso *, Betania Groba and Nereida Canosa

Faculty of Health Sciences, Research Center on Information and Communication Technologies (CITIC), Universidade da Coruña Tecnología Aplicada a la Investigación en Ocupación, Igualdad y Salud (TALIONIS), 15071, A Coruña, Spain
* Correspondence: patricia.concheiro@udc.es
† Presented at the 2nd XoveTIC Conference, A Coruña, Spain, 5-6 September 2019.

Published: 29 July 2019

Abstract: The current study sought to determine the association of sleep with HRQOL and physical function among older nursing home residents. Participants were 37 older adults attending or residing in a semi-urban nursing-home facility in Galicia, Spain (70.3% cognitively normal, 29.7% cognitively impaired, aged 84.1±8.0, 81.1% women) who completed the Pittsburgh Sleep Quality Index (PSQI), the 5-level EuroQol-5D, a measure of HRQOL, and the International Classification of Functioning, Disability and Health (ICF) Core Sets for Sleep, a measure of physical functional. After adjustment for age, poor (PSQI score ≤ 14) and/or worse sleep quality (continuous PSQI score) was associated with several indices of lower HRQOL, including greater immobility (b = 0.19, p = 0.012) difficulty completing self-care (b = 0.23, p < 0.001) and daily activities (b = 0.18, p = 0.004), more severe anxiety/depression (b = 0.10, p = 0.042), and a lower overall health index (b = 0.06, p = 0.001). Further, poor/worse sleep quality was associated with several indices of functional impairment, including greater difficulty maintaining body position (b = 0.32, p = 0.004), walking (b = 0.17, p = 0.001), and moving around (b = 0.45, p = 0.009).

Keywords: Ageing; "Sleep disorders"; "Quality of life" and "Functioning"

1. Introduction

Sleep problems often are associated with difficulties in their daily lives. Several studies have examined associations of poor sleep with health and quality of life (QOL) in the general population of adults, and how sleep might affect health outcomes, including emotional distress, and risk of falls [1,2]. The prevalence of sleep disorders increases with age, and poor sleep is one of the most frequent complaints among older adults [3,4].

However, very few studies have examined the association of sleep with quality of life and physical function among elderly nursing home residents [5,6]. Of those that have, most were conducted in geographical areas outside of Spain with vastly different social cultures, and consequently, may have less generalizability to either the urban or rural environments of Spain [5,7].

Therefore, the primary objective of the current study was to examine the association of subjectively measured sleep disturbance with QOL and physical function among older adults attending or residing in a nursing home facility in Spain, and identify environmental factors that may affect subjectively measured sleep in this population.

2. Material and Methods

A cross-sectional study design was employed. The Autonomous Ethics Committee of Research in Galicia approved the protocol (code: 2017/106).

2.1. Participants and Settings

Participants were nursing home patrons and residents with and without self-report sleep problems or diagnosis of insomnia and/or hypersomnia or drowsiness.

2.2. Procedure

The investigation used several evaluation instruments. Wearables devices were used for the measurement of biomedical parameters of the users, specifically the MiBand2 activity wristbands of the Xiaomi brand [8]. The data collection is automated to through a data capture system that connects directly to the devices and obtains all the information of the wristband without the need to access the manufacturer's application.

3. Results

In the study, 37 people participated. The participants were between 65 and 104 years old and were mostly women (~ 81.1%). More than two thirds of the sample that is a light cognitive (70.3%), 59.5% reported having difficulty sleeping, and 81.1% take medication to sleep.

After adjustment for age, poorer sleep quality (greater PSQI score) was associated with several indices of lower health status, including greater immobility (b = 0.19, p = 0.012) difficulty completing self-care (b = 0.23, p < 0.001) and usual activities (b = 0.18, p = 0.004), more severe anxiety/depression (b = 0.10, p = 0.046), and a lower overall health index (b = -0.06, p = 0.001). Further, poorer sleep quality was associated with several indices of functional impairment, including greater difficulty maintaining body position (b = 0.32, p=0.004), walking (b = 0.17, p = 0.001), and moving around (b = 0.45, p = 0.009).

4. Discussion and Conclusions

The main objective of the current study was to examine the associations of sleep with life quality and daily physical functioning among older nursing home residents in Spain. Our findings revealed that a large proportion of residents suffered from sleep disturbances, which affected their quality of life and daily functioning [9,10].

Among older nursing home residents/patrons in Spain, poorer sleep quality is associated with lower indices of health status and physical function. Longitudinal studies and sleep interventions are necessary to improve health and physical function in this population.

Author Contributions: P.C.-M. and B.G. conceived and designed the experiment; P.C.-M. performed the experiment; B.G. and N.C. analyzed the data; P.C.-M., B.G. and N.C. wrote the paper.

Funding: Cátedra Handrytronic-Grupo Telecon. Universidade da Coruña.

Acknowledgments GERIA-TIC Project, Project co-funded by the Galician Innovation Agency (GAIN) through the Connect PEME Program (3rd edition) (IN852A 2016/10) and EU FEDER funds, Collaborative Genomic Data Integration Project (CICLOGEN). Data mining and molecular docking techniques for integrative data analysis in colon cancer. "Funded by the Ministry of Economy, Industry and Competitiveness. Galician Network of Research in Colorectal Cancer (REGICC) ED431D 2017/23, Galician Network of Medicines (REGID) ED431D 2017/16 funded by the Department of Culture Education and University Planning aids for the consolidation and structuring of competitive research units of the University System of Galicia of the Xunta de Galicia and Singular Centers (ED431G/01) endowed with FEDER funds of the EU.

References

1. Cipriani G; Lucetti C; Danti S; Nuti A. Sleep disturbances and dementia. *Psychogeriatrics* **2015**; *15*, 65–74, doi:10.1111/psyg.12069
2. Wennberg AM; Canham SL; Smith MT; Spira AP. Optimizing sleep in older adults: Treating insomnia. *Maturitas* **2013**, *76*, 247–52, doi:10.1016/j.maturitas.2013.05.007

3. Ynnesdal Haugen LS; Haugland V; Envy A; Borg M, Ekeland TJ,; Anderssen N. Not talking about illness at meeting places in Norwegian community mental health care: A discourse analysis of silence concerning illness-talk. *Health* **2018**, 1–20, doi:10.1177/1363459318785712

4. Crowley K. Sleep and sleep disorders in older adults. *Neuropsychol Rev* **2011**, *21*, 41–53, doi: 10.1007/s11065-010-9154-6

5. Abellán A; Ayala A; Pérez J; Pujol R. Un perfil de las personas mayores en España, *Indicadores estadísticos básicos*. *Inf Envejec en red nº 17* **2018**, 34. Available online: http://envejecimiento.csic.es/documentos/documentos/enred-indicadoresbasicos18.pdf (accessed on 16 November 2016)

6. Centro de Investigaciones sociológicas. 2018. Informe envejecimiento en red. Available online: http://envejecimiento.csic.es/documentos/documentos/enred-estadisticasresidencias2017.pdf (accessed on 16 November 2016)

7. Fetveit A. Late-life insomnia: A review, *Geriatr Gerontol Int.* **2009**, *9*, 220–34. doi:10.1111/j.1447-0594.2009.00537.x

8. Puri A; Kim B; Nguyen O; Stolee P; Tung J; Lee J. User Acceptance of Wrist-Worn Activity Trackers Among Community-Dwelling Older Adults: Mixed Method Study *JMIR mHealth uHealth* **2017**, *5*, e173, doi:10.2196/mhealth.8211

9. Perlick D; Pollak CP; Perlick D. Problems and Institutionalization of the Sleep Elderly Institutionalization. J Geriatr Psychiatry Neurol. **1991**;4, 204–210, doi:10.1177/089198879100400405

10. Fuller JM; Wong KK, Hoyos C; Krass I; Saini B. Dispensing good sleep health behaviours not pills - a cluster-randomized controlled trial to test the feasibility and efficacy of pharmacist-provided brief behavioural treatment for insomnia. *J Sleep Res.* **2016**, *25*, 104–15.

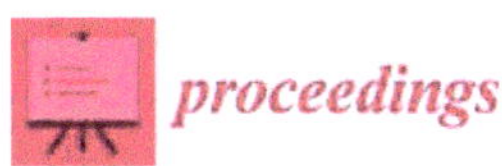 *proceedings*

Proceedings

IoT Platform: Contribution to the Promotion of Mental Health and Wellbeing

António Carlos Correia [1,*], António Marques [1] and Javier Pereira [2]

[1] Psychosocial Rehabilitation Lab, Polytechnic Institute of Porto, 4200-392 Oporto, Portugal
[2] Centre for Information and Communications Technology Research, University of A Coruña, 15071 Coruña, Spain
* Correspondence: antoniocarloscorreia@hotmail.com; Tel.: +351-929091883.
† Presented at the 2nd XoveTIC Conference, A Coruña, Spain, 5–6 September 2019.

Published: 29 July 2019

Abstract: The research intends to gather on a IoT Platform, a set of data existing in the ecosystem - in the universe of things, from sources and types of diverse origin coming from messages, devices, sensors, etc. These structured and related data allow us to generate indicators of anxiety about which we intend to act, either preventively or proactively, through information for an individual's awareness and self-regulation.

Keywords: internet of things (IoT); quality of life; happiness; anxiety; wellbeing

1. Introduction

The purpose of the present study is to provide an online Platform based on the Internet of Things (IoT) concept, which allows to collect, structure and relate a diverse set of data that influences and affects personal mental health conditions. Several sets of events in the global ecosystem generate anxiety, distress and mood disorders; from diverse causes such as individual, social, professional, behavioral, ethical, environmental, among others, with levels of importance relative to each person.

The result of this information aims to generate for an awareness that allows to contribute to the process of cognitive self-regulation, which is, in the first instance, the control vehicle of anxiety for a better mental health and wellbeing of the individual. Improving dynamic self-regulation may be a potential therapeutic method for treating the neurological symptoms of patients with anxiety (Guo Z. et al., 2018) [1].

The holistically structured data are processed in algorithms in order to generate information on a set of health and disease conditions. Such information allows recommendations and forecasts of health states, which contribute to the awareness of the actors.

2. Solution Description

Cognitive-behavioral therapies are techniques recommended by the scientific community (Kropotov J., 2009) [2], and described as treatment in specialized organizations, such as APA [3] and Medical News Today (Felman A., 2018) [4]. In addition, research initiatives with cognitive-behavioral therapies based on the Internet, demonstrate efficacy in the results with significant improvements (Hedman et al., 2011) [5] & (Owens V. et al., 2019) [6].

To achieve this goal, we propose an IoT Platform, with the existing and emerging technological resources for the Internet of Things. The potential of this system allows collecting data from a universe of "things", with a huge amount of information, in permanent growth and that is related multilaterally, analyzed and processed in real time, and finally, securely.

New trends and challenges with Industry 4.0 promote the production of systems, devices, objects and "things" integrated with Wireless Sensor Network (WSN), which benefit from IoT protocols and their heterogeneity. Increasingly, electronic devices integrate APIs—Application Programming Interfaces—with attributes for interoperability and portability between systems. The APIs are the window for the new ecosystem (Iyer B. & Subramaniam M., 2015) [7] and the best way for data to be shared as a service ("Standards for APIs", 2018) [8] in which they stimulate the emergence of innovative groups that, without being clinical, create value tools (Huckman R. & Upallaru M., 2015) [9].

The dynamic IoT ecosystem enables the collection, mapping or processing and distribution of information from a universe of existing data on devices, sensors, software, online services and app's through api's or sdk's and other existing artifacts. These raw data, properly organized and intelligently processed, report the states of health, tension, anxiety, mood, and well-being states of the individual person.

In order to obtain and process these diverse data volumes with an exponential growth, we intend to use a flow-based programming tool for the Internet of Things (IoT), called Node-Red (Figure 1), which supports the features of the IBM Watson Cloud IoT Platform. Node-Red, developed by IBM, allows you to connect, process, and distribute data from diverse systems, devices, sensors, software, online services, messaging in a variety of ways, and execute instructions and functions a broad spectrum of automated, scalable implementations that deliver real-time results.

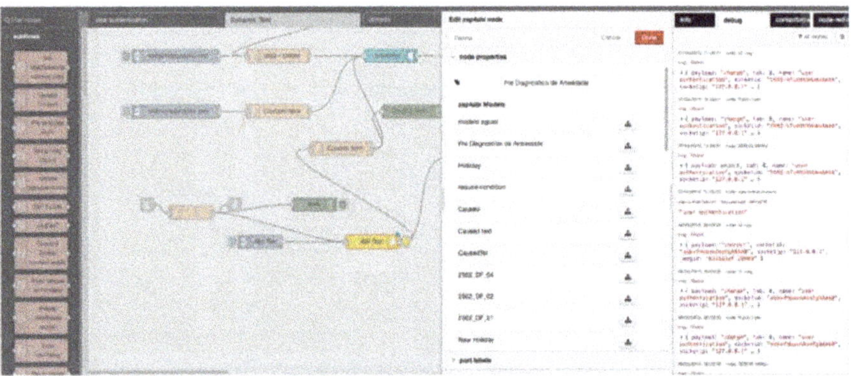

Figure 1. modeling in the Node-Red.

Regarding the proposed technology for the development of the IoT Platform, it is proposed to design in Node.JS [10], through the Node-Red framework [11], which ensures flexibility in allowing to deal with devices that communicate in different ways. Node-Red comes into this system with an API Master that consumes, collects and processes information from any type of data source: apps, web services, sensors, devices, artifacts and Node-Red itself.

In this research context involving multidisciplinary knowledge, with a technical and human dimension, with several possibilities of experimentation, a flow-based programming system such as Node-Red facilitates the interaction between the analyst, programming and the population that interacts with the system. This provide efficiency gains in the scientific progress of testing, trial and error elimination for validation. This condition enables designers and production specialists to be freed, to focus on creativity and innovation, to create new connections, new events and interactions with the "world of things".

The use of IBM Watson IoT Platform [12] will serve in the first phase for concept validation and testing of identified services. The AI (Artificial Intelligence) capabilities provided by the IBM-Watson cloud are certainly of high potential, high availability and security, being an excellent infrastructure for hosting and managing this research project.

3. Conclusions

The great contribution of this research project does not end with the fulfillment of this work plan. Once completed, it will be an important contribute to the continuous advancement between an artificial intelligence relationship with human and emotional intelligence. However, it will be the beginning of a system, potentially open to the environment, with potential of scale horizontally or vertically, with global diffusion, with instruments and functionalities for the integration of new concepts, new scientific production, researchers and specialists.

References

1. Guo, Z.N.; Lv, S.; Liu, J.; Wang, Z.; Jin, H.; Qiu, Q.; Sun, X.; Yang, Y. Compromised dynamic cerebral autoregulation in patients with generalized anxiety disorder: a study using transfer function analysis. *BMC Psychiatry* **2018**, *18*, 164.
2. Kropotov, J.; Quantitative, E.E.G. *Event-Related Potentials and Neurotherapy*, 1st ed.; Elsevier: London, UK, 2019; p. 559.
3. APA, Anxiety and Sadness May Increase on Anniversary of a Traumatic Event. Available online: https://www.apa.org/helpcenter/anniversary (accessed on 25 March 2019).
4. MedicalNewsToday. What to Know about Anxiety. Medical News Today. Available online: https://www.medicalnewstoday.com/articles/323454.php (accessed on 26 March 2019).
5. Hedman, E.; Andersson, G.; Andersson, E.; Ljótsson, B.; Rück, C.; Gordon, J.; Asmundson, G.; Lindefors, N. Internet-based cognitive–behavioural therapy for severe health anxiety: randomised controlled trial. *Br. J. Psychiatry* **2011**, *198*, 230–236.
6. Owens, V.; Hadjistavropoulos, H.; Schneider, L.; Gullickson, K.; Karin, E.; Titov, N.; Dear, B. Transdiagnostic, internet-delivered cognitive behavior therapy for depression and anxiety: Exploring impact on health anxiety. *Internet Intervent.* **2019**, *15*, 60–66, doi:10.1016/j.invent.2019.01.001
7. Iyer, B.; Subramaniam, M. The Strategic Value of APIs, *Harvard Business Review,* **2015**. Available online: https://hbr.org/2015/01/the-strategic-value-of-apis (accessed on 26 March 2019).
8. The Standards for Apis. Promoting the use of Best Practices and Setting Standards for APIs. Available online: http://www.standardsforapis.org/ (accessed on 27 March 2019).
9. Huckman, R.S.; Uppaluru, M. The Untapped Potential of Health Care APIs, *Harvard Business Review,* **2015,** Available online: https://hbr.org/2015/12/the-untapped-potential-of-health-care-apis (accessed on 27 march 2019)
10. Node-RED. Flow-Based Programming for the Internet of Things. Available online: https://nodered.org/ (accessed on 24 March 2019).
11. IBM Watson Plattaform. Available online: https://www.ibm.com/internet-of-things/solutions/iot-platform/watson-iot-platform (accessed on 24 March 2019).

Proceedings

Fast Algorithm for Impact Point Selection in Semiparametric Functional Models [†]

Silvia Novo [1,*] , **Germán Aneiros** [1] and **Philippe Vieu** [2]

1   MODES Research Group, CITIC, Universidade da Coruña, 15071 A Coruña, Spain
2   Institut de Mathématiques, Université Paul Sabatier, 31062 Toulouse, France
*   Correspondence: s.novo@udc.es; Tel.: +34-981-167-000-1301
†   Presented at the 2nd XoveTIC Conference, A Coruña, Spain, 5–6 September 2019.

Published: 31 July 2019

Abstract: A new sparse semiparametric functional model is proposed, which tries to incorporate the influence of two functional variables in a scalar response in a quite simple and interpretable way. One of the functional variables is included trough a single-index structure and the other one linearly, but trough the high-dimensional vector of its discretized observations. For this model, a new algorithm for impact point selection in the linear part and for the model estimation is proposed. This procedure is based on the functional origin of the linear covariates. Some asymptotic results will ensure the good performance of the method. The computational efficiency of the algorithm, without loss of predictive power, will be showed trough a simulation study and a real data application, by comparing its results with those obtained trough the standard PLS method.

Keywords: functional data analysis; multi-functional covariates; dimension reduction; variable selection; functional single-index model; semiparametric model

---

1. Introduction

In the BIG data era, it is more and more frequent having observations of variables measured in a continuous support (data are curves, images). This informative richness provided by the functional variables makes very usual found them in regression problems. In many situations, we have a scalar variable of interest and we want to know which points of a functional variable are the most influential (points of impact) on this scalar variable (see [1]). The problem is that the functional variables usually are observed in many points and standard variable selection methods in the multidimensional context can provide inadequate results. On the one hand, these procedures are affected by the dependence between observations, which in this case is directly derived from its functional origin. On the other hand, the great quantity of observations makes difficult obtaining results in reasonable amount of time.

In this work, we are going to focus on a regression model with scalar response which incorporates the influence of two functional variables: one of them is included trough a single-index type structure (see for details [2,3]) and the other one, linearly, but trough a high-dimensional vector formed by its discretized observations (see [1,4] for details and motivation of this structure). In this way we obtain a very flexible model, which combines interpretable estimations with dimension reduction. For this model, the so-called Multi-functional Partial Linear Single-Index Model (MFPLSIM), we work in the framework where we have a very big number of linear covariates but only a few of them have a real influence in the response (sparse context). Accordingly, we are going to develop an efficient algorithm for impact point selection in the linear part and for the estimation of the model (the Fast Algorithm for Sparse Semiparametric Multifunctional Regression- FASSMR), which takes advantage of the functional origin of these scalar variables included in the linear part. The good practical behaviour of the proposed methodology will be showed trough a simulation study and a real data application. In both cases, we will show its computational efficiency, without loss of predictive power, by comparing its results with the standard PLS procedure. Furthermore, some asymptotic results will support theoretically the FASSMR.

2. The Model

The MFPLSIM is defined by the relationship

$$Y = \sum_{j=1}^{p_n} \beta_{0j} \zeta(t_j) + m\left(\langle \theta_0, \mathcal{X} \rangle\right) + \varepsilon, \tag{1}$$

where Y is a real random response, $\mathcal{X}$ denote a random curve defined on some Hilbert space $\mathcal{H}$ with inner product $\langle \cdot, \cdot \rangle$ and ζ denote another random curve defined on some interval $[c, d]$. The curve ζ is observed in the points $c \leq t_1 < \cdots < t_{p_n} \leq d$ and denote by $\zeta(t_j)$, $j = 1, \ldots, p_n$, its discretized observations; $(\beta_{01}, \ldots, \beta_{0p_n})^{\top}$ is a vector of unknown coefficients, m is an unknown link function and θ_0 denotes an unknown curve in $\mathcal{H}$. Finally, ε is the random error, which verifies $\mathbb{E}\left(\varepsilon | \zeta(t_1), \ldots, \zeta(t_{p_n}), \mathcal{X}\right) = 0$. In model (1), we assume that only a few points of the curve ζ have an effect on the response Y. Then, we denote $S_n = \{j = 1, \ldots, p_n, \quad \text{such that } \beta_{0j} \neq 0\}$, and it is verified that $\sharp S_n = s_n = o(p_n)$.

3. The FASSMR

Our procedure is based on the fact that the variables $\zeta(t_j)$, $j = 1, \ldots, p_n$, come from the discretization of the functional variable ζ. Then, when t_j is close from t_k, the two corresponding variables $\zeta(t_j)$ and $\zeta(t_k)$ roughly contain the same information on the response. As consequence, some variables can be discarded before applying the variable selection procedure.

For presenting the FASSMR, let us assume that we have a statistical sample of size n, $\{(\zeta_i, \mathcal{X}_i, Y_i), \quad i = 1, \ldots, n\}$ i.i.d. as $(\zeta, \mathcal{X}, Y)$. We will consider, without lost of generality, that p_n can be factorized in the following way: $p_n = q_n w_n$ with q_n and w_n integers. The previous considerations allow us present the following set of variables

$$\mathcal{R}_n^1 = \{\zeta(t_k^1) = \zeta(t_{[(2k-1)q_n/2]}), \quad k = 1, \ldots, w_n\},$$

where $[z]$ denotes the smallest integer not less than $z \in \mathbb{R}$. Note that the correlation between consecutive variables inside of $\mathcal{R}_n^1$ is much less important than in the whole set of p_n initial linear covariates. As consequence, the variable selection procedure will be carried out in variables belonging to $\mathcal{R}_n^1$. In other words, we will considerer the following model with only w_n linear covariates

$$Y_i = \sum_{k=1}^{w_n} \beta_{0k}^1 \zeta_i(t_k^1) + m^1\left(\left\langle \theta_0^1, \mathcal{X}_i \right\rangle\right) + \varepsilon_i^1. \tag{2}$$

Then, variable selection task can be developed following the standard procedure described in [5] and detailed in [6], which is based on transforming the model (2) into a linear one and applying the PLS procedure. We denote by $(\widehat{\beta}_0^1, \widehat{\theta}_0^1)$, the estimation of the parameters of model (2) where $\widehat{\beta}_0^1 = (\widehat{\beta}_{01}^1, \ldots, \widehat{\beta}_{0w_n}^1)^{\top}$. Then, $\zeta(t_k^1)$ is selected in $\mathcal{R}_n^1$ if and only if $\widehat{\beta}_{0k}^1 \neq 0$.

Considering the whole set of initial of p_n linear covariates, that is, returning to model (1), a variable $\zeta(t_j) \in \{\zeta(t_1), \ldots, \zeta(t_{p_n})\}$ is selected if and only if it belongs to $\mathcal{R}_n^1$ and its estimated coefficient, which can be denoted by $\widehat{\beta}_{0k_j}^1$, is non null. Then, $\widehat{S}_n = \{j = 1, \ldots, p_n, \quad \text{such that } \zeta(t_j) = \zeta(t_{k_j}^1) \in \mathcal{R}_n^1$ and $\widehat{\beta}_{0k_j}^1 \neq 0\}$ and $\widehat{\beta}_{0j} = \widehat{\beta}_{0k_j}^1$ if $j \in \widehat{S}_n$ and $\widehat{\beta}_{0j} = 0$ otherwise. Finally, $\widehat{\theta}_0 = \theta_0^1$ and an estimator of the function $m_{\theta_0}(\cdot) \equiv m(\langle \theta_0, \chi \rangle)$, denoted by $\widehat{m}_{\widehat{\theta}_0}(\chi)$, can be obtained by smoothing the residuals from the parametric fit (see Appendix A).

4. Theory, Simulation and Real Data Application Conclusions

The good behaviour of the proposed algorithm will be ensured theoretically. Furthermore, from the simulation study it can be seen that the FASSMR allows us to obtain the variable selection and estimation of model (1) in a reasonable amount of time, even for very big values of p_n. As will be derived from the simulation study, the developed algorithm clearly overpasses standard PLS procedure in terms of computational time without loss in prediction power. A real data application will also illustrate the flexibility and applicability of model (1) together with the FASSMR estimation.

Funding: The authors acknowledge partial support by MINECO grants MTM2014-52876-R and MTM2017-82724-R (EU ERDF support included). Additionally, financial support from the Xunta de Galicia (Centro Singular de Investigación de Galicia accreditation ED431G/01 2016-2019 and Grupos de Referencia Competitiva ED431C2016-015) and the European Union (European Regional Development Fund—ERDF), is gratefully acknowledged. The first author also thanks the financial support from the Xunta de Galicia and the European Union (European Social Fund—ESF), the reference of which is ED481A-2018/191.

Conflicts of Interest: The authors declare no conflict of interest. The founding sponsors had no role in the design of the study; in the collection, analyses, or interpretation of data; in the writing of the manuscript, and in the decision to publish the results.

Abbreviations

The following abbreviations are used in this manuscript:

FASSMR	Fast Algorithm for Sparse Semiparametric Multi-functional Regression
i.i.d.	Independent and identically distributed
MFPLSIM	Multi-functional Partial Linear Single-Index Model
PLS	Penalized Least Squares

Appendix A

Denoting by $\widehat{\beta}_0$ the vector of estimated parameters,

$$\widehat{m}_{\widehat{\theta}_0}(\chi) \equiv \widehat{m}\left(\left\langle \widehat{\theta}_0, \chi \right\rangle\right) = \frac{\sum_{i=1}^{n}\left(Y_i - \zeta_i^{\top}\widehat{\beta}_0\right) K\left(d_{\widehat{\theta}_0}\left(\chi, \mathcal{X}_i\right)/h\right)}{\sum_{i=1}^{n} K\left(d_{\widehat{\theta}_0}\left(\chi, \mathcal{X}_i\right)/h\right)},$$

where we have denoted $\zeta_i = \left(\zeta_i(t_1), \ldots, \zeta_i(t_{p_n})\right)^{\top}$, $h > 0$ is a bandwidth, K is a kernel and, for any $\theta \in \mathcal{H}$, $d_{\theta}(\cdot, \cdot)$ is the semimetric defined as $d_{\theta}(\chi, \chi') = |\langle \theta, \chi - \chi' \rangle|$ for each $\chi, \chi' \in \mathcal{H}$.

References

1. Aneiros, G.; Vieu, P. Variable selection in infinite-dimensional problems. *Stat. Probab. Lett.* **2014**, *94*, 12–20.
2. Ait-Saïdi, A.; Ferraty, F.; Kassa, R.; Vieu, P. Cross-Validated Estimations in the Single-Functional Index Model. *Statistics* **2008**, *42*, 475–494.
3. Novo, S.; Aneiros, G.; Vieu, P. Automatic and location-adaptive estimation in functional single-index regression. *J. Nonparametric Stat.* **2019**, *31*, 364–392.
4. Aneiros, G.; Vieu, P. Partial linear modelling with multi-functional covariates. *Comput. Stat.* **2015**, *30*, 647–671.
5. Novo, S.; Aneiros, G.; Vieu, P. Sparse Semi-Functional Partial Linear Single-Index Regression. *Proceedings* **2018**, *2*, 1190.
6. Novo, S.; Aneiros, G.; Vieu, P. Sparse semiparametric regression when predictors are mixture of functional and high-dimensional variables. preprint.

 *proceedings*

Proceedings

Prediction of Peptide Vascularization Inhibitory Activity in Tumor Tissue as a Possible Target for Cancer Treatment [†]

Jose Liñares-Blanco [iD] and Carlos Fernandez-Lozano *[iD]

Department of Computer Science, Faculty of Computer Science, University of A Coruña, CITIC, A Coruña 15071, Spain; j.linares@udc.es
* Correspondence: carlos.fernandez@udc.es; Tel.: +34-881-01-6013
† Presented at the 2nd XoveTIC conference, A Coruña, 5–6 September 2019.

Published: 31 July 2019

Abstract: The prediction of metabolic activities in silico form is crucial to be able to address all research possibilities without exceeding the experimental costs. In particular, for cancer research, the prediction of certain activities can be of great help in the discovery of different treatments. In this work it has been proposed to predict, through Machine Learning, the anti-angiogenic activity of peptides is currently being used in cancer treatment and is giving hopeful results. From a list of peptide sequences, three types of molecular descriptors were obtained (AAC, DC and TC) that offered the possibility of training different ML algorithms. After a Feature Selection process, different models were obtained with a predictive value that surpassed the current state of the art. These results shown that ML is useful for the classification and prediction of the activity of new peptides, making experimental screening cheaper and faster.

Dataset: https://doi.org/10.6084/m9.figshare.6016994

Dataset License: CC0

Keywords: machine learning; feature selection; activity prediction; peptides; cancer; screening

---

1. Introduction

The prediction of metabolic activities in-silico is crucial to address all research possibilities without exceeding the experimental costs. Specifically, in cancer research, there are endless opportunities that may be tested for possible treatment. Among them, one method that is having hopeful results in this field is tumor treatment with anti-angiogenic peptides. Attacking the tumor by destabilizing its micro-environment is crucial to prevent its development. The vast majority of treatments of this type are based on peptides, mainly due to their low toxicity and design possibilities.

Being able to predict the anti-angiogenic activity of these peptides from their amino acid sequence opens the doors to the discovery of new natural peptides or designed in the laboratory with this activity. In this sense, experimental researchers would be able to carry out a previous filter at the time of experimentally validating the treatments and focus only on those that had a previous significance, by means of in-silico techniques.

In this work, Machine Learning techniques were able to predict with high precision if a peptide has anti-angiogenic activity, only from its amino acid sequence. Our work was published before in detail as open access in the Scientific Reports journal [1]. The list of sequences was obtained from the article [2].

2. Results

Previous studies shown that peptides with anti-angiogenic activity have a common structure, presenting mostly folds of beta anti-parallel sheets, with a high incidence of hydrophobic and cationic residues. On the other hand, the composition of these peptides is not fully defined, although it has been observed that these peptides are more prone to present certain amino acid residues in their sequences.

2.1. Baseline Algorithms without Feature Selection

Firstly, a comparative experiment was carried out under the same conditions in order to observe which dataset-algorithm pair achieves the best performance. Four algorithms (SVM [3], RF [4], Glmnet [5] and k-NN [6]) were trained with the three descriptors (AAC, DC and TC) [7] and the union of AAC-DC and AAC-TC. The results obtained in this phase of the experiment do not improve those reported in the literature (0.809 in Accuracy) [2], but they do indicate a certain trend in the data.

2.2. Feature Selection

We ranked the features accordiing with their p-values after performing a Kruskal test of each variable with the dependent variable (Anti-angiogenic and Non Anti-angiogenic). We explored the size of different subgroups, (5, 10 and 15) for AAC, (25, 50, 75, 100) for DC, (75, 100, 125, 150) for TC and (50, 100, 150, 200) for the combination of the three datasets.

In this case, several models exceed the values marked in the literature (red line), all of them with RF and Glmnet algorithms. The best performance was achieved with the Glmnet algorithm trained with the dataset of the union of the three descriptors, using the 200 most significant variables after the action of the statistical test. Furthermore, as can be seen in Figure 1b,d, all the models show great stability, which indicates that they have obtained homogeneous results in all the repetitions.

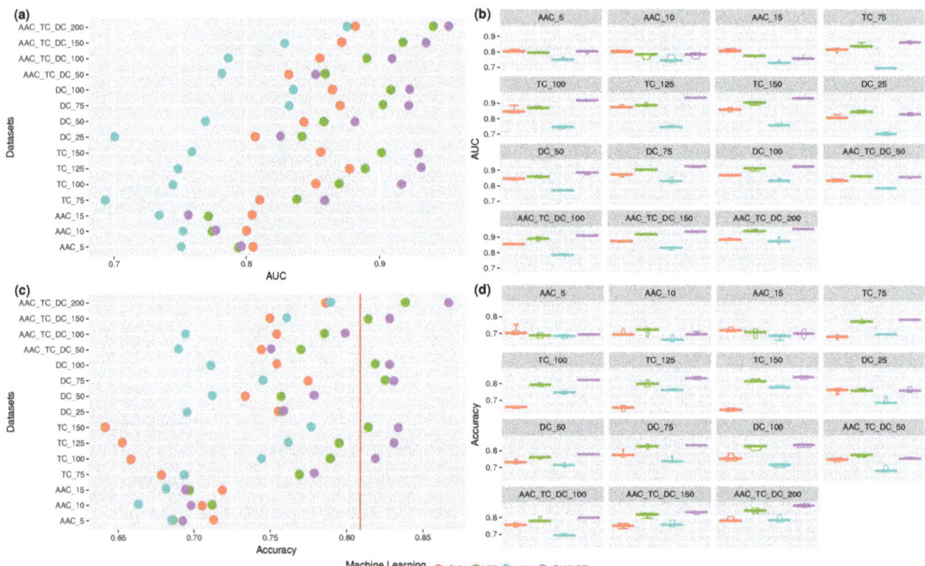

Figure 1. Results obtained in the feature selection process. (**a**) Performance using AUC, (**b**) boxplot using AUC, (**c**) performance using accuracy, and (**d**) boxplot using accuracy. Best previously published value in the literature by Ramaprasad et al. [2] (red line).

3. Discussion

The results obtained in this work reflect the importance of the use of new data analysis technologies to support experimental research. This work reports a set of models that have surpassed previous state of the art models for this type of problem (p-value $= 1.8665 \times 10^{-9}$). A high proportion of amino acids within the sequence such as Alanine, Valine and Cysteine are important for classifying peptides. In addition, it is observed in the higher positions, as di-peptide sequences (SP, VD, ID and CK) and tripeptides (LSL, DIT and PDL) provide significant information to this model.

4. Materials and Methods

Machine Learning Models

The following algorithms were implemented: Support Vector Machines (SVM) [3], Random Forest (RF) [4], k-Nearest Neighbors (k-NN) [6] and Generalized linear model (Glmnet) [5]. A Nested Cross Validation was used for training the models. In other words, there were two validation phases. Firstly, a holdout was used for the selection of the best hyperparameters (2/3 for training and 1/3 for testing) and secondly, a 10-fold CV was used for the validation of the model (we ran 5 times this CV process).

Author Contributions: Conceptualization, C.F.-L.; methodology, C.F.-L.; software, J.L.B. and C.F.-L.; formal analysis, J.L.B. and C.F.-L.; Writing—Original Draft preparation, J.L.B.; Writing—Review and Editing, J.L.B. and C.F.-L.; supervision, C.F-L.

Funding: This research received no external funding.

Acknowledgments: This work is supported by the "Collaborative Project in Genomic Data Integration (CICLOGEN)" PI17/01826 funded by the Carlos III Health Institute from the Spanish National plan for Scientific and Technical Research and Innovation 2013–2016 and the European Regional Development Funds (FEDER)—"A way to build Europe". This project was also supported by the General Directorate of Culture, Education and University Management of Xunta de Galicia (Ref. ED431G/01, ED431D 2017/16), the "Galician Network for Colorectal Cancer Research" (Ref. ED431D 2017/23), and the Spanish Ministry of Economy and Competitiveness via funding of the unique installation BIOCAI (UNLC08-1E-002, UNLC13-13-3503) and the European Regional Development Funds (FEDER) by the European Union and the "Juan de la Cierva" fellowship program supported by the Spanish Ministry of Economy and Competitiveness (Carlos Fernandez-Lozano, Ref. FJCI- 2015-26071).

Conflicts of Interest: The authors declare no conflict of interest.

References

1. Liñares Blanco, J.; Porto-Pazos, A.B.; Pazos, A.; Fernandez-Lozano, C. Prediction of high anti-angiogenic activity peptides in silico using a generalized linear model and feature selection. *Sci. Rep.* **2018**, *8*, 1–11.
2. Ramaprasad, A.S.E.; Singh, S.; Venkatesan, S. AntiAngioPred: a server for prediction of anti-angiogenic peptides. *PLoS ONE* **2015**, *10*, e0136990.
3. Cortes, C.; Vapnik, V. Support-vector networks. *Mach. Learn.* **1995**, *20*, 273–297.
4. Breiman, L. Random forests. *Mach. Learn.* **2001**, *45*, 5–32.
5. Friedman, J.; Hastie, T.; Tibshirani, R. Regularization paths for generalized linear models via coordinate descent. *J. Stat. Softw.* **2010**, *33*, 1.
6. Cover, T.M.; Hart, P. Nearest neighbor pattern classification. *IEEE Trans. Inf. Theory* **1967**, *13*, 21–27.
7. Bhasin, M.; Raghava, G.P. Classification of nuclear receptors based on amino acid composition and dipeptide composition. *J. Biol. Chem.* **2004**, *279*, 23262–23266.

 *proceedings*

Proceedings

Automatic Identification of Diabetic Macular Edema Using a Transfer Learning-Based Approach [†]

Joaquim de Moura [1,2,*], Plácido L. Vidal [1,2], Jorge Novo [1,2] and Marcos Ortega [1,2]

1   Department of Computing, University of A Coruña, 15071 A Coruña, Spain
2   CITIC—Research Center of Information and Communication Technologies, University of A Coruña, 15071 A Coruña, Spain
*   Correspondence: joaquim.demoura@udc.es; Tel.: +34-981-167-000 (ext. 1330)
†   Presented at the 2nd XoveTIC Conference, A Coruña, Spain, 5–6 September 2019.

Published: 31 July 2019

Abstract: This paper presents a complete system for the automatic identification of pathological Diabetic Macular Edema (DME) cases using Optical Coherence Tomography (OCT) images as source of information. To do so, the system extracts a set of deep features using a transfer learning-based approach from different fully-connected layers and different pre-trained Convolutional Neural Network (CNN) models. Next, the most relevant subset of deep features is identified using representative feature selection methods. Finally, a machine learning strategy is applied to train and test the potential of the identified deep features in the pathological classification process. Satisfactory results were obtained, demonstrating the suitability of the presented system to filter those pathological DME cases, helping the specialist to optimize their diagnostic procedures.

Keywords: Computer-Aided Diagnosis; Optical Coherence Tomography; Diabetic Macular Edema; Convolutional Neural Network

1. Introduction

Diabetic Macular Edema (DME) is one of the most prevalent causes of visual loss and blindness in industrialized countries, representing a concerning public health problem. Optical Coherence Tomography (OCT) is a non-invasive diagnostic technique that provides a high-resolution cross-sectional view of the retina, being commonly used for the diagnosis, monitoring and treatment of the DME disease [1,2]. In this way, a precise and automatic classification of OCT scans between normal or pathological DME cases allows the clinical specialists to make a more accurate diagnosis and treatment of this relevant ocular disease. Figure 1 shows representative examples of OCT scans with and without the presence of DME where we can observe a considerable level of deterioration of the main retinal tissues and the consequent thickening of the retina.

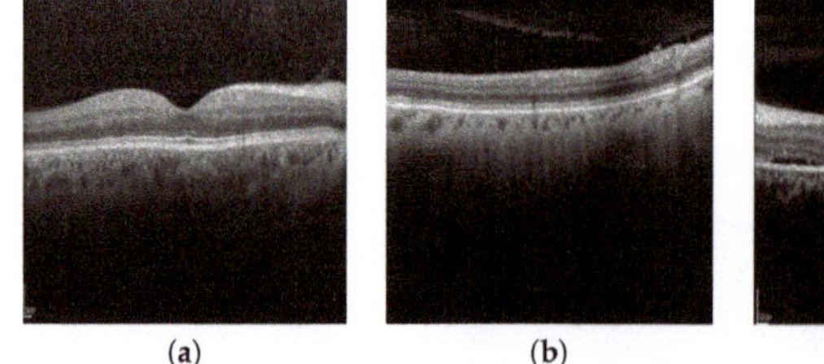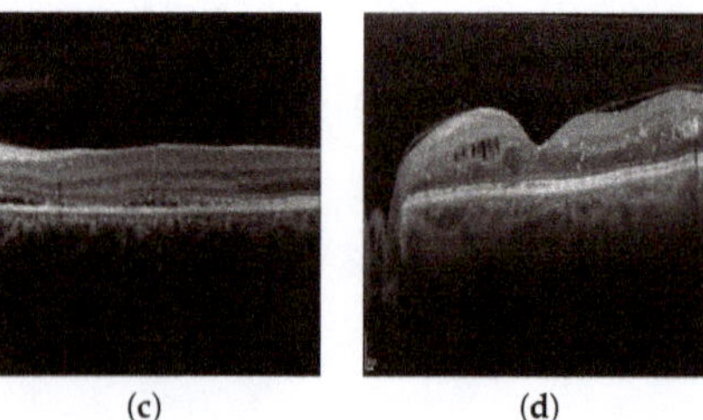

(a)   (b)   (c)   (d)

Figure 1. Representative examples of OCT scans. (a,b) OCT scans without the presence of DME. (c,d) OCT scans with the presence of DME.

2. Methodology

The presented methodology receives, as input, a set of cross-sectional OCT scans centered in the macular region of the retina. As illustrated in Figure 2, the designed pipeline is composed by 3 main stages. Firstly, the method extracts a set of deep features from the OCT scans using a transfer learning-based approach from different fully-connected layers and different pre-trained Convolutional Neural Network (CNN) models [3]. Then, the method identifies the most relevant subset of deep features using different feature selection approaches. Then, a machine learning strategy is applied to generate a classification model. Finally, the method presents, as output, a labelled OCT image with the classification between normal or pathological DME cases.

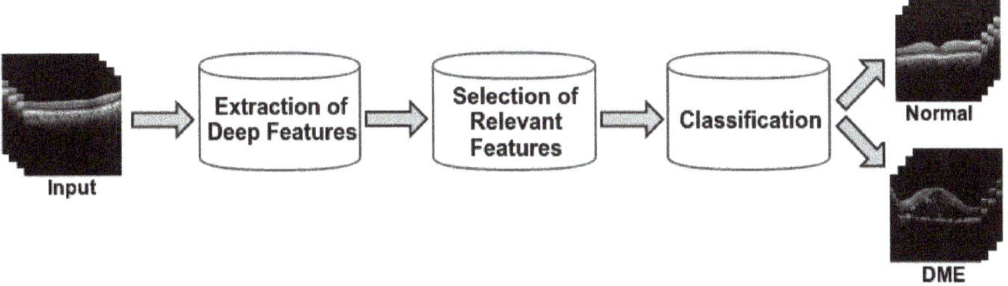

Figure 2. Main structure of the proposed methodology.

3. Results and Conclusions

In this paper, we propose a complete methodology for the automatic identification of pathological DME cases using the OCT images as source of information. Satisfactory results were obtained, demonstrating the suitability of the presented system and consequently helping the clinical specialists in their diagnostic procedures, reducing healthcare costs and improving the quality of life of patients with diabetes.

Author Contributions: J.d.M., P.L.V. and J.N. contributed to the analysis and design of the computer methods and the experimental evaluation methods. J.N. and M.O. contributed with domain-specific knowledge. All the authors performed the result analysis. J.d.M. was in charge of writing the manuscript, and all the authors participated in its critical revision and final approval.

Funding: This work is supported by the Instituto de Salud Carlos III, Government of Spain and FEDER funds through the DTS18/00136 research project and by Ministerio de Ciencia, Innovación y Universidades, Government of Spain through the DPI2015-69948-R and RTI2018-095894-B-I00 research projects. Also, this work has received financial support from the European Union (European Regional Development Fund—ERDF) and the Xunta de Galicia, Centro singular de investigación de Galicia accreditation 2016–2019, Ref. ED431G/01; and Grupos de Referencia Competitiva, Ref. ED431C 2016-047.

Conflicts of Interest: The authors declare no conflict of interest.

References

1. Samagaio, G.; Estévez, A.; de Moura, J.; Novo, J.; Fernández, M.; Ortega, M.; Automatic macular edema identification and characterization using OCT images. *Comput. Methods Programs Biomed.* **2018**, *163*, 47–63.
2. Vidal, P.L.; de Moura, J.; Novo, J.; Penedo, M.G.; Ortega, M. Intraretinal fluid identification via enhanced maps using Optical Coherence Tomography images. *Biomed. Opt. Express* **2018**, *9*, 4730–4754.
3. De Moura, J.; Novo, J.; Ortega, M. Deep Feature Analysis in a Transfer Learning-based Approach for the Automatic Identification of Diabetic Macular Edema. In Proceedings of the 2019 International Joint Conference on Neural Networks (IJCNN), Budapest, Hungary, 14–19 July 2019; pp. 1–8.

 *proceedings*

Proceedings

Efficient PRNU Matching in the Encrypted Domain [†]

Alberto Pedrouzo-Ulloa [1,*], Miguel Masciopinto [1], Juan Ramón Troncoso-Pastoriza [2] and Fernando Pérez-González [1]

[1] Theory and Communications Department, University of Vigo,36310 Vigo, Spain
[2] École Polytechnique Fédérale de Lausanne, School of Computer and Communication Sciences, CH-1015 Lausanne, Switzerland
* Correspondence: apedrouzo@gts.uvigo.es
[†] Presented at the 2nd XoveTIC, A Coruña, Spain, 5–6 September 2019.

Published: 31 July 2019

Abstract: Photoresponse Non-Uniformity (PRNU) is becoming particularly relevant within digital media forensics, as a means to effectively determine the source camera of a given image. Most of the practical applications in digital media forensics involve dealing with highly sensitive data whose content must be protected. In this context, several secure frameworks have been proposed to perform PRNU-based camera attribution while preserving the privacy of both the testing images and the PRNU fingerprint. The two most recent and relevant ones, independently proposed in 2018, are (a) Mohanty et al.'s, who combine the use of a trusted environment (ARM TrustZone) to compute the PRNU fingerprint, with the Boneh-Goh-Nissim (BGN) cryptosystem to perform the matching, and (b) Pedrouzo-Ulloa et al.'s, who propose a more flexible solution which can be fully implemented on a general purpose architecture and does not require access to a trusted environment. In this work, we revisit the existing frameworks and propose a general formulation for PRNU matching based on lattice cryptosystems which improves on the BGN-based solution in terms of efficiency, flexibility and privacy.

Keywords: Photoresponse Non-Uniformity; lattice-based cryptosystems; digital media forensics; camera attribution forensic analyzer

---

1. Introduction

Photoresponse Non-Uniformity (PRNU) is a specific noise pattern inherent to digital imaging sensors [1]. It is becoming especially relevant in digital media forensics as, due to its random nature, can be used as a fingerprint of the underlying device.

In particular, PRNU has a great protential within image forensics, as it can help to determine whether a given image was taken by a certain camera [2]. Actually, several commercial applications are already able to identify acquisition devices, but they present two apparently contradictory needs:

- *High Computational Demands:* Outsourcing is an appealing solution for digital media forencis because the involved operations are computationally intensive and they must also deal with very large databases.
- *Privacy issues:* Forensic data is especially privacy-sensitive and it must be protected when outsourced. Actually, not only while outsourced, but it should be protected even when it is inside our own infrastructure to prevent non-authorized parties from accessing the content.

In view of the above restrictions, several works have proposed solutions for the secure evaluation of PRNU-based camera attribution [3–5]: (1) In [3,4], Mohanty et al. combine the use of a trusted environment (ARM TrustZone) to compute the PRNU fingerprint, and the Boneh-Goh-Nissim (BGN) cryptosystem to perform the matching. (2) In [5], we proposed a more general formulation based on lattice cryptosystems. On the contrary to the previous method, our solution can be fully implemented on a general purpose arquitecture, and does not need to have access to a trusted environment because the involved images are encrypted along the whole computing chain.

Structure and Objectives: Our main objective in this work is to provide a brief overview of the existing secure schemes for PRNU-based camera attribution. With this in mind, we revisit the existing schemes and showcase how lattice-based cryptosystems are more convenient to perform the PRNU matching, improving the BGN-based solution in terms of efficiency, flexibility and privacy.

The structure is as follows: Section 2 describes the high-level structure of the two main existing secure approaches. Finally, Section 3 includes a discussion regarding the convenience of lattice-based cryptosystems for the case of PRNU matching, highlighting the flexibility of our solution.

2. Main Approaches

This section includes a high-level description of the two main methods for secure PRNU-based camera attribution: (a) Mohanty et al.'s scheme [3,4], and (b) our fully unattended solution from [5].

2.1. Previous Methods

In [3,4], Mohanty et al. describe their solution to securely compute the PRNU extraction/detection. It is composed of two main blocks:

- The Wavelet-based denoising is computed in a trusted environment (ARM TrustZone).
- The correlation test is homomorphically evaluated by means of the BGN cryptosystem.

The availability of a trusted environement enables to work very efficiently with the data in the clear. However, their use of the BGN cryptosystem introduces a high overhead (they report runtimes of 1.2 ms for the encryption of one number). To mitigate this effect, they resort to a fingerprint digest by removing some values of the fingerprint. This icreases the efficiency but also worsens the performance.

2.2. Our Fully Unattended Solution

In [5], we proposed a fully unattended solution, based on RLWE (Ring Learning with Errors) cryptosystems [6], which is able to homomorphically evaluate the PRNU extraction/detection without the need of the intervention of the secret key owner in the middle of the process. To this aim, we resort to the pre-/post processing introduced in [7] and the homomorphic Wavelet-denoising proposed in [8].

A complete diagram of our proposed scheme in [5] is included in Figure 1. The main challenge is the homomorphic evaluation of the threshold operation inside the denoising block. This threshold operation is implemented by the use of the "lowest digita removal" polynomials introduced in [9,10].

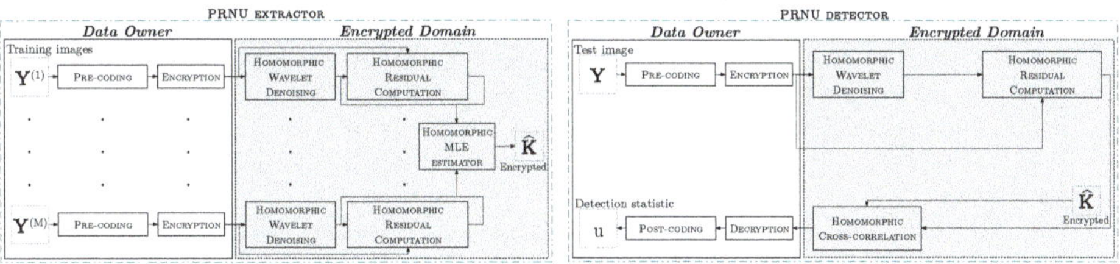

Figure 1. The secure PRNU extractor/detector proposed in [5].

We include some runtimes for the encrypted PRNU detection in Table 1. To obtain the given runtimes, images of size 2048 × 2048 and a PRNU of 16 Mpixels were considered.

The obtained results (see [5] for a much more detailed analysis) are promising as for all the conducted experiments, a True Acceptace Rate (TAR) of at least 95% was obtained for values of False Alarm Rate (FAR) above 0.5%.

Table 1. Performance of Encrypted PRNU detection (bit security > 128).

Parallelization	8	16
Encryption + Pre-coding (s)	3.6	
Decryption + Post-coding (ms)	27	
Encrypted Detection (min)	16.05	8.03

3. A Discussion: Efficient Encrypted Matching

This work reviews the existing methods in the literature for secure camera attribution based on PRNU. Even though the Mohanty et al.'s scheme is evaluating most of the computation in the clear, their runtimes do not outperform the runtimes obtained with our fully unattended proposed solution in [5]. This fact highlights the versatility of our scheme, which can be implemented in a more general arquitecture and does not need a trusted environment. Even so, if a trusted environement is available, we could make use of it to have important efficiency improvements on the scheme.

It is worth noting that the BGN scheme seems to add a high overhead in the Mohanty et al.'s solution. By making use of an RLWE-based cryptosystem combined with a pre-/post-coding [11], the correlation runtimes are improved, while also avoiding to have to discard values of the fingerprint.

Funding: This research was funded by the Agencia Estatal de Investigación (Spain) and the European Regional Development Fund (ERDF) under projects WINTER (TEC2016-76409-C2-2-R) and COMONSENS (TEC2015-69648-REDC). Also funded by the Xunta de Galicia and the European Union (European Regional Development Fund - ERDF) under projects Agrupación Estratéxica Consolidada de Galicia accreditation 2016-2019 and Grupo de Referencia ED431C2017/53, and also by the FPI grant (BES-2014-069018).

Conflicts of Interest: The authors declare no conflict of interest. The funders had no role in the design of the study; in the collection, analyses, or interpretation of data; in the writing of the manuscript, or in the decision to publish the results.

References

1. Holst, G.C. *CCD Arrays, Cameras, and Displays,* 2nd ed.; SPIE Optical Engineering Press: Bellingham, WA, USA, 1998.

2. Chen, M.; Fridrich, J.; Goljan, M.; Lukáš, J. Determining Image Origin and Integrity Using Sensor Noise. *IEEE Trans. Inf. Forensics Secur.* **2008**, *3*, 74–90.

3. Mohanty, M.; Zhang, M.; Asghar, M.R.; Russello, G. PANDORA: Preserving Privacy in PRNU-Based Source Camera Attribution. In Proceedings of the 2018 17th IEEE International Conference on Trust, Security and Privacy in Computing and Communications/12th IEEE International Conference on Big Data Science and Engineering (TrustCom/BigDataSE), New York, NY, USA, 1–3 August 2018; pp. 1202–1207.

4. Mohanty, M.; Zhang, M.; Asghar, M.R.; Russello, G. e-PRNU: Encrypted Domain PRNU-Based Camera Attribution for Preserving Privacy. *IEEE Trans. Dependable Secur. Comput.* **2019**, *1*, doi:10.1109/TDSC.2019.2892448.

5. Pedrouzo-Ulloa, A.; Masciopinto, M.; Troncoso-Pastoriza, J.R.; Pérez-González, F. Camera Attribution Forensic Analyzer in the Encrypted Domain. In Proceedings of the 2018 IEEE International Workshop on Information Forensics and Security (WIFS), Hong Kong, China, 1–13 December 2018; pp. 1–7.

6. Lyubashevsky, V.; Peikert, C.; Regev, O. On Ideal Lattices and Learning with Errors over Rings. *J. ACM* **2013**, *60*, 43:1–43:35.

7. Pedrouzo-Ulloa, A.; Troncoso-Pastoriza, J.R.; Pérez-González, F. Number Theoretic Transforms for Secure Signal Processing. *IEEE Trans. Inf. Forensics Secur.* **2017**, *12*, 1125–1140.

8. Pedrouzo-Ulloa, A.; Troncoso-Pastoriza, J.R.; Pérez-González, F. Image Denoising in the Encrypted Domain. In Proceedings of the WIFS 2016: 8th IEEE International Workshop on Information Forensics and Security (WIFS), Abu Dhabi, UAE, 4–7 December 2016; pp. 1–6.

9. Griffin, M. Lowest Degree of Polynomial That Removes the First Digit of an Integer in Base. Available online: https://mathoverflow.net/q/269282 (accessed on 12 July 2019).

10. Chen, H.; Han, K. Homomorphic Lower Digits Removal and Improved FHE Bootstrapping. In Proceedings of the 37th Annual International Conference on the Theory and Applications of Cryptographic Techniques (EUROCRYPT), Tel Aviv, Israel, 29 April–3 May 2018; pp. 315–337.
11. Pedrouzo-Ulloa, A.; Troncoso-Pastoriza, J.R.; Pérez-González, F. Revisiting Multivariate Lattices for Encrypted Signal Processing. In Proceedings of the 2018 ACM Conference on Economics and Computation, Ithaca, NY, USA, 18–22 June 2018; pp. 161–172.

Proceedings

Cyberphysical Network Applied to Fertigation Agricultural Processes [†]

Higor Vendramini Rosse [1,*,‡] and **João Paulo Coelho** [1,2,*,‡]

1   Instituto Politécnico de Bragança, Campus de Santa Apolónia, 5301-857 Bragança, Portugal
2   Centro de Investigação em Digitalização e Robótica Inteligente (CeDRI), Campus de Santa Apolónia, 5300-253 Bragança, Portugal
*   Correspondence: higorvendraminirosse@gmail.com (H.V.R.); jpcoelho@ipb.pt (J.P.C.)
†   Presented at the 2nd XoveTIC conference, A Coruña, 5–6 September 2019.
‡   These authors contributed equally to this work.

Published: 31 July 2019

Abstract: Fertigation is a widely used crop growing method that consists on the precise injection of a nutrient solution that commonly consists on a mixture of three basis components (nitrogen, phosphorus and potassium) diluted in water. This nutritive suspension is delivered to the plants with a frequency and relative basis contents that depends on the plant's type, its vegetative state and actual environmental conditions. This production process is becoming increasingly popular due to several advantages over more traditional approaches such as more control on the plant fertilisers and an increasing reduction of irrigation water. This is achieved by an increase complexity on the crop growing process management which requires a technological layer responsible for mixing the nutrients and monitoring the local environmental conditions. Despite this technical component, the short and long term management decisions depend almost exclusively on the grower's experience and intuition. This type of human-on-the-loop control can lead to a suboptimal use of resources wish can translate into reduction of economic profit and an can lead to waste of water and fertilisers. In this context, decision support mechanisms based on artificial intelligence and machine learning algorithms can be of extreme relevance in order to steer the grower decisions and increase the overall production process efficiency. The performance of those types of approaches strongly relies on the availability of data which can be both local and global. This work deals with the architecture of a sensor network which will be responsible to gather local information on the actual growing conditions. Those conditions are usually not homogeneous within the complete production plant and must be taken into consideration. In particular, the current architecture vision will consider those clusters, where the environmental conditions are similar, as cyberphysical devices. These devices will consist on vegetative production area, sensor networks and local control of irrigation state.

Keywords: agriculture; fertigation; cyberphysical devices; sensor network

---

1. Introduction

Fertigation is a cultivation technique that relies on the precise injection of the nutrient solution according to plant requirements, environmental and soil/substrate conditions. The use of fertigation systems has become popular as an alternative to more classical cultivation techniques. Indeed, more than 11 million hectares of area are associated with fertigation-based production schemes. This mark tends to increase due to the advantages promoted by this method, among which are the reduction of fertilisers, phytopharmaceuticals and water consumption. However, these advantages are achieved at the expense of rigorous monitoring of the nutrient solution, environmental conditions and vegetative state of the crop. Maintaining rigid management of these conditions is a difficult process due to several factors: first, the high area of cultivation normally at stake requires a large number of human resources to achieve the necessary monitoring accuracy and second, the information on the current crop state is taken on average, even if there is heterogeneity in the vegetative state of some plant clusters within the universe of the total production. For these reasons, complete automation of the irrigation process should be considered in order to characterise, in real-time, the actual state of the crops and promote the adjustment of nutrient according to fluctuations in environmental conditions and low frequency deviations due to vegetative evolution of the crop. Thus, it is proposed the incorporation of artificial intelligence and machine learning mechanisms merged with cyberphysical units as a way to create a decision support system.

This approach considers the fertigation crop growing system equivalent to an industrial production line where the raw material enters, a set of operations is performed and the final product is created. In this case, the mixture of fertigation, solar radiation and relevant environmental variables are the raw input material. The photosynthesis and other biological functions are compared to the operations performed and the vegetable matter generated the final output. Due to the similarity between common industrial processes and the production scheme based on fertigation, it makes sense to migrate some of the concepts presented in the Industrie 4.0 paradigm to this agricultural production reality. In particular, those that lead to an increase in robustness, adaptability, lean and waste reduction. Among other approaches, the use of decentralised agent-based control methods has proven to be an efficient solution in the management of complex industrial systems. Those agents will responsible to locally manage each cyberphisical cluster. Each cyberphysical elements is composed of areas of vegetative production, sensor networks and local control of the state of irrigation. In a typical fertigation production system, there will be a large number of cyberphysical elements that must be scaled up or down according to the production schedule. Notice that, although each cyberphysical element is considered to have local processing capacity, these will be vertices in an integrated system that will take place on a cloud computing platform (FIWIRE). This work deals with the cyberphisical element architecture which will be present in the next section.

2. The Cyberphysical Ecosystem

The full crop production area will be divided into cyberphysical elements. Each cyberphysical element will be composed by a set of neighbour crop growing lines that share common environmental conditions. A set of measurement nodes (MOTES) will be distributed along the growing stands gathering information on substrate moisture, air temperature, solar radiation, pH, electrical conductivity, nitrites and nitrates. Artificial vision is also being considered in order to estimate the vegetative state of the crop. But at this point, the sensor network only involves data from environmental and substrate conditions.The overall architecture of one of such cyberphysical elements is presented in Figure 1.

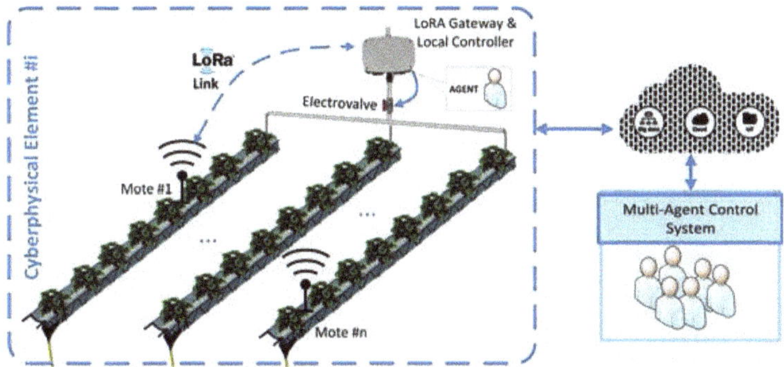

Figure 1. Schematic diagram of the cyberphysical fertigation element architecture.

Each MOTE consists of a local low power processor, a set of sensors such as temperature, solar radiation, soil moisture and water level, and a transceiver. The information sent by the MOTES will be filtered and organised by a software agent which is also responsible to communicate with the FIWIRE platform. The communication between the virtual agent and the motes is carried out through a Gateway connected to the motes by using a wireless point-to-multipoint LoRAWAN based network architecture. Whenever required, the agent sends a message to the MOTES requesting the sensors information. At the present time, we are engaged in developing the MOTES hardware and firmware and evaluate the sensors technologies to be used.

Author Contributions: The original idea and concept was put forward by J.P.C and both the methodology and paper writing were carried out by H.V.R and J.P.C.

Funding: This research received no external funding.

Conflicts of Interest: The authors declare no conflict of interest.

Proceedings

Gene Signatures Research Involved in Cancer Using Machine Learning †

Jose Liñares-Blanco and **Carlos Fernandez-Lozano** *

Department of Computer Science, Faculty of Computer Science, University of A Coruña, CITIC,
A Coruña 15071, Spain; j.linares@udc.es
* Correspondence: carlos.fernandez@udc.es; Tel.: +34-881-01-6013
† Presented at the 2nd XoveTIC Conference, A Coruña, Spain, 5–6 September 2019.

Published: 31 July 2019

Abstract: With the cheapening of mass sequencing techniques and the rise of computer technologies, capable of analyzing a huge amount of data, it is necessary nowadays that both branches mutually benefit. Transcriptomics, in this case, is a branch of biology focused on the study of mRNA molecules, among others. The quantification of these molecules gives us information about the expression that a gene is having at a given moment. Having information on the expression of the approximately 20,000 genes harbored by human beings is a really useful source of information for the study of certain conditions and/or pathologies. In this work, patient expression -omic data data have been used to offer a new analysis methodology through Machine Learning. The results of this methodology were compared with a conventional methodology to observe how they differed and how they resembled each other. These techniques, therefore, offer a new mechanism for the search of genetic signatures involved, in this case, with cancer.

Keywords: machine learning; cancer; transcriptomics; TCGA; RNA-seq

1. Introduction

Having access to the expression of the whole spectrum of genes of an individual gives us the possibility to identify specific expression patterns of a condition and/or pathology. Nowadays, with the use of Machine Learning (ML) techniques, and with the large amount of data available for free, it is possible to use these techniques to extract new knowledge from the analysis. ML is able to identify expression patterns and/or gene subgroups that conventional techniques are not able to detect. For this reason, the detection of differential genetic expression patterns has been proposed for two groups of patients: patients with colon cancer and patients with lung cancer. The analysis will be carried out using two different approaches: conventional statistics and ML. Our work was published before in "Machine Learning Paradigms. Learning and Analytics in Intelligent Systems" [1].

2. Results

In this paper, a new way of analyzing gene expression data is proposed. The use of ML offer the possibility of widening the search space in terms of genes of interest. Unlike conventional analysis techniques, ML techniques allow working with hundreds and thousands of variables. The final objective of the analysis is to find those genes that have a differential expression between two patient populations, labeled as COAD and LUAD.

2.1. Conventional Analysis of Differential Gene Expression

In order to decide whether, for a given gene, there is a significant statistical difference in the number of mapped readings of that gene for different biological conditions, a statistical test should be performed, where the count of readings should be modeled to a certain distribution. Once the distribution that follow the data has been defined, and in this case, the dispersion of the data has been calculated, the differential expression of the transcripts is determined by the corresponding statistical tests for hypothesis contrast. Today there are different implementations in several statistical software that execute all this analysis in a simple way for the researcher. In this work we have used one of the most used in the field, called edgeR [2] package. According with a classical approach, Table 1 shows the 10 genes that have obtained the most significant values through classical analysis.

Table 1. Classical approach. ten genes with the higher impact between conditions.

Gene Name	p-Value
ITGA6	$2.605237 \times 10^{-245}$
AXIN2	$4.065388 \times 10^{-203}$
NOS2	$1.848360 \times 10^{-185}$
MYC	$4.409724 \times 10^{-171}$
TCF7	$3.930353 \times 10^{-163}$
COL4A3	$2.205117 \times 10^{-162}$
COL4A4	$1.548193 \times 10^{-138}$
TCF7L1	$2.527959 \times 10^{-110}$
PIK3R2	$6.857479 \times 10^{-103}$
BBC3	2.481885×10^{-99}

2.2. Data Analysis Using Machine Learning

On the other hand, the development of Machine Learning algorithms has greatly benefited the analysis of complex data, such as genomic data. In this work we have used ML to solve a classification problem (COAD vs LUAD), providing in this way, a new way to model transcriptomic data and thus to be able to extract new knowledge and search for new genetic signatures involved in cancer. The analysis of the importance of the variables gives us a fairly realistic approximation of what is happening. In Figure 1 we can see how the genes COL4A3 and NOS2 are the most important. On the other hand, PIK3CD and COL4A4 have hardly any weight in the model. If we compare the Top 10 genes of both approximations we observe coincidences in 7 genes and differences in 3 of them. As far as the conventional approximation is concerned, this presents significant results for the TCF7L1, PIK3R2 and BBC3 genes that the ML has not detected among the Top 10. For its part, ML techniques added NFKBIA, RASSF5 and PIK3CD genes among its Top 10.

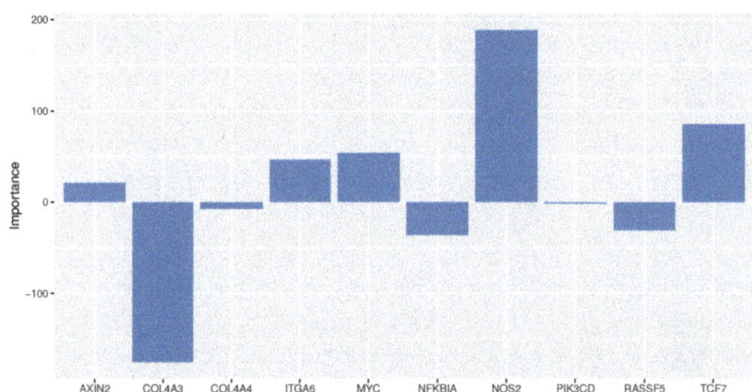

Figure 1. Variable importance according with the glmnet algorithm.

3. Discussion

The results obtained in this work indicate that ML offer coherent results in comparison with conventional techniques. The results that are observed shown that for a simple classification problem, both approaches reach almost the same results, although it is true that ML techniques may offer different possibilities when searching for new genetic marks. It is for this reason that the use of these techniques is considered useful when problems increase in complexity and the spectrum of genes involved in the pathology, such as cancer, is unknown.

4. Materials and Methods

The data has been downloaded from The Cancer Genome Atlas (TCGA) repository [3] from colon cancer patients (COAD) and lung cancer patients (LUAD). Due to the great dimensionality of the data (around 20,000), those genes belonging to specific cellular pathways were selected. In this case, genes were selected that had been previously identified in the routes related to colon cancer and lung cancer. For this purpose, the repository KEGG [4] was used, through the package KEGGREST [5] of R [6]. Specifically, the identifiers of pathways hsa05222, hsa05223 and hsa05210 were used, thus reducing the dimensionality to 173 genes. An univariate method (Kruskal test) were used to rank the genes. As for the classical approach, the edgeR package [2] has been taken as a reference. A Nested Cross Validation was used for training the models. In other words, there were two validation phases. Firstly, a holdout was used for the selection of the best hyperparameters (2/3 for training and 1/3 for testing) and secondly, a 10-fold CV was used for the validation of the model (we ran 5 times this CV process).

Author Contributions: Conceptualization, C.F.-L.; methodology, C.F.-L.; software, J.L.B. and C.F.-L.; formal analysis, J.L.B.; Writing—Original Draft preparation, J.L.B.; Writing—Review and Editing, J.L.B. and C.F.-L.; supervision, C.F.-L.

Funding: This research received no external funding.

Acknowledgments: This work is supported by the "Collaborative Project in Genomic Data Integration (CICLOGEN)" PI17/01826 funded by the Carlos III Health Institute from the Spanish National plan for Scientific and Technical Research and Innovation 2013–2016 and the European Regional Development Funds (FEDER)—"A way to build Europe". This project was also supported by the General Directorate of Culture, Education and University Management of Xunta de Galicia (Ref. ED431G/01, ED431D 2017/16), the "Galician Network for Colorectal Cancer Research" (Ref. ED431D 2017/23), and the Spanish Ministry of Economy and Competitiveness via funding of the unique installation BIOCAI (UNLC08-1E-002, UNLC13-13-3503) and the European Regional Development Funds (FEDER) by the European Union and the "Juan de la Cierva" fellowship program supported by the Spanish Ministry of Economy and Competitiveness (Carlos Fernandez-Lozano, Ref. FJCI- 2015-26071).

Conflicts of Interest: The authors declare no conflict of interest.

References

1. Liñares Blanco, J.; Gestal, M.; Dorado, J.; Fernandez-Lozano, C. Differential Gene Expression Analysis of RNA-seq Data Using Machine Learning for Cancer Research. In *Machine Learning Paradigms. Learning and Analytics in Intelligent Systems*; Springer: Cham, Switzerland, 2019; pp. 27–65.

2. McCarthy, D.J.; Chen, Y.; Smyth, G.K. Differential expression analysis of multifactor RNA-Seq experiments with respect to biological variation. *Nucleic Acids Res.* **2012**, *40*, 4288–4297.

3. Tomczak, K.; Czerwińska, P.; Wiznerowicz, M. The Cancer Genome Atlas (TCGA): An immeasurable source of knowledge. *Contemp. Oncol.* **2015**, *19*, A68.

4. Kanehisa, M.; Goto, S. KEGG: Kyoto encyclopedia of genes and genomes. *Nucleic Acids Res.* **2000**, *28*, 27–30.

5. Tenenbaum, D. KEGGREST: Client-side REST access to KEGG. *R Package Vers.* **2016**, *1*, DOI: 10.18129/B9.bioc.KEGGREST.

6. R Core Team. *R: A Language and Environment for Statistical Computing*; R Foundation for Statistical Computing: Vienna, Austria, 2019.

 *proceedings* 

Proceedings

Priors for Diversity and Novelty on Neural Recommender Systems [†]

Alfonso Landin *[iD], **Daniel Valcarce** [iD], **Javier Parapar** [iD] and **Álvaro Barreiro** [iD]

Information Retrieval Lab, Centro de Investigación en Tecnoloxías da Información e as Comunicacións (CITIC), Universidade da Coruña, Elviña, 15071 A Coruña, Spain
* Correspondence: alfonso.landin@udc.es; Tel.: +34-881-01-1276
† Presented at the 2nd XoveTIC Conference, A Coruña, Spain, 5–6 September 2019.

Published: 31 July 2019

Abstract: PRIN is a neural based recommendation method that allows the incorporation of item prior information into the recommendation process. In this work we study how the system behaves in terms of novelty and diversity under different configurations of item prior probability estimations. Our results show the versatility of the framework and how its behavior can be adapted to the desired properties, whether accuracy is preferred or diversity and novelty are the desired properties, or how a balance can be achieved with the proper selection of prior estimations.

Keywords: recommender systems; neural models; item priors; diversity; novelty

1. Introduction

In recent years, there has been a shift in the way users interact with the information services, from a proactive approach, where users looked actively for content, to one where users take a more passive role and content is suggested to them. Recommender Systems have played a pivotal role in this transformation. The advances in this field have driven increases in user engagement and revenue.

Among the properties of a recommender, accuracy is usually the more desirable one. However, there are other properties, such as novelty and diversity [1], that are also important and that, depending on the task, can be of higher priority. Diversity is the ability of the system to produce recommendations that include items from the whole catalog. This property is usually desirable for the vendors [2,3]. Novelty is the ability of the system to produce unexpected recommendations and is associated with serendipity, a property associated with higher user engagement and satisfaction [4]. These properties are related to accuracy insofar that increasing the later lowers the best achievable numbers in those metrics [5].

Recently a neural based recommendation method was presented, PRIN [6], that allows the incorporation of prior knowledge about the items into the recommendation process. This previous work was focused on the accuracy of the system. In this work we focus on studying the behavior of the system in terms of diversity and novelty and how the choice of prior information affects the performance of the system in these metrics.

2. Materials and Methods

We conducted a series of experiments in order to analyze the trade-off between accuracy, diversity and novelty when choosing different configurations of item prior probabilities with the PRIN recommender framework.

2.1. PRIN and Prior Probabilities of Items

PRIN [6] is a recommendation framework composed of two components: a neural model trained to predict the probability of a user given an item, $p(u|i)$, and a graph model of the data where centrality measures are applied to calculate the prior probability distribution of the items, $p(i)$. The objective of the system is to produce a ranking of items for a user. We cannot use $p(u|i)$ to produce such ranking as $p(u|i)$ and $p(u|j)$ for two items i and j, $i \neq j$, are not comparable as they are in different event spaces. Bayes' rule can be used to obtain $p(i|u), \forall i \in \mathcal{I}$, which is used to produce a ranking.

Previously reported results focused on the accuracy of the system [6]. In this work we analyze the behavior of the system with respect to diversity and novelty. We take the neural model that gets the best results in accuracy and explore how the system responds with different prior probability estimations. This showcases how the same model can be reused depending on the particular needs without the need to train a new model. We report the results obtained when using indegree, PageRank [7], Katz's Index [8], eigenvector, HITS [9] and closeness [10] centrality measures. We also report the result obtained when using an uniform prior and the complement of indegree. Lastly, we report the results of PRIN's dual model, PRN [6], that is trained to estimate $p(i|u)$, which is used directly to produce a ranking.

2.2. Evaluation Protocol

We report our results on the MovieLens 20M dataset, a popular public dataset. It contains 20,000,263 ratings that 138,493 users gave to 26,744 items. We split the data into training and test sets, with 80% of the ratings of each user in the train set and the remaining 20% in the test set.

To evaluate the accuracy of the recommendations we used the Normalized Discounted Cumulative Gain (nDCG), using the standard formulation as described in [11], with ratings as graded relevance judgments. We only considered items with a rating of 4.0 or more as relevant during evaluation. We used the inverse of the Gini index [2] to assess diversity and mean self-information (MSI) [12] to evaluate novelty. All metrics are evaluated at a cut-off of 100 because of its better robustness to sparsity and popularity biases and greater discriminative power with respect to shallower cut-offs [13].

3. Results

Results for all the centrality measures and other prior estimations, including also the results for PRN, can be seen in Figure 1. The systems are ordered by their accuracy result, except for PRN, that is the last bar in the graphs.

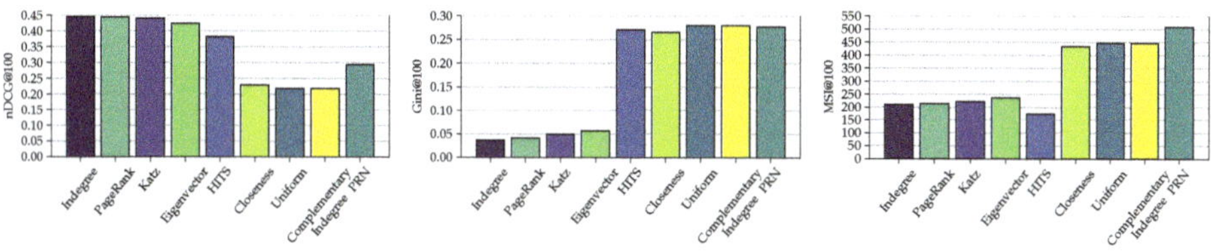

Figure 1. Values of nDCG@100, Gini@100 and MSI@100 for the MovieLens 20M dataset with different item prior configurations and for PRN.

We can see that as accuracy decreases we get better results in novelty and diversity. An exception to this in the HITS centrality measure, that has the worst results in novelty. Uniform prior and complementary indegree obtain similar results in all the metrics. This can be explained by the long tail distribution of the items that leads to similar estimations for most of the items.

The results of PRIN dual model, PRN, are also noteworthy. It obtains competitive results in diversity and has the best result in novelty while having better accuracy than the systems with similar behavior in those metrics.

4. Discussion

We have shown how the properties of the recommendations produced by PRIN can be adjusted by the selection of the estimation of the prior probabilities of the items. This is done without the need to train the neural model with a different configuration of hyper-parameters. It should be possible to fine tune even more the trade-off between accuracy and novelty/diversity by tuning the hyper-parameters of the neural model independently, but this process is computationally intensive.

The behavior of the system when using HITS shows that while usually increases in diversity and novelty are paired, it is not always necessarily true. In this particular case we can see that the results in diversity are competitive with the best systems in this metric, while having greater accuracy. On the other hand, the results in terms of novelty are the worst of all the prior configurations.

Funding: This work was supported by project RTI2018-093336-B-C22 (MCIU & ERDF), project GPC ED431B 2019/03 (Xunta de Galicia & ERDF) and accreditation ED431G/01 (Xunta de Galicia & ERDF). The first and second authors also acknowledge the support of grants FPU17/03210 and FPU014/01724 (MCIU), respectively.

References

1. McNee, S.M.; Riedl, J.; Konstan, J.A. Being Accurate is Not Enough: How Accuracy Metrics have hurt Recommender Systems. In Proceedings of the CHI EA '06, CHI '06 Extended Abstracts on Human Factors in Computing Systems, Montréal, QC, Canada, 22–27 April 2006; ACM Press: New York, New York, USA, 2006; pp. 1097–1101, doi:10.1145/1125451.1125659.
2. Fleder, D.; Hosanagar, K. Blockbuster Culture's Next Rise or Fall: The Impact of Recommender Systems on Sales Diversity. *Manag. Sci.* **2009**, *55*, 697–712, doi:10.1287/mnsc.1080.0974.
3. Valcarce, D.; Parapar, J.; Álvaro Barreiro. Item-based relevance modelling of recommendations for getting rid of long tail products. *Knowl.-Based Syst.* **2016**, *103*, 41–51, doi:10.1016/j.knosys.2016.03.021.
4. Ge, M.; Delgado-Battenfeld, C.; Jannach, D. Beyond Accuracy: Evaluating Recommender Systems by Coverage and Serendipity. In Proceedings of the RecSys '10, Fourth ACM Conference on Recommender Systems, Barcelona, Spain, 26–30 September 2010; pp. 257–260, doi:10.1145/1864708.1864761.
5. Landin, A.; Suárez-García, E.; Valcarce, D. When Diversity Met Accuracy: A Story of Recommender Systems. *Proceedings* **2018**, *2*, 1178, doi:10.3390/proceedings2181178.
6. Landin, A.; Valcarce, D.; Parapar, J.; Álvaro Barreiro. PRIN: A Probabilistic Recommender with Item Priors and Neural Models. In Proceedings of the 41st European Conference on IR Research, ECIR 2019, Cologne, Germany, 14–18 April 2019; Part I, pp. 133–147, doi:10.1007/978-3-030-15712-8_9.
7. Page, L.; Brin, S.; Motwani, R.; Winograd, T. *The PageRank Citation Ranking: Bringing Order to the Web*; Technical Report; Stanford InfoLab: Stanford, CA, USA, 1999.
8. Katz, L. A new status index derived from sociometric analysis. *Psychometrika* **1953**, *18*, 39–43.
9. Kleinberg, J.M. Authoritative Sources in a Hyperlinked Environment. *J. ACM* **1999**, *46*, 604–632.
10. Bavelas, A.; Barrett, D. *An Experimental Approach to Organizational Communication*; American Management Association: New York, NY, USA, 1951.
11. Wang, Y.; Wang, L.; Li, Y.; He, D.; Chen, W.; Liu, T.Y. A Theoretical Analysis of NDCG Ranking Measures. In Proceedings of the 26th Annual Conference on Learning Theory (COLT '13), Princeton, NJ, USA, 12–14 June 2013; pp. 1–30.
12. Zhou, T.; Kuscsik, Z.; Liu, J.G.; Medo, M.; Wakeling, J.R.; Zhang, Y.C. Solving the apparent diversity-accuracy dilemma of recommender systems. *Proc. Natl. Acad. Sci. USA* **2010**, *107*, 4511–4515, doi:10.1073/pnas.1000488107.
13. Valcarce, D.; Bellogín, A.; Parapar, J.; Castells, P. On the robustness and discriminative power of information retrieval metrics for top-N recommendation. In Proceedings of the 12th ACM Conference on Recommender Systems (RecSys '18); Vancouver, BC, Canada, 2–7 October 2018; ACM: New York, NY, USA, 2018; pp. 260–268, doi:10.1145/3240323.3240347.

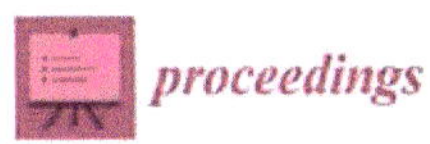 *proceedings*

Proceedings

Using Artificial Vision Techniques for Individual Player Tracking in Sport Events [†]

Roberto López Castro * and Diego Andrade Canosa

Departamento de Ingeniería de Computadores, Universidade da Coruña, Campus de Elviña, 15071 A Coruña, Spain; diego.andrade@udc.es
* Correspondence: roberto.lopez.castro@udc.es; Tel.: +34-981-167-000
† Presented at the 2nd XoveTIC Congress, A Coruña, Spain, 5–6 September 2019.

Published: 31 July 2019

Abstract: We introduce a hybrid approach that can track an individual football player in a video sequence. This solution achieves a good balance between speed and accuracy, combining traditional object tracking techniques with Deep Neural Networks (DNN). While traditional techniques lack accuracy, the main shortcoming of DNN is performance. Both types of techniques complement to each other to provide an accurate and fast object tracking approach that does not require human intervention. The accuracy of our solution has been validated using the SoccerNet Dataset against hand annotated video sequences. For the tracking of 4 different players of 2 different teams our approach has achieved an Area Under Curve (AUC) of 0.66, in terms of accuracy, and a frame rate of 91.75 FPS, in terms of performance, running on a Nvidia GTX 1080Ti GPU.

Keywords: artificial vision; object tracking; object detection; machine learning; deep learning; real time

---

1. Introduction

The tracking of individual players in sport events is really interesting for coaches, personal trainers, fans and media. One of the best ways to do it automatically is using computer vision [1]. However, the sport case is particularly challenging due to several factors: some players have a very similar aspect, the jersey number is not always visible, the video codification algorithms frequently generate blurry video segments, the player is often partially or totally occluded, etc.

Object tracking algorithms can be classified in two main classes:

- Traditional algorithms based on mathematical and machine learning principles usually suffer lack of accuracy, caused by: the accumulation of tracking errors, which makes the bounding box (area which the algorithm uses to delimit the object) to lose progressively the tracked object, and partial or total occlusions of the tracked individual with others. Additionally, it needs a human operator that makes the initial identification and selection of the tracked individual. A good example of these algorithms are Discriminative Correlation Filters (DCF) [2].
- Deep Neural Networks that can track an object by detecting it in each frame. Specifically, Convolutional Neural Networks (CNNs) [3] are used to solve this problem. A properly trained network can achieve a very good accuracy but at the cost of high computational cost, which makes them often unusable to process high definition video sequences at real-time.

The solution proposed in this work combines two CNNs with one DCF algorithm to perform a fast and accurate tracking of a football player in a video sequence. Besides, the initial position of the individual to be tracked does not have to be selected by a human operator. The solution is fast enough to process video sequences of 60 fps (or more) at real-time, and it is sufficiently accurate to recover from temporary tracking errors, and to support camera movements and switches from one camera to another.

2. Hybrid Solution

The two CNNs models used in our hybrid solution are Faster-RCNN [4] and SSD [5]. Faster-RCNN is a highly accurate detector but which needs near 45 ms to process a single frame of the video sequence, this means that it can only process 22 fps. On the other hand, SSD is less accurate but has an affordable performance. These two networks are combined in the following manner: Faster-RCNN is executed on the whole frame, but only processes one of every λ frames. In the $\lambda - 1$ frames in between, SSD is applied on a sub-frame cropped around the area where Faster-RCNN detected the tracked individual.

This combination of both CNNs increases performance, but loses accuracy with respect to using Faster-RCNN for every frame. To increase the accuracy of our hybrid approach we add a DCF algorithm, specifically KCF (Kerneralized Correlation Filter) [6], to the workflow. This traditional algorithm is good at tracking a previously selected object for some time, but it suffers the aforementioned accuracy problems of this type of algorithms. In our proposal, the two CNNs can play the role of a human operator which is constantly informing KCF of the position of the tracked object. Figure 1 shows the execution diagram of our approach. Faster-RCNN is executed in one of every λ frame playing the role of the guide of the other two algorithms (KCF and SSD). In the remaining $\lambda - 1$ iterations, these other two algorithms collaborate to track the object, SSD constantly correcting, if necessary, the possible tracking errors introduced by KCF.

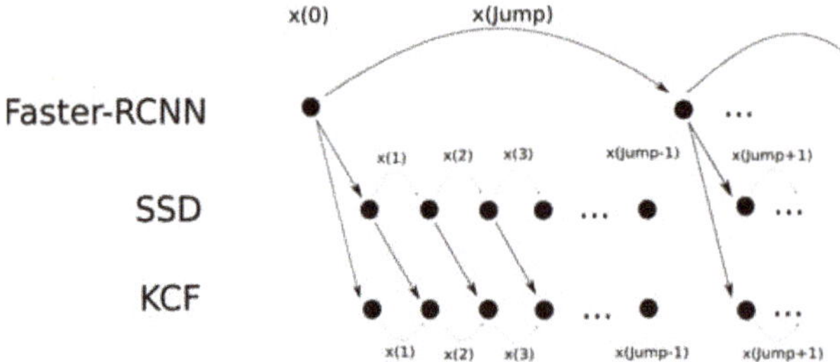

Figure 1. Execution diagram.

3. Results

Our approach has been trained for tracking 4 different players of 2 different teams, using the SoccerNet Dataset [7]. Table 1 shows the average accuracy and performance results obtained when running the algorithm on a NVidia GTX 1080Ti GPU.

Table 1. Average hybrid algorithm performance.

	Avg. Accy	Avg. Fps	Avg. AUC	*Lost Frames*
Player 1	0.620	91.75	0.610	2
Player 2	0.653	84.98	0.651	0
Player 3	0.650	86.65	0.660	0
Player 4	0.600	87.36	0.600	0
TOTAL AVG.	0.6308	87.685	0.6302	0.5

The performance results show that the approach can process around 87 FPS on average. Regarding the accuracy, the average AUC is 0.6302, a similar value to the one obtained by state-of-the-art algorithms on generic datasets [8].

References

1. Manafifard, M.; Ebadi, H.; Moghaddam, H.A. A survey on player tracking in soccer videos. *Comput. Vis. Image Underst.* **2017**, *159*, 19–46.
2. Lukezic, A.; Vojir, T.; Cehovin Zajc, L.; Matas, J.; Kristan, M. Discriminative correlation filter with channel and spatial reliability. *Proc. IEEE Conf. Comput. Vis. Pattern Recognit.* **2017**, 6309–6318.
3. Géron, A. *Hands-on Machine Learning with Scikit-Learn and TensorFlow: Concepts, Tools, and Techniques to Build Intelligent Systems*; O'Reilly Media, Inc.: Sebastopol, CA, USA, 2017.
4. Ren, S.; He, K.; Girshick, R.; Sun, J. Faster r-cnn: Towards real-time object detection with region proposal networks. *Adv. Neural Inf. Process. Syst.* **2015**, 91–99.
5. Liu, W.; Anguelov, D.; Erhan, D.; Szegedy, C.; Reed, S.; Fu, C.-Y.; Berg, A.C. Ssd: Single shot multibox detector. In *European Conference on Computer Vision*; Springer: Berlin, Germany, 2016; pp. 21–37.
6. Henriques, J.F.; Caseiro, R.; Martins, P.; Batista, J. High-speed tracking with kernelized correlation filters, *IEEE Trans. Pattern Anal. Mach. Intell.* **2014**, *37*, 583–596.
7. Giancola, S.; Amine, M.; Dghaily, T.; Ghanem, B. SoccerNet: A Scalable Dataset for Action Spotting in Soccer Videos. *arXiv* **2018**. arXiv:1804.04527.
8. Li, Y.; Zhang, X. SiamVGG: Visual Tracking using Deeper Siamese Networks. *arXiv* **2019**. arXiv:1902.02804.

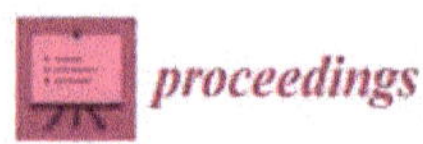 *proceedings*

Proceedings

Minish HAT: A Tool for the Minimization of Here-and-There Logic Programs and Theories in Answer Set Programming [†]

Rodrigo Martin * and Pedro Cabalar

CITIC, University of Corunna, 15001 A Coruña, Spain; pedro.cabalar@udc.es
* Correspondence: r.martin1@udc.es
† Presented at the 2nd XoveTIC Conference, A Coruña, Spain, 5–6 September 2019.

Published: 31 July 2019

Abstract: When it comes to the writing of a new logic program or theory, it is of great importance to obtain a concise and minimal representation, for simplicity and ease of interpretation reasons. There are already a few methods and many tools, such as Karnaugh Maps or the Quine-McCluskey method, as well as their numerous software implementations, that solve this minimization problem in Boolean logic. This is not the case for *Here-and-There logic*, also called *three-valued logic*. Even though there are theoretical minimization methods for logic theories and programs, there aren't any published tools that are able to obtain a minimal equivalent logic program. In this paper we present the first version of a tool called that is able to efficiently obtain minimal and equivalent representations for any logic program in Here-and-There. The described tool uses an hybrid method both leveraging a modified version of the Quine-McCluskey algorithm and Answer Set Programming techniques to minimize fairly complex logic programs in a reduced time.

Keywords: logic minimization; knowledge representation; answer set programming; here-and-there logic

1. Introduction

In the field of *logic programming* it has always been f great importance to reduce the formulae and expressions to their minimal conjunctive or disjunctive normal forms (*CNF* and *DNF* respectively), as this reduces the number of logic OR and AND gates needed to implement the function as a circuit. This topic has been broadly studied for *Boolean Logic* and well known methods such as the Karnaugh Maps [1] and Quine-McCluskey algorithm [2,3] have served as base for powerful tools such as ESPRESSO [4] and BOOM [5]. Despite this being the case for Boolean Logic, it is not for Here-and-There logic (i.e., three-valued logic). There is a modified version of the Quine-McCluskey algorithm that takes in account the particularities of this specific logic [6] but there aren't any available tools implementing it. In this paper we describe a first approach to a tool that is able to minimize logic programs and theories in Here-and-There logic leveraging both the Quine-McCluskey algorithm alongside the power of Answer Set Programming.

2. Materials and Methods

The Quine-McCluskey algorithm aims to obtain a minimal normal form equivalent to any propositional theory. It can obtain either a minimal *DNF* from the set of models of the theory or a minimal *CNF* from its countermodels. The algorithm computes the set of prime implicates of a given theory given its countermodels. To obtain the minimal CNF we also need a coverage algorithm (Usually *Petrick's Method* [7]) to select the elements of the minimal subset of prime implicates that cover all of the initial countermodels of the theory.

In the logic of *here-and-there* (HT), a *formula* is defined in the usual way as a well-formed combination of the operators $\bot, \wedge, \vee, \rightarrow$ with atoms in a propositional signature *At*. We also define $\varphi \overset{\text{def}}{=} \varphi \rightarrow \bot$, and $\top \overset{\text{def}}{=} \bot$. A theory is a set of formulas.

An HT-interpretation $\langle H, T \rangle$ is a model of a given theory if satisfies all formulas in that theory. A formula true in all models is said to be valid or a tautology, while an *Equilibrium Model* of a theory is any total model $(H = T)$ $\langle T, T \rangle$ of that theory such that no $\langle H, T \rangle$ with $H \subset T$ is model of the theory. *Equilibrium Logic* is the logic induced by equilibrium models.

As shown in [8], logic programs constitute a CNF for HT. A logic program is a conjunction of *clauses*, called *rules* with a positive and negative bodies and positive and negative heads in the form:

$$B_r^+ \wedge B_r^- \rightarrow Hd_r^+ \vee Hd_r^- \tag{1}$$

2.1. Implementation

Fundamental rules are rules in which all pairwise intersections of the head and body sets are empty with the possible exception of $Hd_r^+ \cap Hd_r^-$. Said rules can be translated to a minterm-like notation. Such rules can be transformed into minterm-like labels using a set of six symbols $\{0, 1, 2, \bar{2}, \bar{0}, -\}$

These rules are then codified to octal and compared in a pairwise manner by using bit-by-bit operations, which allows us to perform the prime implicate generation taking in account the set of adjacent values for HT. This octal codification uses each one of the three bits for each symbol to describe which values are used (e.g., the symbol $\bar{2}$, meaning "not 2" having all bit positions set to 1 except the one corresponding to 2).

Value	2	1	0	Value	2	1	0
0	0	0	1	$\bar{2}$	0	1	1
1	0	1	0	$\bar{0}$	1	1	0
2	1	0	0	-	1	1	1

On top of the modified version of the Quine-McCluskey method, we add a previous step that allows us to work with the direct translation of the rules, instead of having to expand all of the possible minterms that each aggregated rule contains. Instead of comparing which labels are totally adjacent, we check that all positions are *compatible* except the adjacent one. This means that every position should subsum each other, or in the best case, be equal. Since we only expand the partially adjacent labels, in the worst case scenario it will be equal to expanding all of the labels into the possible minterms and in the average case will be logarithmically smaller. Finally, for the minimal coverage step, since this is a well studied case in ASP we leverage the ASP solver *clingo* to obtain the set of minimal versions of the original program, thus avoiding the implementation of the Petrick's method.

2.2. Tests

For a minimal program to be correct, it has to verify three conditions:

- **Size**: The minimal program has to be smaller, or at least equal in number of rules to the original program.
- **Subsumption**: The rules of the minimal program subsume all of the rules of the original program.
- **Strong Equivalence**: Both the original program and the minimal program have exactly the same models.

The size condition check is straightforward, only in the case that the number of rules remain the same (i.e., the original program is already minimal) we have to check that any rewriting of the original rules is valid regarding the other two conditions.

The subsumption condition is further detailed in [6] but to summarize, every rule of the minimal program has to subsume at least a rule of the original program and there can't be any rule of the original program that is not subsumed by the rules of the minimal program. This condition is checked with a program in ASP that compares both the original and the minimal programs to verify the condition by checking which parts of each rules of the latter are a subset of the ones of the original one.

For the strong equivalence condition, the objective is to transform both the original and minimal programs to classical logic by applying a set of transformations. By comparing the classical models obtained for the transformations of the original program and the minimal version we can ensure the strong equivalence property.

3. Conclusions

We have developed a novel tool that implements the modified version of Quine-McCluskey's method for HT, while also using the capabilities of Answer Set Programming to perform the minimal coverage of the initial countermodels, as well as using it to test and validate the results.

This first version of the tool is able to minimize the samples used in [6] in better times than the proof-of-concept Prolog script provided by the authors, since it doesn't rely on the calculation of all of the countermodels for a logic program, being able to work directly with the rules of the program as input by checking which rules can be potentially subsumed and only expanding those into minterms.

As for future work, we are already studying the *splitting properties* of logic programs in terms of minimization, which would allow us to separately minimize parts of a given logic program, greatly minimizing the number of atoms and rules that have to be dealt with at a single time in the current approach.

The currently *in-development* version of the scripts can be found at https://github.com/Trigork/minish-hat alongside examples and usage guidelines.

Funding: This research received no external funding.

Conflicts of Interest: The funders had no role in the design of the study; in the collection, analyses, or interpretation of data; in the writing of the manuscript, or in the decision to publish the results.

References

1. Karnaugh, M. The map method for synthesis of combinational logic circuits. *Trans. Am. Inst. Electr. Eng. Part I* **1953**, *72*, 593–599.
2. Quine, W.V.O. The problem of simplifying truth functions. *Am. Math. Mon.* **1952**, *59*, 521–531.
3. McCluskey, E.J. Minimization of boolean functions. *Bell Syst. Tech. J.* **1956**, *35*, 1417–1444.
4. McGeer, P.; Sanghavi, J.V.; Brayton, R.K.; Sangiovanni-Vincentelli, A. Espresso-Signature: A New Exact Minimizer for Logic Functions. *IEEE Trans. VLSI Syst.* **1993**, *1*, 618–624.
5. Fiser, P.; Hlavička, J. BOOM, A Heuristic Boolean Minimizer. *Comput. Inform.* **2003**, *22*, 19–51.
6. Cabalar, P.; Pearce, D.; Valverde, A. Minimal Logic Programs. In *Logic Programming*; Dahl, V., Niemelä, I., Eds.; Springer Berlin Heidelberg: Berlin/Heidelberg, Germany, 2007; pp. 104–118.
7. Petrick, S.R. *A Direct Termination of the Irredundant Forms of a Boolean Functionfrom the Set of Prime Implicants*; Technical Report AFCRC-TR-56-110; Air ForceCambridge Res. Center: Cambridge, MA, USA, 1956.
8. Cabalar, P.; Ferraris, P. Propositional theories are strongly equivalent to logic programs. *Theory Pract. Logic Program.* **2007**, *7*, 745–759.

 *proceedings*

Proceedings

The Role of Software-Defined Networking in Cellular Networks [†]

Pablo Fondo-Ferreiro * and **Felipe Gil-Castiñeira**

atlanTTic Research Center, University of Vigo, 36310 Vigo, Pontevedra, Spain
* Correspondence: pfondo@gti.uvigo.es; Tel.: +34-986-818-684
† Presented at the XoveTIC Conference, A Coruña, Spain, 5–6 September 2019.

Published: 31 July 2019

Abstract: In this paper, we discuss how SDN can contribute to enhance future cellular networks. We first present SDN and describe its characteristics. Then, we explore how SDN can be used to improve current cellular networks, analyzing the advantages and disadvantages, while highlighting some use cases. Finally, we conclude this work exposing some challenges that still require further research to take full advantage of SDN in cellular networks.

Keywords: cellular networks; mobile networks; mobile core network architecture; software-defined networking; SDN

1. Introduction

Since the advent of mobile phones, cellular networks became one of the most relevant communication systems. Moreover, cellular networks are embracing more applications, supporting a wide range of connectivity typologies with different types of requirements, such as those coming from Internet of Things (IoT), Industry 4.0 or connected cars. The growing demand for ubiquitous connectivity is leading operators to enhance their current networks in terms of scalability, adaptability and performance. Yet many efforts are being focused on the evolution of the radio access network (RAN) by exploring new frequencies, antennas and modulation techniques, the core network (CN) also needs to be evolved, in order to properly manage the increased amount of traffic.

New network architectures such as Network Slicing and Multi-Access Edge Computing (MEC) have been identified to play a key role in satisfying the diverse requirements brought by the new use cases. However, in order to implement such architectures it is essential to have flexible and programmable networks. Two networking paradigms, namely Software-Defined Networking (SDN) and Network Function Virtualization (NFV), are key enablers to build these networks.

2. Software-Defined Networking

Software-Defined Networking (SDN) [1] is an architecture that decouples the control plane from the data plane in networking devices. Besides, the control plane is centralized in a logical entity named the SDN controller. The network is then programmable through software applications running on top of the SDN controller.

This paradigm enables flexibility by breaking the vertical integration in traditional IP networks where control and data planes are combined inside the same networking device. In SDN, controllers follow policies specified by SDN applications to decide where packets should be forwarded (i.e., the control plane), whereas SDN enabled devices, such as switches or routers, execute the forwarding actions (i.e., data plane), as shown in Figure 1.

In SDN networks forwarding decisions are now flow-based, where a flow is defined as an artificial logical equivalent to a call or connection [2]. Thus, SDN networks can define complex sets of rules (which can be modified dynamically at the controller) that match different packet header fields to establish a set of actions that will handle the network traffic.

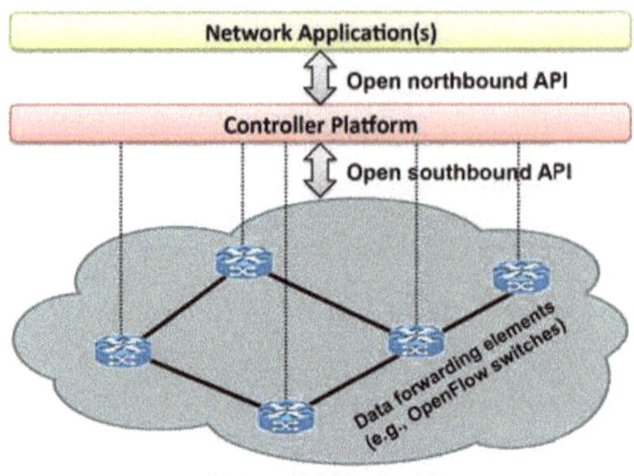

Figure 1. SDN architecture. Retrieved from [1].

3. SDN in Mobile Cellular Networks

The SDN technology enables flexible networks that will be the key to implement the functionalities that are expected to be provided by the Core Network (CN) of the future cellular networks. In this section, we present the major directions for introducing SDN in the core of the mobile network architecture. There are three main ways to re-architect the Evolved Packet Core (EPC) of the mobile cellular networks according to [3]: the first one consists in virtualizing the EPC using NFV techniques, the second one separates the control and user planes in the EPC using SDN, and the third one consists in a "clean-slate" fully SDN based architecture.

The first approach consists in migrating conventional EPC entities to Virtual Machines (VMs) or containers. This way, the protocols and interfaces standardized by the 3GPP are maintained. This approach introduces benefits such as cost reduction, flexibility, and simplicity in the deployment, since it does not require any major change, and it is interoperable with current deployments. However, this approach presents several limitations: difficult management, orchestration, scaling and resilience problems. This approach was, for example, discussed in [4].

The second group of proposals put their focus on the data plane entities of the core network, that is, the Serving Gateway (SGW) and Packet Data Network Gateway (PGW) in 4G cellular networks. These entities are divided into control plane (SGW-C and PGW-C) and data plane (SGW-U and PGW-U), following the decoupling proposed by the SDN paradigm. Some proposals maintain the data plane entities as hardware elements (for performance purposes) while others virtualize them. All of these proposals employ an SDN controller for configuring the forwarding rules of the data plane devices. The main advantages of these architectures are the flexibility introduced by SDN and also the independent scalability of control and data planes. On the other hand, the introduction of the SDN controller slightly increases the latency in the control plane of the network. Besides, keeping 3GPP protocols in the architecture maintains the overhead that they introduce. This type of architecture was initially proposed in [5].

The third approach proposes a clean-slate SDN based revolutionary architecture, not influenced by the entities, interfaces and protocols standardized by the 3GPP. Most of these proposals depict the following simplified architecture: a control plane implemented as SDN applications running on top of an SDN controller, and a data plane composed of SDN switches and middleboxes. The main benefits are the improved flexibility and reduced overhead due to the elimination of the specific protocols such as GTP. However, despite the simplicity of the architecture, the complexity of the control plane and

QoS enforcing policies imposes challenges in the implementation. In addition, it should also be noted that this approach is not interoperable with current deployments. Further information can be found in [6].

Furthermore, we can also consider using an SDN network as the transportation network interconnecting the elements of the EPC. The main advantage of this simple approach is that it can be quickly deployed without the need to modify any entity, while being interoperable with existing deployments. Besides, it introduces some flexibility in the traffic management, facilitating the balancing of traffic among different EPC entities. On the contrary, the main drawback is the remaining overhead due to the operation of conventional EPC entities.

Finally, Network Slicing is a practical use case that can clearly take advantage of the application of the SDN paradigm to the core of the cellular networks. SDN can be used in the transport network to redirect traffic to the appropriate Network Slice, just by programming the SDN controller to manage traffic flows according to their slice.

4. Conclusions

Current and future cellular networks can benefit from the application of some recent networking paradigms such as SDN and NFV. For example, MEC and Network Slicing paradigms will require flexible CNs, as the ones that can be built with SDN. Furthermore, we have summarized the proposals of different authors who have considered using SDN to reinvent the cellular network architecture by taking advantage of the flexibility and programmability provided by SDN. As future work, we will continue exploring how new networking paradigms can be used to optimize and improve cellular networks.

Author Contributions: Conceptualization, F.G.-C.; investigation, P.F.-F.; writing—original draft preparation, P.F.-F.; writing—review and editing, F.G.-C.; supervision, F.G.-C.; funding acquisition, P.F.-F. and F.G.-C.

Funding: This work has been supported by "la Caixa" Foundation (ID 100010434) fellowship code LCF/BQ/ES18/11670020.

Conflicts of Interest: The authors declare no conflict of interest. The founding sponsors had no role in the design of the study; in the collection, analyses, or interpretation of data; in the writing of the manuscript, or in the decision to publish the results.

References

1. Kreutz, D.; Ramos, F.M.; Verissimo, P.; Rothenberg, C.E.; Azodolmolky, S.; Uhlig, S. Software-defined networking: A comprehensive survey. *Proc. IEEE* **2015**, *103*, 14–76.
2. Carpenter, B.E.; Deering, D.S.E.; Rajahalme, J.; Conta, A. *IPv6 Flow Label Specification*; RFC 3697; Internet Engineering Task Force (IETF): Fremont, CA, USA, 2014, doi:10.17487/RFC3697
3. Nguyen, V.G.; Brunstrom, A.; Grinnemo, K.J.; Taheri, J. SDN/NFV-based mobile packet core network architectures: A survey. *IEEE Commun. Surv. Tutor.* **2017**, *19*, 1567–1602.
4. Yousaf, F.Z.; Lessmann, J.; Loureiro, P.; Schmid, S. SoftEPC—Dynamic instantiation of mobile core network entities for efficient resource utilization. In Proceedings of the 2013 IEEE International Conference on Communications (ICC), Budapest, Hungary, 9–13 June 2013; pp. 3602–3606.
5. Kempf, J.; Johansson, B.; Pettersson, S.; Lüning, H.; Nilsson, T. Moving the mobile evolved packet core to the cloud. In Proceedings of the 2012 IEEE 8th International Conference on Wireless and Mobile Computing, Networking and Communications (WiMob), Barcelona, Spain, 8–10 October 2012; pp. 784–791.
6. Jin, X.; Li, L.E.; Vanbever, L.; Rexford, J. Softcell: Scalable and flexible cellular core network architecture. In Proceedings of the Ninth ACM Conference on Emerging Networking Experiments and Technologies, Santa Barbara, CA, USA, 9–12 December 2013; pp. 163–174.

Proceedings

Flexible Spectral Precoding for OFDM Systems [†]

Khawar Hussain * and Roberto López-Valcarce (iD)

atlanTTic Research Center, University of Vigo, 36310 Vigo, Spain
* Correspondence: khawar@gts.uvigo.es
† Presented at the 2nd XoveTIC Conference, A Coruña, Spain, 5–6 September 2019.

Published: 31 July 2019

Abstract: Spectral precoding is a popular approach to reduce out-of-band radiation (OBR) in multicarrier systems in order to avoid adjacent channel interference. However, it introduces distortion in the data, appropriate decoding is required at the receiver side. Thus, trading off between implementation complexity, OBR reduction and error rate is important. We present a novel linear precoder design with flexibility to trade off OBR reduction, precoding/decoding complexity, and error rate at the receiver. Moreover, the constraint can be imposed on each subcarrier individually to provide more flexibility. The precoding matrices have low rank, which translates into significant computational savings. In this way, the requirements of different systems can be satisfied with varying complexity levels.

Keywords: OFDM; spectral precoding; out-of-band radiation ; sidelobe supression

1. Introduction

Orthogonal frequency division multiplexing (OFDM) is a mature technology with significant advantages: it is spectrally efficient, robust against multipath effects, and well matched to multiple input multiple output (MIMO) implementation. Due to these, the Third Generation Partnership Project (3GPP) has agreed on cyclic prefix (CP)-based OFDM as the modulation technique for 5G phase 1. Nevertheless, OFDM also has drawbacks, such as large spectrum side lobes, causing high out-of-band radiation (OBR) and adjacent channel interference. Traditionally, OBR has been mitigated via guard-band insertion, filtering, and/or pulse shaping. These techniques are straightforward, but they either degrade spectral efficiency or decrease the effective CP length.

Over the years, new OBR reduction approaches have been proposed. Constellation expansion and multiple choice sequences[1] require transmitting side information, causing system overhead. Subcarrier weighting [2] and adaptive symbol transition techniques are data dependent, i.e., they require solving an optimization problem for each OFDM symbol.

Spectral precoding is a popular method to reduce OBR in multicarrier systems. A number of precoder designs have been proposed according to different criteria, e.g., smoothing the time-domain waveform, introducing out-of-band notches, contrast energy ratio, or other heuristics. In general, these methods suffer from high complexity at both transmitter and receiver, where the precoding and decoding operations are respectively implemented.

We present a novel linear precoder design with flexibility to trade off OBR reduction, precoding/decoding complexity, and error rate at the receiver. The design directly minimizes OBR over a given frequency range without specifying the notch frequencies. The amount of distortion on data subcarriers, which determines the complexity of the decoder at the receiver, is controlled through a user-selectable parameter, in terms of normalized mean squared error (NMSE). Moreover, it is possible to set different NMSE constraints on each data subcarrier [3,4]. In this way, a user-selectable NMSE profile can be specified, providing more flexibility and control in the tradeoff between OBR reduction and the required number of decoder iterations. The precoding matrices have low rank, which translates into significant computational savings.

2. Results

Numerical results are presented to illustrate the performance of the proposed technique. Power spectral density (PSD) and symbol error rate (SER) are the performance metrics used for comparison. Complexity of the system, which can be a bottleneck for some systems, is also considered.

The proposed technique provides the flexibility to control the trade-off between OBR reduction and system complexity. Figure 1a shows the PSD obtained with the proposed design for a 5-MHz CP-OFDM system with 1/8 CP and $N = 256$ subcarriers, of which $N_d = 206$ transport 16-QAM data. At the lower and upper spectrum edges, 25 subcarriers are reserved for OBR reduction. Clearly, increasing the value of distortion (ϵ) improves OBR performance, but as shown in Figure 1b (which considers an AWGN channel), this is at the cost of either SER degradation or increased receiver complexity. With $\epsilon = 0.002$, distortion is small and even without decoding, the SER is close to that of an uncoded system; the small gap can be bridged with a single iteration of the proposed decoder. With $\epsilon = 0.02$, OBR is significantly improved at the expense of computational complexity.

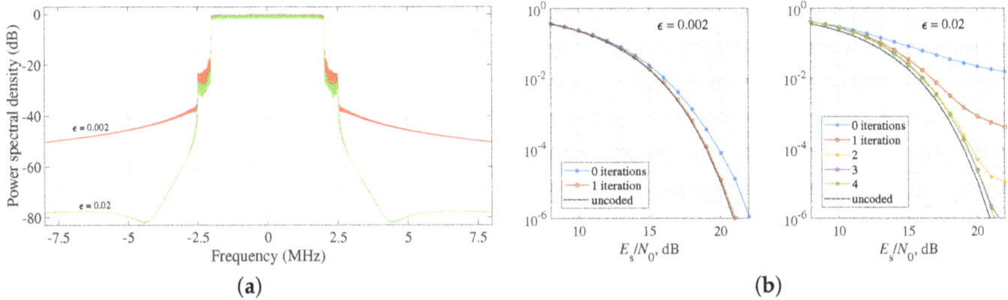

Figure 1. Proposed precoder design with $N = 256$, $N_c = 50$. (**a**) PSD for different values of ϵ. (**b**) SER in AWGN channel for the proposed iterative decoder

For performance comparison against other techniques, we have considered the parameters of the IEEE 802.22 standard for 16-QAM transmission in TV White Spaces with 6-MHz TV channels. The system uses 1/32 CP, subcarrier spacing $\Delta_f = 3.347$ kHz, and has a total of $N = 2048$ subcarriers, out of which $N_d = 1680$ are used to transmit data. Of the remaining subcarriers, $N_c = 100$ are used for active OBR reduction and the rest are turned off.

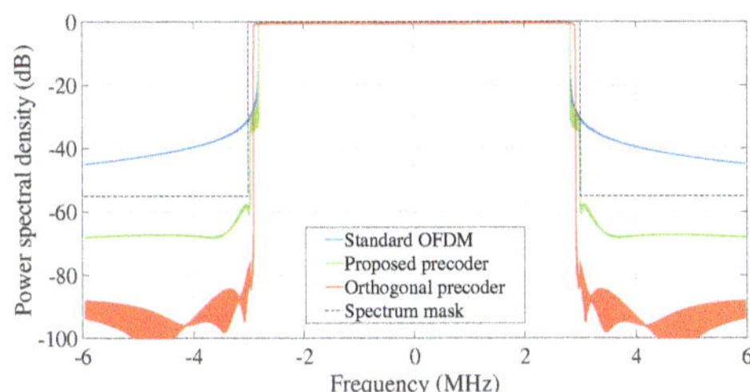

Figure 2. PSD of various designs and IEEE spectral emission mask.

The proposed design was applied to this setting, taking $\epsilon = 0.002$. Figure 2 shows the resulting PSD together with that of plain OFDM (all non-data subcarriers turned off) and with the orthogonal precoder design from [5]; the IEEE 802.22 spectral emission mask for USA is also shown. It is seen that both precoder designs are mask compliant. The SER of the proposed iterative decoder in an AWGN channel requires a single iteration. The complexity at transmitter and receiver of orthogonal precoder is $2,990,400$ cmults/symb and $346,000$ cmults/symb using Clarkson's reduced complexity, while the proposed technique reduce the complexity to 58,120 cmults/symb at transmitter and 40,320 cmults/symb at receiver. In fact, the complexity of the proposed precoder is only 2% of that of the direct method, and 17% of that of Clarkson's method. At the decoder the figures are 1.3% and 11.6% respectively.

In the third example, we consider a bandwidth-limited scenario with only $N_c = 4$ cancellation subcarriers available. In this case, the orthogonal precoder requires 4080 cmults/symb at both transmitter and receiver. The OBR reduction obtained by orthogonal precoding can be improved if one uses IDC (individual distortion constraint) precoding instead, at the cost of additional complexity. Figure 3 shows an example with $\epsilon_i = 0.007 \ \forall i$. In this case, the decoder requires a single iteration. The complexity incurred is 9160 and 7112 cmults/symb at the transmitter and receiver, respectively.

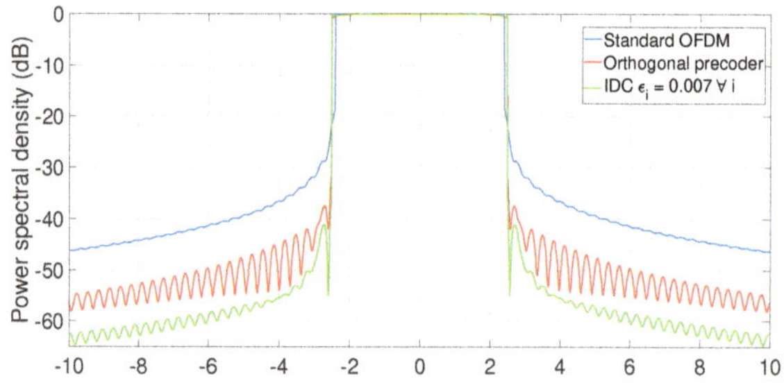

Figure 3. PSD for different systems with $N = 512$, $N_c = 4$.

3. Conclusions

The proposed spectral precoder designs provide significant flexibility when achieving a tradeoff between out-of-band radiation reduction and computational complexity. The fact, that the maximum distortion experienced by data subcarriers can either be specified overall subcarriers or on a per-subcarrier basis can be exploited in order to reduce the number of iterations required by the decoder, significantly reducing the computational complexity of the receiver.

Funding: Supported by Agencia Estatal de Investigación (Spain) and the European Regional Development Fund (ERDF) under project WINTER (TEC2016-76409-C2-2-R, BES-2017-080305), and by Xunta de Galicia (Agrupación Estratéxica Consolidada de Galicia accreditation 2016-2019; Red Temática RedTEIC 2017-2018).

References

1. Cosovic, I.; Janardhanam, V. Sidelobe Suppression in OFDM Systems. In *Multi-Carrier Spread-Spectrum*; Fazel, K., Kaiser, S., Eds.; Springer: Dordrecht, The Netherlands, 2006; pp. 473–482.
2. Cosovic, I.; Brandes, S.; Schnell, M. Subcarrier weighting: A method for sidelobe suppression in OFDM systems. *IEEE Commun. Lett.* **2006**, *10*, 444–446, doi:10.1109/LCOMM.2006.1638610.
3. Hussain, K.; Lojo, A.; López-Valcarce, R. Flexible Spectral Precoding for Sidelobe Suppression in OFDM Systems. In Proceedings of the 2019 IEEE International Conference on Acoustics, Speech and Signal Processing (ICASSP 2019), Brighton, UK, 12–17 May 2019; pp. 4789–4793, doi:10.1109/ICASSP.2019.8683162.
4. Hussain, K.; López-Valcarce, R. OFDM Spectral Precoding with Per-Subcarrier Distortion Constraint. In Proceedings of the 27th European Signal Processing Conference (EUSIPCO), A Coruña, Spain, 2–6 September 2019; accepted.
5. Xu, R.; Chen, M. A Precoding Scheme for DFT-Based OFDM to Suppress Sidelobes. *IEEE Commun. Lett.* **2009**, *13*, 776–778.

 *proceedings*

Proceedings

Parallelization of ARACNe, an Algorithm for the Reconstruction of Gene Regulatory Networks [†]

Uxía Casal *, Jorge González-Domínguez and María J. Martín

Grupo de Arquitectura de Computadores, CITIC, Universidade da Coruña, 15071 A Coruña, Spain; jgonzalezd@udc.es (J.G.-D.); mariam@udc.es (M.J.M.)

* Correspondence: uxia.casal.baldomir@udc.es

† Presented at the 2nd XoveTIC Conference, A Coruña, Spain, 5–6 September 2019.

Published: 31 July 2019

Abstract: Gene regulatory networks are graphical representations of molecular regulators that interact with each other and with other substances in the cell to govern the gene expression. There are different computational approaches for the reverse engineering of these networks. Most of them require all gene-gene evaluations using different mathematical methods such as Pearson/Spearman correlation, Mutual Information or topology patterns, among others. The Algorithm for the Reconstruction of Accurate Cellular Networks (ARACNe) is one of the most effective and widely used tools to reconstruct gene regulatory networks. However, the high computational cost of ARACNe prevents its use over large biologic datasets. In this work, we present a hybrid MPI/OpenMP parallel implementation of ARACNe to accelerate its execution on multi-core clusters, obtaining a speedup of 430.46 using as input a dataset with 41,100 genes and 108 samples and 32 nodes (each of them with 24 cores).

Keywords: network reconstruction; ARACNe; High Performance Computing; MPI; OpenMP

---

1. Introduction

A Gene Regulatory Network (GRN) is a network that has been inferred from gene expression data, explaining how a collection of molecular regulators interact with each other and with other substances in the cell, to govern the gene expression levels and it is crucial for understanding normal cell physiology and complex pathological phenotypes. The importance of this kind of networks can be seen in [1], where the authors explain the concept of GRNs and its relevance in different fields.

The Algorithm for the Reconstruction of Accurate Cellular Networks (ARACNe) [2] represents one of the most used methods in the scientific community to reconstruct GRNs. It is based on information theory and a network pruning process called Data Processing Inequality (DPI) theorem, which is used to infer direct regulatory relationships among transcriptional factors and their genes. ARACNe has been extensively used for real-data biological works such as the ones shown in [3,4]. However, its main drawback is its quadratic complexity with the number of genes, resulting in a high computational cost that prevents its use for large datasets.

The aim of this work is to provide biologists a new version of ARACNe faster than the original one which will be able to infer GRNs of large datasets. The approach to decrease the runtime consists in parallelizing the code using MPI routines and OpenMP directives so that the new implementation increases performance in clusters of multi-core nodes, a type of systems that nowadays are widely used by biologists as each day it is easier to have access to them through a supercomputing center.

2. Parallel ARACNe

The ARACNe framework receives as input a matrix where rows represent genes or variables and columns represent samples. It returns as output an adjacency matrix that indicates gene-gene interactions. In this work, we have developed a hybrid OpenMP/MPI parallel implementation that works with the same input/output formats and guarantees the same results as the original tool but at significantly lower runtime. In our implementation, all MPI processes read the input matrix but the workload to calculate the adjacency matrix is distributed among them. We apply a cyclic distribution by rows. Moreover, our implementation uses a second level of parallelization so that the rows assigned to each process are distributed among the different OpenMP threads following a dynamic scheduling.

Once all processes have finished their work, they use MPI communications to store the whole output matrix in the memory of Process 0 (the only process that writes into the output file). Remark that we also needed to modify the datatype used to represent the output adjacency matrix because that datatype cannot be used for MPI communications.

3. Results and Conclusions

The performance analysis of the new version of ARACNe was carried out in 32 nodes of the Finis Terrae 2 (FT2) supercomputer, a computational system based on Intel Haswell processors (each node has 24 cores) that is installed in the Centro de Supercomputatión de Galicia (CESGA). We have used three datasets, GDS2767 (14,170 genes and 108 samples), GDS6248 (45,281 genes and 51 samples) and GDS5037 (41,000 genes and 108 samples). All of them have been downloaded from the Geo Expression Omnibus (GEO) Dataset Browser available at the National Center for Biotechnology Information (NCBI) website (https://www.ncbi.nlm.nih.gov/sites/GDSbrowser).

Table 1 shows the runtime and speedup (in brackets) for different number of nodes. In all the cases the parallel code was run using one MPI process per node and 24 threads per process, one per core. The tool was run using the default parameters except for the p-value, which was explicitly set to 0.01 to remove non-significant interactions. As can be observed, the performance is high, as the runtime decreases when the number of cores increases. For instance, for the dataset GDS5037 using the original framework the execution time is more than 38 h, while it is reduced to less than 6 minutes using 768 cores (32 processes, each one with 24 threads).

Table 1. Runtime (in seconds) and speedup of the parallel version of ARACNe using up to 32 nodes of the FT2.

Nodes	Cores	GDS2767	GDS6248	GDS5037
Original ARACNe		16552	41452	139077
1	24	801.56 (20.65)	1979.09 (20.95)	6563.16 (21.19)
2	48	415.84 (39.80)	1033.60 (40.10)	3343.16 (41.60)
4	96	223.25 (74.14)	561.39 (73.84)	1763.04 (80.11)
8	192	126.49 (130.86)	323.82 (128.01)	931.15 (149.36)
16	384	88.34 (187.36)	231.16 (179.33)	608.10 (228.71)
32	768	53 (312.31)	144.93 (286.02)	323.09 (430.46)

Author Contributions: conceptualization, J.G.-D. and M.J.M.; methodology, U.C., J.G.-D. and M.J.M.; software, U.C.; validation, U.C.; writing–original draft preparation, U.C.; writing–review and editing, J.G-D. and M.J.M.

Funding: This research was supported by the Ministry of Economy and Competitiveness of Spain and FEDER funds of the EU [Project TIN2016-75845-P (AEI/FEDER, UE)]; the Xunta de Galicia and FEDER funds of the EU (Centro Singular de Investigación de Galicia) [grant number ED431G/01]; and Consolidation Program of Competitive Research [grant number ED431C 2017/04].

Acknowledgments: We gratefully thank Galicia Supercomputing Center for providing access to the Finis Terrae 2 supercomputer.

Conflicts of Interest: The authors declare no conflict of interest.

References

1. Emmert-Streib, F.; Dehmer, M.; Haibe-Kains, B. Gene regulatory networks and their applications: understanding biological and medical problems in terms of networks. *Front. Cell Dev. Biol.* **2014**, *2*, 38.
2. Margolin, A.A.; Nemenman, I. ; Basso, K.; Wiggins, C.; Stoolovitzky, G.; Dalla Favera, R.; Califano, A. ARACNE: An Algorithm for the Reconstruction of Gene Regulatory Networks in a Mammalian Cellular Context. *BMC Bioinform.* **2006**, *7*, S1.
3. Mao, X.; Xue, X. ; Wng, L.; Wang , L.; Li, L.; Zhang, X. Hypoxia Regulated Gene Network in Glioblastoma Has Special Algebraic Topology Structures and Revealed Communications Involving Warburg Effect and Immune Regulation. *Cell. Mol. Neurobiol.* **2019**, 1–22, doi:10.1007/s10571-019-00704-5.
4. Clark, J.E.; Ng, W.-F.; Rushton, S.; Watson, S.; Newton, J.L. Network structure underpinning (dys)homeostasis in chronic fatigue syndrome; Preliminary findings. *Cancer Discov.* **2019**, *3*.

proceedings  

Proceedings

Spatial Modulation for Beyond 5G Communications: Capacity Calculation and Link Adaptation [†]

Anxo Tato *[iD] and **Carlos Mosquera**[iD]

AtlanTTic Research Center, Universidade de Vigo, 36310 Vigo, Spain; mosquera@gts.uvigo.es
* Correspondence: anxotato@gts.uvigo.es
† Presented at the 2nd XoveTIC Conference, A Coruña, Spain, 5–6 September 2019.

Published: 31 July 2019

Abstract: Spatial Modulation (SM) is a candidate modulation scheme for beyond 5G communications systems due to its reduced hardware complexity and good trade-off between energy and spectral efficiency. This paper proposes two Machine Learning based solutions for easing the implementation of adaptive SM systems. On the one hand, a shallow neural network is shown to be an accurate and simple method for obtaining the capacity of SM. On the other hand, a deep neural network is proposed to select the coding rate in practical adaptive SM systems.

Keywords: link adaptation; adaptive coding and modulation; spatial modulation; 5G; neural networks; machine learning; deep learning

---

1. Introduction

Future mobile cellular networks need not only to increase their capacity, to be able to transport all the future data traffic; but also to improve their energy efficiency, to save battery and reduce the high power consumption of base stations. One key technology at the physical layer level in 5G is MIMO (Multiple Input Multiple Output), which leverages several antennas at both transmitter and receiver. One modulation scheme for this multiantenna scenario is Spatial Modulation (SM) and its many variants. SM increases the capacity compared with single antenna systems and, in addition, a significant enhancement in the energy efficiency is achieved compared with other MIMO techniques. For this reason, SM scheme is considered for future 5G systems.

All modern digital communication systems allow to tune some transmission parameters in order to adapt to the changing channel conditions and provide the highest throughput to the users. A technology named Link Adaptation or Adaptive Coding and Modulation (ACM) is behind this adaptation, allowing to change the bit rate offered to the users dynamically. This work presents some novel ACM techniques which can be used in beyond 5G systems which make use of SM.

2. System Description

SM is a family of multi-antenna modulation schemes where information is transmitted not only by modulating the amplitude, phase and/or frequency of a sinusoidal carrier, but also by selecting the antenna or group of antennas employed to transmit the modulated symbols. In the simplest scheme, there is just one Radio Frequency (RF) chain, and only one antenna is activated at each time instant, reducing both the transmitter complexity and the power consumption. Despite of this, it allows to transmit information using also all the rest of silent antennas. The more antennas you have, the higher the bit rate you can achieve at a lower energy cost. If M denotes the size of the constellation and N_t the number of transmit antennas, a spectral efficiency of $\eta = \log_2 N_t + \log_2 M$ bits/s/Hz can be achieved with SM.

Figure 1 shows a block diagram of a 2 × 2 adaptive SM system with ACM which allows to change both the coding rate r of the channel encoder and the modulation order M. The adaptation of the physical layer parameters allows to follow the time variant channel with the aim of approaching the transmission bit rate as much as possible to the instantaneous channel capacity.

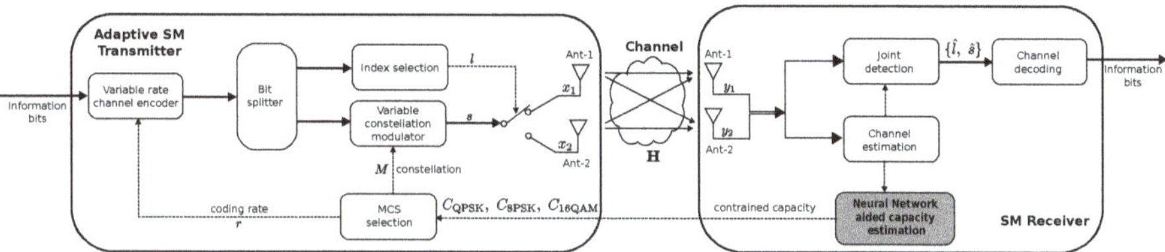

Figure 1. Block diagram of an adaptive SM system with ACM.

3. Capacity Calculation of SM Systems

The capacity of SM depends on the SNR γ and the channel matrix **H**. Therefore, whilst a mobile user is moving with his smartphone around the city, the strength of the received signal and the environment surrounding the gNB and the UE antennas will impact the capacity and, in consequence, the maximum bit rate that the user can get.

There is not a closed form expression for the SM capacity although this can be calculated by means of Monte Carlos simulations. To reduce its computation time, some analytical approximations of the SM capacity constrained to a given constellation were proposed. However, those expressions still entail a high complexity and, in addition, they have a problem of overestimation of the true capacity for some channels.

To avoid these issues, a Machine Learning (ML) approach was applied successfully to compute the SM capacity [1]. A Multilayer Feedforward Neural Network (MFNN) was trained with supervised learning to perform the mapping between the channel conditions, $(\gamma, \mathbf{H})$, and the constrained capacity of SM for several constellations. A single hidden layer MFNN with a specif set of input features extracted from the SNR and the channel matrix was enough to outperform previous analytical approximations, both in terms of accuracy and complexity, as can be seen in Figure 2.

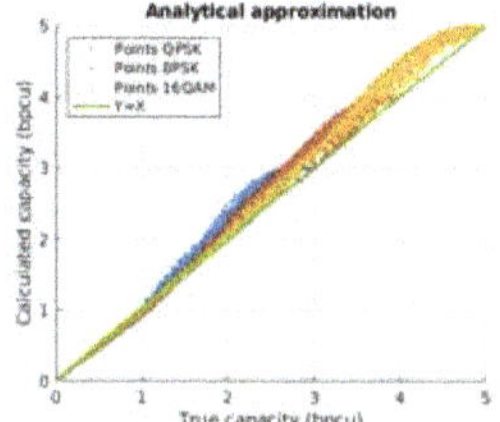

		Taylor approx.	MFNN	Factor
	Real products	7,168	368	$\div$ 20
Complexity	**Non linear op.**	2,128	23	$\div$ 92
	Execution time	5.47 ms	0.107 ms	$\div$ 51
Accuracy	3σ	0.392	0.018	$\times$ 22

(**a**) Prior approximation   (**b**) Comparison between MFNN and prior analytical approx.

Figure 2. Performance comparison of the previous analytical approximations and the MFNN for obtaining the contrained capacity of SM with three constellations (QPSK, 8PSK and 16QAM).

4. Coding Rate Selection with a Deep Neural Network

The coding rate selection in a practical SM system can be done with the capacity calculated by the neural network if a proper back-off margin Δ is subtracted from the theoretical capacity. In Figure 3b the throughput achieved with this ACM mechanism is referred as capacity based. Nevertheless, a neural network can be trained for making the coding rate selection directly [2]. In this Deep Learning

(DL) based approach, a MFNN of three hidden layers learns the mapping from the channel conditions to the optimum coding rate.

Figure 3b compares the throughput of different adaptive and non adaptive SM systems. For bounding the error rate, a non adaptive system should use a low coding rate that, as can be seen in the plot, limits considerably the achievable throughput. On the other hand, the selection based on the calculated capacity represents clearly a great improvement. However, the DL based mechanism outperforms all the other methods, achieving the highest throughput and being very closed to the ideal genie-aided coding rate selection.

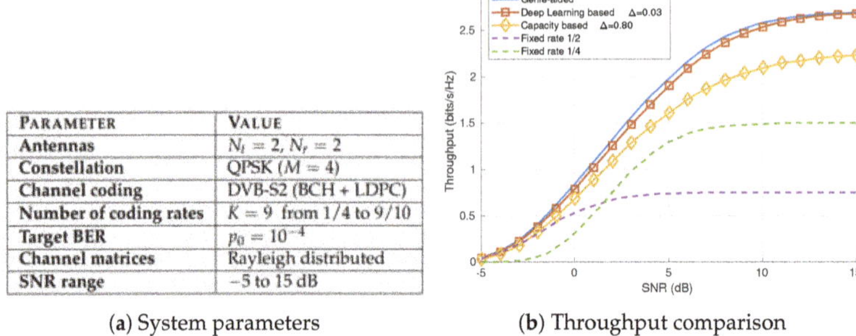

Parameter	Value
Antennas	$N_t = 2,\ N_r = 2$
Constellation	QPSK ($M = 4$)
Channel coding	DVB-S2 (BCH + LDPC)
Number of coding rates	$K = 9$ from $1/4$ to $9/10$
Target BER	$p_0 = 10^{-4}$
Channel matrices	Rayleigh distributed
SNR range	-5 to 15 dB

(**a**) System parameters

(**b**) Throughput comparison

Figure 3. System parameters, classification performance of the DL-based coding rate selection and throughput obtained with different adaptive and non adaptive SM coding rate selection mechanisms.

5. Conclusions

In this article our recent contributions regarding the adaptation of SM systems were briefly presented. These embrace the capacity calculation of SM by means of a neural network and the coding rate selection in practical SM systems with a deep neural network. Thus, a link adaptation method is proposed for SM, a sort of modulation scheme considered for beyond 5G systems due to is good trade-off between complexity and spectral and energy efficiency.

Funding: This work was funded by the Xunta de Galicia (Secretaria Xeral de Universidades) under a predoctoral scholarship (co-funded by the European Social Fund).

Conflicts of Interest: The authors declare no conflict of interest.

References

1. Tato, A.; Mosquera, C.; Henarejos, P.; Pérez-Neira, A. Neural Network Aided Computation of Mutual Information for Adaptation of Spatial Modulation. *arXiv* **2019**, arXiv:1904.10844.
2. Tato, A.; Mosquera, C. Deep Learning Assisted Rate Adaptation in Spatial Modulation Links. In Proceedings of the 16th International Symposium on Wireless Communications Systems (ISWCS), Oulu, Finland, August, 2019.

Proceedings

Nonparametric Regression Estimation for Circular Data [†]

Andrea Meilán-Vila [1],* , **Mario Francisco-Fernández [1]**, **Rosa M. Crujeiras [2] and Agnese Panzera [3]**

[1]   Department of Mathematics, Universidade da Coruña, 15071 A Coruña , Spain
[2]   Department of Statistics, Mathematical Analysis and Optimization, Universidade de Santiago de Compostela, 15705 Santiago de Compostela, Spain
[3]   Department of Statistics, Computer Science, Applications "Giuseppe Parenti", Università degli Studi di Firenze, 50134 Florence, Italy
*   Correspondence: andrea.meilan@udc.es; Tel.: +34-981-167000
†   Presented at the 2nd XoveTIC Conference, A Coruña, Spain, 5–6 September 2019.

Published: 31 July 2019

Abstract: Non-parametric regression with a circular response variable and a unidimensional linear regressor is a topic which was discussed in the literature. In this work, we extend the results to the case of multivariate linear explanatory variables. Nonparametric procedures to estimate the circular regression function are formulated. A simulation study is carried out to study the sample performance of the proposed estimators.

Keywords: circular data; nonparametric methods; multidimensional data analysis

---

1. Introduction

Circular data can be regarded as points whose support is on a circle (with unit radius) measured in degrees or radians and with periodic nature. Examples of circular data arise in many applied fields such as biology (orientation of animals), meteorology (wind direction), oceanography (ocean currents), among others. Comprehensive reviews on circular statistics are provided by [1] and [2].

Nonparametric regression with circular response and univariate linear predictor was studied by [3]. They defined local estimators for the circular regression function. The aim of this work is to propose and study nonparametric procedures to estimate the circular regression function, assuming a multivariate linear-circular regression model (circular responses and multivariate linear predictors). Simulation studies are carried out to check the finite sample performance of the considered estimators.

2. The Model

Let $\{(\mathbf{X}_i, \Theta_i)\}_{i=1}^n$ be a random sample of $(\mathbf{X}, \Theta)$, where Θ is an angular or circular random variable taking values on $\mathbb{T} = [0, 2\pi)$, and $\mathbf{X}$ is a random variable taking values in $D \subseteq \mathbb{R}^d$. The following regression model is assumed:

$$\Theta_i = (m(\mathbf{X}_i) + \varepsilon_i)(\mathrm{mod}\,2\pi), \quad i = 1, \ldots, n, \tag{1}$$

where the random angles ε_i have zero mean direction, finite concentration, and are independent of the $\mathbf{X}_i$. This implies that $\mathbb{E}[\sin(\varepsilon) \mid \mathbf{X} = \mathbf{x}] = 0$ and $\mathbb{E}[\cos(\varepsilon) \mid \mathbf{X} = \mathbf{x}] < \infty$. Additionally, it is supposed that $\mathrm{Var}[\sin(\varepsilon) \mid \mathbf{X} = \mathbf{x}] < \infty$, $\mathrm{Var}[\cos(\varepsilon) \mid \mathbf{X} = \mathbf{x}] < \infty$ and $\mathrm{Cov}[\sin(\varepsilon), \cos(\varepsilon) \mid \mathbf{X} = \mathbf{x}] < \infty$.

3. Kernel-Type Estimators

In order to construct an estimator for the regression circular function m, the risk measure $\mathbb{E}(1 - \cos(\Theta - m(\mathbf{x})))$ can be used. Defining $m_1(\mathbf{x}) = E[\sin(\Theta) \mid \mathbf{X} = \mathbf{x}]$ and $m_2(\mathbf{x}) = E[\cos(\Theta) \mid \mathbf{X} = \mathbf{x}]$, then the minimizer of the risk function is $m(\mathbf{x}) = \text{atan2}(m_1(\mathbf{x}), m_2(\mathbf{x}))$, where the function $\text{atan2}(y, x)$ returns the angle between the x-axis and the vector from the origin to (x, y). Therefore, the proposed estimator for the circular regression function $m(\mathbf{x})$ is given by:

$$\hat{m}_{\mathbf{H}}(\mathbf{x}; p) = \text{atan2}(\hat{m}_{1,\mathbf{H}}(\mathbf{x}; p), \hat{m}_{2,\mathbf{H}}(\mathbf{x}; p)), \tag{2}$$

where $\hat{m}_{1,\mathbf{H}}(\mathbf{x}; p)$ and $\hat{m}_{2,\mathbf{H}}(\mathbf{x}; p)$ denote the p-th order local polynomial estimators of $m_1(x)$ and $m_2(x)$, respectively. Although theoretical results are omitted here, the asymptotic properties of the estimator given in (2) were derived in terms of bias and variance.

4. Simulation Study

In order to explore the performance of the estimators proposed in Section 3, a simulation study considering different scenarios is carried out. Only the case $d = 2$ is analyzed in the study. For each scenario, 500 samples of size n ($n = 64, 100, 225$ and 400) are generated on a bidimensional regular grid in the unit square considering the following regression models:

R1. $\Theta = (\text{atan2}(6X_1^5 - 2X_1^3 - 1, -2X_2^5 - 3X_2 - 1) + \varepsilon)(\text{mod}2\pi)$

R2. $\Theta = (\text{acos}(X_1^5 - 1) + \dfrac{3}{2}\text{asin}(X_2^3 - X_2 + 1) + \varepsilon)(\text{mod}2\pi)$

where $\mathbf{X} = (X_1, X_2)$ denote the bidimensional covariate and the circular errors, ε_i, are drawn from a von Mises distribution $vM(0, \kappa)$ with different values of κ (5, 10 and 15). For each sample the estimator (2) is computed, assuming $p = 0$ (Nadaraya-Watson estimator) and $p = 1$ (local linear estimator). In both cases, the smoothing parameter $\mathbf{H}$ is chosen by cross-validation, minimizing $\sum_{i=1}^{n}\{1 - \cos[\Theta_i - \hat{m}^{(i)}(\mathbf{X}_i)]\}$, where $\hat{m}^{(i)}(\mathbf{X}_i)$ represents the Nadaraya-Watson or the local linear estimator, computed using all observations except $(\mathbf{X}_i, \Theta_i)$, and evaluated at $\mathbf{X}_i$. The results of errors $\frac{1}{n}\sum_{i=1}^{n}\{1 - \cos[m(\mathbf{X}_i) - \hat{m}(\mathbf{X}_i)]\}$ are shown in Table 1 for models R1 and R2. It can be observed that the local linear estimator gives a smaller error than the Nadaraya-Watson estimator in most cases. On the other hand, as expected, considering a larger sample size, the error is smaller. Further, smaller errors are also obtained if the concentration parameter κ is larger (less *variance*).

Table 1. Means of errors $\frac{1}{n}\sum_{i=1}^{n}\{1 - \cos[m(\mathbf{X}_i) - \hat{m}(\mathbf{X}_i)]\}$ over 500 simulations, for models R1 and R2, using Nadaraya-Watson and local linear fits.

| | | Model R1 | | | Model R2 | | |
| | | κ | | | κ | | |
Estimator	n	5	10	15	5	10	15
Nadaraya-Watson	64	0.0226	0.0121	0.0089	0.0367	0.0213	0.0165
	100	0.0171	0.0108	0.0080	0.0388	0.0024	0.0152
	225	0.0058	0.0049	0.0038	0.0185	0.0125	0.0108
	400	0.0056	0.0035	0.0026	0.0129	0.0080	0.0062
Local linear	64	0.0234	0.0125	0.0089	0.0283	0.0144	0.0107
	100	0.0165	0.0086	0.0061	0.0209	0.0013	0.0083
	225	0.0050	0.0039	0.0029	0.0103	0.0061	0.0047
	400	0.0050	0.0026	0.0018	0.0074	0.0043	0.0033

5. Conclusions

Nonparametric procedures to estimate the the circular regression function were proposed and studied. The new estimators were based on local polynomial fits as part of their construction. Simulation studies were carried out justifying the correct performance of the proposed estimators.

Funding: This research has received financial support from the Xunta de Galicia and the European Union (European Social Fund—ESF). This research has been partially supported by MINECO grant MTM2016-76969-P and MTM2017-82724-R and by the Xunta de Galicia (ED481A-2017/361, Grupos de Referencia Competitiva ED431C-2016-015 and Centro Singular de Investigación de Galicia ED431G/01), all of them through the ERDF.

Conflicts of Interest: The authors declare no conflict of interest.

References

1. Fisher, N.I. *Statistical Analysis of Circular Data*; Cambridge University Press: Cambridge, UK, 1995.
2. Mardia, K.V.; Jupp, P.E. *Directional Statistics*; John Wiley & Sons: New York, NY, USA, 2009.
3. Di Marzio, M.; Panzera, A.; Taylor, C.C. Non-parametric Regression for Circular Responses. *Scand. J. Stat.* **2013**, *40*, 142–149.

 *proceedings* 

Proceedings

System for Automatic Assessment of Alzheimer's Disease Diagnosis Based on Deep Learning Techniques †

Alejandro Puente-Castro *, **Cristian Robert Munteanu** and **Enrique Fernandez-Blanco**

Faculty of Computer Science, CITIC, University of A Coruna, 15071 La Coruña, Spain
* Correspondence: a.puentec@udc.es
† Presented at the 2nd XoveTIC Conference, A Coruna, Spain, 5–6 September 2019.

Published: 1 August 2019

Abstract: Automatic detection of Alzheimer's disease is a very active area of research. This is due to its usefulness in starting the protocol to stop the inevitable progression of this neurodegenerative disease. This paper proposes a system for the detection of the disease by means of Deep Learning techniques in magnetic resonance imaging (MRI). As a solution, a model of neuronal networks (ANN) and two sets of reference data for training are proposed. Finally, the goodness of this system is verified within the domain of the application.

Keywords: Alzheimer; Deep learning; MRI; sagittal; ANN; transfer learning

---

1. Introduction

The progressive and constant aging of the population causes a higher incidence of neurodegenerative diseases associated with age. Among these diseases, the Alzheimer's has a prevalence of 5.05% in Europe as early as 2016 [1]. Early palliative diagnosis and treatment continue to be the best alternatives for improving the patient's quality of life and their environment. To make this diagnosis, various cognitive, psychological or clinical tests are used. Within the group of clinical tests, one of the most widely used is the analysis of brain images obtained by magnetic resonance imaging (MRI), as changes in brain morphology can be seen such as contraction of the hippocampus and cerebral cortex, or elongation of the ventricles [2].

The objective of this work is the use of Deep Learning techniques to support an early diagnosis of Alzheimer's disease through the analysis of conventional sagittal MRI images from two reference sets of data.

2. Materials and Methods

This section describes the datasets and computer models proposed in this work, each of which is described in its corresponding subsection.

2.1. Materials

This work makes the MRI images dataset ADNI [3]. Both sets are collections of correctly labeled MRI images of 255 × 255 pixels, which are two of the most common in the literature.

2.2. Proposed Model

The proposed method uses the classical pipeline to solve a problem on any kind of signal, and in particular in this case images. This pipeline has a pre-established set of stages, being: pre-processing phase, feature extraction phase and a regression or classification phase based on the features extracted from the images.

The proposed model is based on the use of a pre-trained model which, in this particular case is ResNet [4]. The idea behind this is to take advance of features extration phase of the model while the classification is droped or ajusted for a new problem. This squema known under the name of transfer learning has been used many times in the related literature. In the proposed model, the classifier has been replaced by a Support Vector Machine (SVM) [5]. Thus, the speed of experimentation can be accelerated by adapting to this problem, successful models in other different problems.

3. Results

In this paper, the results for the ADNI dataset are presented. The results shown on Table 1 are average of 50 repretitions of a Hold-Out training strategy. The table showns the test result comparison between a reference work and two developed developped models, one with ResNet as base and one with MobileNet [6]. The dataset was splited in 80% for training and 20% for testing, while a 1% of the training data set was used for validation purposes. The advantages of the ResNet approach are noticeable being the best one in precision and recall which are our main objective.

Table 1. Best results for ADNI.

Model	Image	Accuracy	Precision	Recall	Specificity	f1-Score	AUC
Inception [7]	PET hor.	-	63.66%	64.67%	79.00%	64.00%	76.00%
ResNet	**MRI sag.**	**81.46%±1.9%**	**82.48%±2.2%**	**93.09%±1.9%**	**55.19%±4.1%**	**87.44%±1.5%**	**74.14%±2.2%**
MobileNet	MRI sag.	51.08%±19.1%	37.56%±34.7%	52.4%±49.7%	47.73%±40.7%	43.16%±40.7%	50.01%±0.1%

4. Discussion

As a main conclusion the identification of Alzheimer's disease in sagittal MRI images from ADNI dataset is accessible using Deep Learning techniques. These results are comparable to those proposed by the horizontal cuts in the literature. Despite the high imbalance of both data sets and the small OASIS set, the proposed model presents satisfactory results because of its simplicity.

Based on the authors' experience in the field of Alzheimer's disease, the sagittal plane also shows characteristic deformations of the disease. Traditionally, specialists use the horizontal plane. This opens up new ways for experimentation. New characteristics of Alzheimer's disease can be found in them in other regions. These new features may make the diagnosis of Alzheimer's a more precise task.

Author Contributions: Conceptualization, A.P.-C.; methodology, A.P.-C.; experiment design, C.M.; software, A.P.-C. and E.F.-B.; validation, A.P.-C.; formal analysis, A.P.-C.; investigation, A.P.-C.; resources, A.P.-C.; data curation, A.P.-C.; writing—original draft preparation, A.P.-C.; writing—review and editing, E.F.-B.; visualization, A.P.-C.; supervision, C.M. and E.F.-B.

Funding: This research received no external funding.

Acknowledgments: The authors would like to thank the support from NVidia corp., which granted the GPU used in this work. They also acknowledge the support from the CESGA, where many of the preliminary tests were run.

Conflicts of Interest: The authors declare no conflict of interest.

Abbreviations

The following abbreviations are used in this manuscript:

ANN	Artificial Neural Network
MRI	Magnetic Resonance Imaging
AUC	Area Under Curve ROC
ROC	Receiver Operating Characteristic

References

1. Niu, H.; Álvarez-Álvarez, I.; Guillén-Grima, F.; Aguinaga-Ontoso, I. Prevalencia e incidencia de la enfermedad de Alzheimer en Europa: Metaanálisis. *Neurología* **2017**, *32*, 523–532.
2. Sarraf, S.; Tofighi, G. DeepAD: Alzheimer's disease classification via deep convolutional neural networks using MRI and fMRI. *BioRxiv* **2016**, p. 070441.
3. ADNI | Alzheimer's Disease Neuroimaging Initiative. Avaialble online: http://adni.loni.usc.edu (accessed on 27 June 2019).
4. He, K.; Zhang, X.; Ren, S.; Sun, J. Deep residual learning for image recognition. In Proceedings of the IEEE Conference on Computer Vision and Pattern Recognition, Las Vegas, NV, USA, 27–30 June 2016; pp. 770–778.
5. Joachims, T. Text categorization with support vector machines: Learning with many relevant features. In *European Conference on Machine Learning*; Springer: Berlin/Heidelberg, Germany, 1998; pp. 137–142.
6. Howard, A.G.; Zhu, M.; Chen, B.; Kalenichenko, D.; Wang, W.; Weyand, T.; Andreetto, M.; Adam, H. Mobilenets: Efficient Convolutional Neural Networks for Mobile Vision Applications. *arXiv* **2017**, arXiv:1704.04861 .
7. Ding, Y.; Sohn, J.H.; Kawczynski, M.G.; Trivedi, H.; Harnish, R.; Jenkins, N.W.; Lituiev, D.; Copeland, T.P.; Aboian, M.S.; Mari Aparici, C.; et al. A Deep learning model to predict a diagnosis of alzheimer disease by using 18F-FDG PET of the brain. *Radiology* **2018**, *290*, 456–464.

 *proceedings*

Proceedings

Mouse Behavior Analysis Based on Artificial Intelligence as a Second-Phase Authentication System [†]

Daniel Garabato *, **Jorge Rodríguez García**, **Francisco J. Novoa** and **Carlos Dafonte**

Centro de investigación CITIC, Universidade da Coruña, Campus de Elviña s/n, 15071 A Coruña, Spain

* Correspondence: daniel.garabato@udc.es

† Presented at the 2nd XoveTIC Conference, A Coruna, Spain, 5–6 September 2019.

Published: 1 August 2019

Abstract: Nowadays, a wide variety of computer systems use authentication protocols based on several factors in order to enhance security. In this work, the viability of a second-phase authentication scheme based on users' mouse behavior is analyzed by means of classical Artificial Intelligence techniques, such as the Support Vector Machines or Multi-Layer Perceptrons. Such methods were found to perform particularly well, demonstrating the feasibility of mouse behavior analytics as a second-phase authentication mechanism. In addition, in the current stage of the experiments, the classification techniques were found to be very stable for the extracted features.

Keywords: authentication; computer security; artificial intelligence

---

1. Introduction

Computer security has been one of the main issues and areas of interest and research since the origin of Information Technology. A wide variety of security measures have been developed over the years in order to try to protect different type of assets, from physical systems to software services and data [1]. Authentication systems can be considered a key component of these security models, becoming the basis for access control systems and the first barrier against threats. Nowadays, almost every computer system or service relies on an authentication process in order to check the identity of the users and to determine the access permissions that should be granted according to the users' specific profiles.

Such an authentication process can be performed by means of different methods or factors [2]. The most common ones are based on knowledge, such as a password or a personal identification number, or some device or item that the user owns, such as an identity card or a bank card. More sophisticated methods based on users' biometric properties, such as fingerprint, retina or voice, have evolved over the last years, so that they can verify users' identity in a very precise and robust manner. These methods have become more and more popular along with the use of smartphones and tablets, which use them to grant access to the device features. In addition, behavioral biometrics have arisen from the analysis of users' behavior during their interaction with computer systems as an alternative way of authentication. Different behavioral features, such as keyboard typing and mouse usage, have been widely studied as possible authentication factors [3], but their high variability over time make them unstable to become a primarily authentication method.

During the last years, classical authentication schemes have moved towards a two-step verification process in order to strengthen authentication. Under this scheme, users must prove their identity in two different and complementary ways, typically a password-based method is used as primary verification and, then, a generated code which is sent to the user's phone is also required to successfully complete the process.

The second verification step could be extended so that it is periodically repeated all along the users' session to verify their identities in a transparent manner, so that they are not continuously bothered and required to identify themselves. To this purpose, behavioral authentication methods could be useful as they do not require any specific device and they just monitor users' activity. Therefore, in this work we conduct an analysis of a mouse-based authentication mechanism in order to be used as a continuous second step verification process. Such a method aims to create a specific profile for each user by means of Artificial Intelligence (AI) techniques, and it requires the application of Big Data and Data Mining techniques in order to handle the enormous volume of data gathered from the users' interaction with the computer environment.

2. Methods

In order to conduct this experiment, mouse movement data were collected from a variety of test cases oriented to frequent user interactions with a computer, such as closing a window, forced waiting periods, or even locating the mouse pointer on the screen. To this purpose, an ad-hoc application was developed to guide the user across these test cases, while the mouse movement data were being collected in a transparent manner to the user. Due to the high variability of behavioral biometry, the entire process was repeated over three different sessions for each one of the twenty test volunteers, resulting in more than one million records of data.

Users' identity must be verified in order to make the authentication process feasible. A number of features related to different spatial-temporal measurements on mouse usage were originally proposed in [4], and they were used in this work. Since the users' behavior may significantly vary due to particular circumstances (i.e. emotional state or distractions), outlier measurements were filtered out, and then the data was scaled to the interval $[0, 1]$ prior to any further processing. Due to the temporal and sequential basis in which the events are captured, two different data scenarios were proposed for analysis: in the first one, data were grouped in windows of 100, 200, and 500 events, respectively; and, in the second one, data were grouped in time windows of one, two and five seconds, respectively.

The analysis conducted in this work addresses the authentication process by means of two different widely used AI classification algorithms: Support Vector Machines [5] (SVM) and Multi-Layer Perceptrons [6] (MLP). User-specific profiles were built upon the three data scenarios proposed, searching for an appropriate model hyperparameterization using a grid search procedure, which also takes cross-validation into account, so that the generalization of the trained models can be assessed.

3. Results

The performance of the proposed experiments was measured in order to analyze whether it is possible to authenticate users according to their behavior when they are interacting with computers by means of mouse devices (Table 1). To this purpose, four different common metrics have been computed: precision, recall, F_1-score, and AUC-ROC [7].

Table 1. Average and standard deviation performance.

		Event-Based Windows			Time-Based Windows		
		100 events	200 events	500 events	1 second	2 seconds	5 seconds
MLP	Precision	0.82 ($\pm$0.06)	0.83 ($\pm$0.07)	0.85 ($\pm$0.09)	0.79 ($\pm$0.07)	0.80 ($\pm$0.08)	0.80 ($\pm$0.09)
	Recall	0.91 ($\pm$0.05)	0.89 ($\pm$0.07)	0.87 ($\pm$0.10)	0.86 ($\pm$0.07)	0.85 ($\pm$0.07)	0.82 ($\pm$0.10)
	F_1-score	0.86 ($\pm$0.05)	0.86 ($\pm$0.06)	0.85 ($\pm$0.08)	0.82 ($\pm$0.06)	0.82 ($\pm$0.06)	0.81 ($\pm$0.08)
	AUC-ROC	0.90 ($\pm$0.04)	0.91 ($\pm$0.05)	0.91 ($\pm$0.06)	0.87 ($\pm$0.06)	0.88 ($\pm$0.06)	0.87 ($\pm$0.08)
SVM	Precision	0.80 ($\pm$0.06)	0.81 ($\pm$0.07)	0.83 ($\pm$0.09)	0.78 ($\pm$0.08)	0.79 ($\pm$0.08)	0.79 ($\pm$0.09)
	Recall	0.94 ($\pm$0.04)	0.94 ($\pm$0.06)	0.93 ($\pm$0.07)	0.89 ($\pm$0.06)	0.90 ($\pm$0.06)	0.88 ($\pm$0.08)
	F_1-score	0.86 ($\pm$0.04)	0.87 ($\pm$0.05)	0.87 ($\pm$0.07)	0.83 ($\pm$0.06)	0.84 ($\pm$0.06)	0.83 ($\pm$0.07)
	AUC-ROC	0.91 ($\pm$0.04)	0.92 ($\pm$0.04)	0.92 ($\pm$0.06)	0.88 ($\pm$0.06)	0.88 ($\pm$0.06)	0.89 ($\pm$0.07)

The overall performance is similar for all the experiments conducted, obtaining for most users values around 0.84 and 0.89 for F_1-score and AUC-ROC, respectively. On the one hand, it was found that the usage of time windows performed slightly worse than using a fixed number of events for each chunk. The underlying cause may be the variable number of records available for each user: some of them impulsively move the mouse, whereas others use the mouse in a smoother manner. On the other hand, MLPs achieved a higher precision rate, so that it should be favored for authentication purposes rather than SVMs.

4. Conclusions and Future Work

Through the analysis conducted in this work, it has been demonstrated that users' mouse-based behavior can be used for authentication purposes. Although the obtained performance may not be suitable for a single-primary authentication mechanism, it could be perfectly used as a second-phase authentication method that continuously monitors users' activity seeking after behavior anomalies, similarly to an intrusion detection system. In case of a security issue detection, the authentication monitor could decide to close users' sessions, or to report such an issue to the system administrators for further investigation.

On the basis of these results, a mouse behavior monitoring system could be developed and tested under a real environment, so that the stability of these models over time could be assessed. In addition, further analysis based on different approaches or techniques, such as deep learning, could be conducted to improve the overall performance.

Funding: The manpower of this work was funded by the Spanish MECD FPU16/03827, and CITIC–ACATIA contract.

Acknowledgments: This work was also supported by the Xunta de Galicia (Potencial Crecemento ED431B 2018/42) and the European Union (European Social Fund – ESF); we also used IT infrastructure that was acquired through the RTI2018-095076-B-C22 and ESP2016-80079-C2-2-R projects, financed by the Spanish Ministry of Science, Innovation and Universities and the Ministry of Economy, Industry and Competitiveness.

Conflicts of Interest: The authors declare no conflict of interest.The funders had no role in the design of the study; in the collection, analyses, or interpretation of data; in the writing of the manuscript, or in the decision to publish the results.

References

1. Stallings, W.; Brown, L. *Computer Security: Principles and Practice*, 2nd ed.; Pearson Education Limited: London, UK, 2012.
2. Barkadehi, M.H.; Nilashi, M.; Ibrahim, O.; Fardi, A.Z.; Samad, S. Authentication systems: A literature review and classification. *Telemat. Inform.* **2018**, *35*, 1491–1511.
3. Bhatnagar, M.; Jain, R.K.; Khairnar, N.S. A Survey on Behavioral Biometric Techniques: Mouse vs Keyboard Dynamics. *IJCA* **2013**, *975*, 8887.
4. Sayed, B.; Traoré, I.; Woungang, I.; Obaidat, M.S. Biometric Authentication Using Mouse Gesture Dynamics. *IEEE Syst. J.* **2013**, *7*, 262–274.
5. Cortes, C.; Vapnik, V. Support-Vector Networks. *Mach. Learn.* **1995**, *20*, 273–297.
6. Rumelhart, D.E.; Hinton, G.E.; Williams, R.J. Learning Internal Representation by Error Propagation. In *Parallel Distributed Processing: Explorations in the Microstructure of Cognition*; MIT Press: Cambridge, MA, USA, 1986; Volume 1.
7. Tharwat, A. Classification assessment methods. *Appl. Comput. Inform.* **2018**. doi:10.1016/j.aci.2018.08.003.

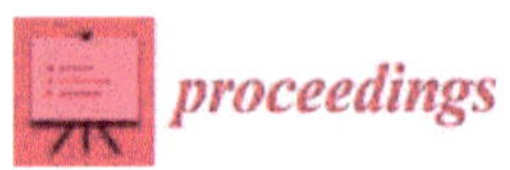 *proceedings*

Proceedings

Internationalization of the ClepiTO Web Platform †

Eloy Naveira Carro [1,*], María del Carmen Miranda-Duro [1], Patricia Concheiro-Moscoso [1], Alejandro Puente Castro [1], Paula Cristina Costa Portugal Cardoso [2] and Tiago Filipe Mota Coelho [2]

[1] Faculty of Health Sciences, Research Center on Information and Communication Technologies (CITIC), Universidade da Coruña Tecnología Aplicada a la Investigación en Ocupación, Igualdad y Salud (TALIONIS), 15071 A Coruña, Spain

[2] Universidade Politécnica do Porto, Laboratório de Reabilitação Psicossocial, 4200-465 Porto, Portugal

* Correspondence: eloy.naveira@udc.es

† Presented at the 2nd XoveTIC Conference, A Coruña, Spain, 5–6 September 2019.

Published: 1 August 2019

Abstract: This adaptation consists of the translation from Spanish into Portuguese of the different contents offered by the ClepiTO web platform to be able to carry out a pilot test with a larger population in Portugal and thus be able to compare the results obtained among the Spanish and Portuguese population

Keywords: internationalization; globalization; localization

1. Introduction

This work arises as a continuation of a research project in the field of health that focuses on the study of the use of technologies in elderly people to promote the health of this population. This project was carried out during 3 years, during which a technological solution was investigated and developed that offers services oriented to the evaluation and intervention with older people in three areas of action: increase urinary continence, the detection and prevention of falls and the sleep control [1].

As a result of this project, a web platform called ClepiTO was implemented, which was used in a pilot study with the Spanish population.

2. Objective

The main objective of this web internationalization is the adaptation of the ClepiTO website to Portuguese-Speaking countries. The internationalization process enabled to deploy in a production environment to its later use at international level, and to be able to compare different populations with similar characteristics.

3. Material and methods

3.1. Design

The first step was to do some guides that represent the contents and the functionalities of the website to translate through collaboration with experienced health practitioners from Portugal that participates in the pilot test.

The second step was to develop the changes in the project with some technical considerations that are described in the next subsection.

Lastly, the website will be used in a pilot study in the Oporto area, with the collaboration of research groups from the Porto Polytechnic Institute.

3.2. Technical considerations

- Because of lexicon similarities between both languages there have been no longitudinal variations in the contents and, consequently, there have been no major changes in the interfaces.
- The proximity between both languages avoid the adaptation of the typography in the website contents.
- An evaluation of changes to be introduced in the design of the database was made. The chosen strategy was based on the introduction of language columns because many more translations are not expected in the future nor a critical loss of performance in the system.
- The rest of the contents to be translated have been collected in a structure of resource files, in which the content is mapped according to the location from which it is accessed by the browser.

4. Results and Conclusions

Since the pilot study has not yet been carried out using the adapted tool, it will be necessary to wait for the final results with the analysis performed, as well as future tests with larger samples, to determine if the project has a real impact on the quality of life.

Author Contributions: P.C.M. and M.d.C.M.D conceived and designed the experiments; P.C.M. performed the experiments; A.P.C. and E.N.C. contributed with technical changes; E.N.C. and M.d.C.M.D wrote the paper.

Funding: Project GERIA-TIC, co-funded by the Galician Innovation Agency (GAIN) through the Connect PEME Program (3rd edition) (IN852A 2016/10) and EU FEDER funds, Collaborative Genomic Data Integration Project (CICLOGEN). Data mining techniques and molecular docking for analysis of integrative data in colon cancer. "Funded by the Ministry of Economy, Industry and Competitiveness. Galician Network of Research in Colorectal Cancer (REGICC) ED431D 2017/23, Galician Network of Medicines (REGID) ED431D 2017/16 funded by the Department of Culture Education and University Planning aids for the consolidation and structuring of competitive research units of the University System of Galicia of the Xunta de Galicia and Singular Centers (ED431G/01) endowed with FEDER funds of the EU. Financial support from the Xunta de Galicia and the European Union (European Social Fund—ESF), is gratefully acknowledged."

References

1. Nieto-Riveiro, L.; Groba, B.; Miranda, M.C.; Concheiro, P.; Pazos, A.; Pousada, T.; Pereira, J. Technologies for participatory medicine and health promotion in the elderly population. *Medicine* **2018**, *97*, e10791. doi:1097/MD.0000000000010791.

 *proceedings*

Proceedings

Dataset for the Aesthetic Value Automatic Prediction †

Nereida Rodriguez-Fernandez *, Iria Santos and Alvaro Torrente

Department of Computer Science, Faculty of Computer Science, University of A Coruña, 15071 A Coruña, Spain; iria.santos@udc.es (I.S.); alvaro.torrente@udc.es (A.T.)
* Correspondence: nereida.rodriguezf@udc.es
† Presented at 2nd XoveTIC Conference, A Coruña, Spain, 5–6 September 2019.

Published: 1 August 2019

Abstract: One of the most relevant issue in the prediction and classification of the aesthetic value of an image is the sample set used to train and validate the computational system. In this document the limitations found in different datasets used to classificate and predict aesthetic values are exposed, and a new dataset is proposed with images from the DPChallenge.com portal, with evaluations of three different populations.

Keywords: dataset; aesthetics; quality; prediction; classification; artificial intelligence; assessment

---

1. Introduction

Different research groups have tried to create computer systems capable of learning the aesthetic perception of a group of human beings as part of a generative system, with the intention of being used in the selection or automatic ordering of images. Due the subjective nature of the aesthetic problem, the selection of the dataset with which the system is trained is especially relevant. After analyzed, in previous research [1,2], the generalization degree of some datasets, it has been concluded that it is not enough to take them as a reference in the training of automatic image classification and prediction systems. In order to providing a solution to the problems detected, this paper describes the creation of a new dataset from the DPChallenge.com portal, with greater statistical coherence. In addition, this new dataset has been evaluated according to aesthetic and quality criteria by a human group in controlled experimental conditions and by another American group through online surveys.

2. Limitations Found in the Datasets Available

There are some datasets that have been used in several times for the images classification. Among them, Photo.net [3–5], DPChallenge.com [6,7] and the one created by Cela-Conde et al. [8–10] However, when its generalization capacity is studied, it has been detected that they cannot be considered as representative for the realization of image experiments. In some cases, the correlation is greater when the validation set belongs to the same data source as the training set, and this correlation drops markedly when the validation source set is different from that of the training. In addition, the sample sets trained with evaluations from the photographic portals have some defects: the evaluation system does not have the same control as a psychological test because it is not possible to obtain all the information about the evaluators or about the evaluation conditions; the number of images could be insufficient, since there is no justified reason to choose a sample size and there is a very high difference between the number of people who value each image; user ratings can be easily conditioned by personal tastes, personal relationships with the work creator, or by the momentary boom or popularity of certain styles. Lastly, in one of the cases [3] it has been shown that the users of these portals do not have sufficient grounds to differentiate between aesthetics and originality criteria, with a Pearson correlation coefficient of 0.891. In the dataset created by Ke et al. [6] is another limitation: the web portal DPChallenge.com works as a photo contest and does not specify any criteria to evaluate the images with their own judgment and nothing related with that of other users. On the other hand, in the dataset created by Cela-Conde et al. [8] the number of images presented by category is not equitable, so the results obtained cannot be considered as representative of the set. In addition, it part of a considerable amount of subsets of images, which results in the dataset is eventually converted into several independent datasets, smaller and with less internal consistency.

3. A New Dataset

After the detection of the limitations described above, the construction of a new dataset for the aesthetic prediction of images has been carried out. This new creation method allows us to build a dataset with greater statistical coherence from the evaluation results collected on the DPChallenge.com photography website. Later, it is evaluated by two different population types. With this, we obtained the possibility of analyzing the correlation between the results obtained with subjects in controlled circumstances and those obtained through online surveys. First, a set of images has been compiled from the DPChallenge.com photo portal. This portal has been used previously to obtain data for aesthetic classification experiments [6,7]. Those images with a minimum of 100 ratings have been selected. In this way, it is intended that the average value that will be assigned to each image will be as little biased as possible. Once this selection is made, the images are organized in groups according to the average evaluation received in DPChallenge.com. The images of our selection have been classified in 9 scoring ranges, one for each whole value of evaluation allowed. Then, all groups are expected to have a minimum number of images, which in our case was 200. There are not sufficiently large groups of images with average evaluations lower than 3 or higher than 8, so the groups used were those collected in the range [≥3, <8]. Of these groups, the 200 images with the smallest standard deviation were selected, that is, those that present votes with greater internal coherence. This process provides a set of images with the same number of elements in each range and with high voting coherence.

4. Evaluation

The dataset proposed above was evaluated by a group of Spanish humans under controlled experimental conditions. The evaluations were carried out by student volunteers from the Universidade da Coruña, Spain. Ninety-nine participants (33 men and 66 women) were part of this study, with an average age of 18.7 years, in an age range of 18–30. Each participant evaluated at least 200 images in the members of the research group presence and under the same viewing conditions. For each image, users assessed their aesthetics and their quality independently. Later, another experiment was conducted through online surveys with the USA population. This experiment was carried out through the Amazon Mechanical Turk tool. 525 people evaluated the images, 39% men and 61% women, with an average age of 32.6 years, in a range of 18–70 years. The same images were used as in the on-site experiment and the evaluators had to score, in the same way, the aesthetics and quality criteria, independently.

5. Results

The correlation between the evaluations made in person and those recorded on the DPChallenge.com platform has been calculated. The Pearson correlation between the average score of DPChallenge.com and the average evaluation according to the aesthetic value is 0.692, and of 0.69 according to Spearman. The average correlation between DPChallenge.com and the average according to the quality value is 0.748 according to Pearson and 0.756 according to Spearman. Finally, the correlation between the two measurements obtained in the on-site experiment (aesthetics/quality) is 0.787 according to Pearson and 0.786 according to Spearman. When it analyzes the correlation between the on-site evaluations and the USA online survey, a correlation of 0.76 was detected between the aesthetic criteria of both experiments, and of 0.85 between the quality criteria. The correlation between the aesthetic and the quality criteria in the USA evaluations is 0.89, the same correlation that exists between criteria in the experiment carried out by Datta et al. [3] With this new dataset, different models based on Machine Learning have been trained using different metrics for automatic prediction of aesthetic and quality value. The highest correlation obtained with these models is 0.58 using SVM [11].

6. Conclusions

The correlation results suggest that the evaluation of DPChallenge.com is closer to a quality criteria than aesthetics and that, in the same way, all evaluators coincide with greater precision when evaluating the quality criteria than aesthetics. In addition, it can be deduced that the evaluators better differentiate the criteria to be evaluated when the difference can be explained to them in person. It should be noted that the complex systems used predict better quality results than aesthetic ones, perhaps due to their lower subjective component and their greater relationship with the intrinsic characteristics of the images.

Acknowledgments: This work is supported by the General Directorate of Culture, Education and University Management of Xunta de Galicia (Ref. GRC2014/049) and the European Fund for Regional Development (FEDER) allocated by the European Union, the Portuguese Foundation for Science and Technology for the development of project SBIRC (Ref. PTDC/EIA– EIA/115667/2009), Xunta de Galicia (Ref. XUGA-PGIDIT-10TIC105008-PR) and the Spanish Ministry for Science and Technology (Ref. TIN2008-06562/TIN). We gratefully acknowledge the support of NVIDIA Corporation with the donation of the Titan Xp GPU used for this research.

Conflicts of Interest: The authors declare no conflict of interest.

References

1. Carballal, A.; Castro, L.; Rodríguez-Fernández, N.; Santos, I.; Santos, A.; Romero, J. Approach to minimize bias on aesthetic image datasets. In *Interface Support for Creativity, Productivity, and Expression in Computer Graphics*; IGI Global: Hershey, PA, USA, 2019; pp. 203–219.
2. Carballal, A.; Castro, L.; Perez, R.; Correia, J. Detecting bias on aesthetic image datasets. *Int. J. Creat. Interfaces Comput. Graph.* **2014**, *5*, 62–74.
3. Datta, R.; Joshi, D.; Li, J.; Wang, J.Z. Studying aesthetics in photographic images using a computational approach. In *European Conference on Computer Vision*; Springer: Berlin/Heidelberg, Germany, 2006; pp. 288–301.
4. Wang, W.; Cai, D.; Wang, L.; Huang, Q.; Xu, X.; Li, X. Synthesized computational aesthetic evaluation of photos. *Neurocomputing* **2016**, *172*, 244–252.
5. Wong, L.K.; Low, K.L. Saliency-enhanced image aesthetics class prediction. In Proceedings of the 2009 16th IEEE International Conference on Image Processing (ICIP), Cairo, Egypt, 7–10 November 2009; pp. 997–1000.
6. Ke, Y.; Tang, X.; Jing, F. The design of high-level features for photo quality assessment. In Proceedings of the 2006 IEEE Computer Society Conference on Computer Vision and Pattern Recognition (CVPR'06) 2006, New York, NY, USA, 17–22 June 2006; Volume 1, pp. 419–426.
7. Tang, X.; Luo, W.; Wang, X. Content-based photo quality assessment. *IEEE Trans. Multimed.* **2013**, *15*, 1930–1943.
8. Cela-Conde, C.J.; Ayala, F.J.; Munar, E.; Maestú, F.; Nadal, M.; Capó, M.A.; del Río, D.; López-Ibor, J.J.; Ortiz, T.; Mirasso, C.; et al. Sex-related similarities and differences in the neural correlates of beauty. *Proc. Natl. Acad. Sci. USA* **2009**, *106*, 3847–3852.
9. Forsythe, A.; Nadal, M.; Sheehy, N.; Cela-Conde, C.J.; Sawey, M. Predicting beauty: Fractal dimension and visual complexity in art. *Br. J. Psychol.* **2011**, *102*, 49–70.
10. Nadal, M.; Munar, E.; Marty, G.; Cela-Conde, C.J. Visual complexity and beauty appreciation: Explaining the divergence of results. *Empir. Stud. Arts* **2010**, *28*, 173–191.

11. Carballal, A.; Fernandez-Lozano, C.; Rodriguez-Fernandez, N.; Castro, L.; Santos, A. Avoiding the inherent limitations in datasets used for measuring aesthetics when using a machine learning approach. *Complexity* **2019**, *2019*, 4659809.

Proceedings

Signal Processing Techniques Intended for Peculiar Star Detection in APOGEE Survey [†]

Raul Santovena [1,*], Arturo Manchado [2] and Carlos Dafonte [1]

[1] Centro de investigación CITIC, Universidade da Coruña, Campus de Elviña s/n, 15071 A Coruña, Spain
[2] Instituto de Astrofísica de Canarias, E-38206 La laguna, Tenerife, Spain
* Correspondence: raul.santovena@udc.es
† Presented at the 2nd XoveTIC Congress, A Coruña, Spain, 5–6 September 2019.

Published: 1 August 2019

Abstract: Like other disciplines, Astronomy faces the era of Big Data, where the analyses and discovery of specific objects is a significant and non-trivial matter. The APOGEE survey and Gaia mission are good examples of how these kind of projects have increased the amount of data to be managed. In this context, we have developed an algorithm to search for specific features in the APOGEE database. The main purpose is to seek spectral lines both in absorption or emission, in the whole APOGEE database, in order to find chemically-peculiar stars. We propose an algorithm which has been validated using cerium lines and we have applied it to the search for other chemical compounds.

Keywords: apogee survey; chemically peculiar stars; spectral line detection; signal processing

---

1. Introduction

The Apache Point Observatory Galactic Evolution Experiment (APOGEE) [1] is a galactic survey focused on the structure and evolution of the Milky Way galaxy using high-resolution infrared spectroscopy. It aims to observe a very extensive star dataset in a late stage of stellar evolution to study its chemical composition and physical structure. APOGEE is a phase of a wider project, named Sloan Digital Sky Survey (SDSS), whose objective is to create the most detailed three-dimensional map of our galaxy [2].

We have used the fourth spectroscopic release from APOGEE, called Data Release 14 (DR14), which contains data for approximately 263.000 APOGEE targets. Each star includes spectra, derived stellar parameters, as well as elemental abundances for most of the stars. To develop our algorithm we have only used spectra data.

Our aim is to develop an algorithm to search for peculiar targets. To achieve this objective, we have applied signal processing techniques to stellar spectra, which can reveal many features of stars such as their chemical composition. We focused on detect spectral lines, which are used to identify the presence of atoms and molecules in stellar objects. For each chemical element present in a galactic target, there will be spectral lines in one or several wavelengths. The algorithm searches for these lines in the wavelengths of interest, and it has been developed to be able to seek any chemical compound.

2. Methods

The algorithm uses methods to detect specific features, categorizing and filtering each detection by means of different thresholds defined based on the local values of the signal.

For each wavelength where there can be located a spectral line, a window for local analysis is created. We apply morphological analysis for their extraction. First, we look for peaks—or valleys—close to these wavelengths, defining a threshold calculated from the signal continuum and their variance to avoid the detection of false positives due to noise or very rippled spectra. Secondly, the area of the candidate line is calculated and normalized according to continuum, with the aim of filtering lines with little width and/or height. The detection of a line is considered positive when both steps are achieved. Furthermore, the algorithm is configurable, in order to allow the user to define a great deal of parameters to search for different types of objects. The user can:

- Search for any list of lines of interest from their wavelengths.
- Search for emission or absorption lines.
- Choose the minimum number of lines which should be detected over the total to consider a positive case
- Determine critical lines which must be detected in all objects. If these lines are not detected in the spectrum, it would not be a positive case, even though the number of the other detections exceeded the minimum.
- Define the size of the local analysis window.
- Establish the minimum value of the normalized area that the lines must satisfy.

As it can be seen in Figure 1, spectra present two gaps without flux. These absences of data are the result of the wavelength coverage in APOGEE detectors, since spectra are recorded onto three separate detectors, which do not cover the full infrared H band. Some lines could appear within these gaps but, as the range of the gaps can vary slightly, sometimes they are added as an optional lines to seek. If they are distinctly located within these bands, we discard them.

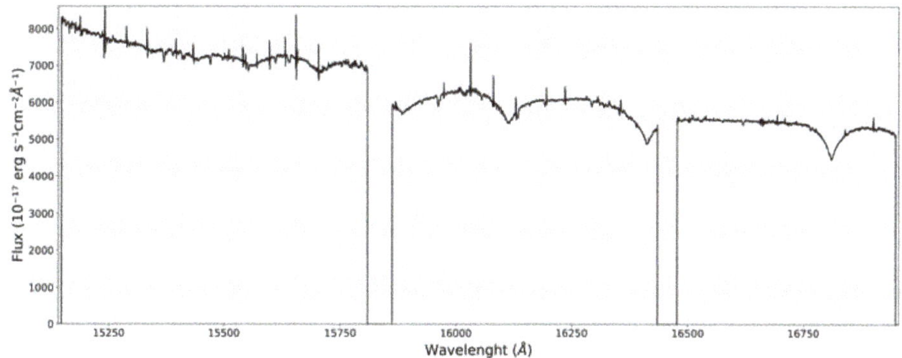

Figure 1. APOGEE Spectrum.

3. Results

We tested the algorithm searching for cerium III compound (Ce III), which can present several lines in a spectrum. In order to validate it, we have compared our result with the detections of Chojnowski et al., who report 157 chemically-peculiar stars with Ce III absorption lines [3]. Our exploration detected 105 stars in common with measurements taken by Chojnowski. In addition, we detected 975 new objects with presence of cerium. The results were obtained using the parameters shown below:

- Lines: 15,961.157, 15,964.928, 16,133.170, 16,292.642 Å.
- Type of lines: Absorption lines.
- Minimum number of lines: 4 (All lines are considered critical).
- Window size: 30 Å.
- Minimum area: 0.020.
- Total detections: 1080 stars.

In Figure 2 it is shown several stars with Ce III lines.

After validation, the algorithm has been used to find other chemically peculiar stars. In order to ensure the quality of the search and in accordance with the nature of each chemical compound, it has been mandatory to adjust individually the parameters of the algorithm.

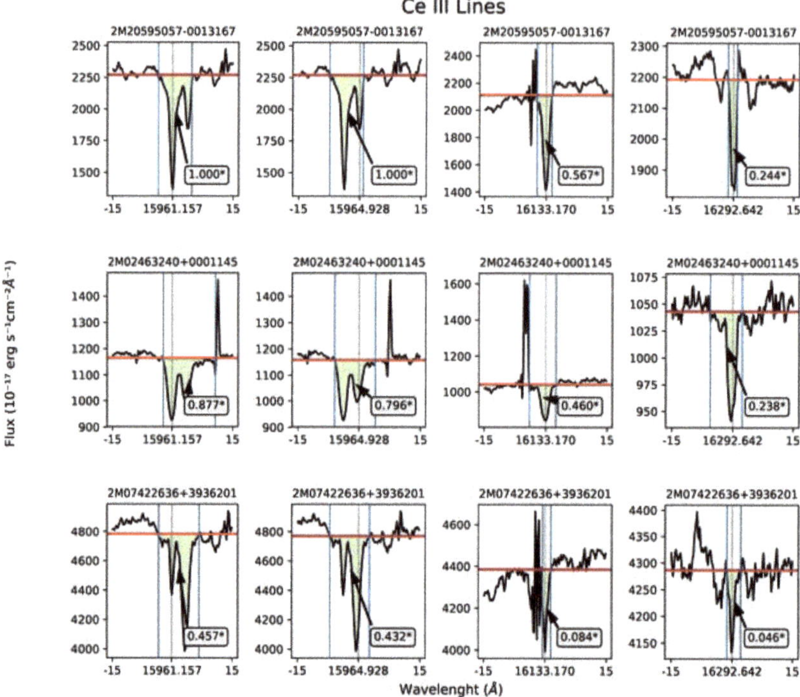

Figure 2. Ce III Lines. Each row shows a single target with cerium lines.

4. Conclusions

On balance, we have designed and tested an algorithm whose aim is provide a useful tool to help in the search of chemically peculiar stars as it has been seen in more detail above. We are working to improve the calibration in the validation stage in order to achieve better and more reliable results and to avoid false positive cases. Moreover, we have obtained promising results searching for rarer elements, which have to be studied in detail and may be important enough to be published in the future. Also, we want to combine morphological analysis with Artificial Intelligence techniques to enhance feature extraction, allowing to discover new peculiar stars.

Funding: This work was supported by the Spanish Ministry of Science Innovation and the Ministry of Economy, Industry and Competitiveness (RTI2018-095076-B-C22 and ESP2016-80079-C2-2-R) and by the Xunta de Galicia (Potencial Crecemento ED431B 2018/42) and the European Union (European Social Fund—ESF).

Conflicts of Interest: The authors declare no conflict of interest. The funders had no role in the design of the study; in the collection, analyses, or interpretation of data; in the writing of the manuscript, or in the decision to publish the results.

References

1. Majewski, S.R.; Schiavon, R.P.; Frinchaboy, P.M.; Prieto, C.A.; Barkhouser, R.; Bizyaev, D.; Blank, B.; Brunner, S.; Burton, A.; Carrera, R.; et al. The Apache Point Observatory Galactic Evolution Experiment (APOGEE). *Astron. J.* **2017**, *154*, 94, doi:10.3847/1538-3881/aa784d.

2. Blanton, M.R.; Bershady, M.A.; Abolfathi, B.; Albareti, F.D.; Prieto, C.A.; Almeida, A.; Alonso-García, J.; Anders, F.; Anderson, S.F.; Andrews, B.; et al. Sloan Digital Sky Survey IV: Mapping the Milky Way, Nearby Galaxies, and the Distant Universe. *Astron. J.* **2017**, *154*, 28, doi:10.3847/1538-3881/aa7567.

3. Chojnowski, S.D.; Hubrig, S.; Hasselquist, S.; Castelli, F.; Whelan, D.G.; Majewski, S.R.; Nitschelm, C.; García-Hernández, D.A.; Stassun, K.G.; Zamora, O.; et al. Discovery of Resolved Magnetically Split Lines in SDSS/APOGEE Spectra of 157 Ap/Bp Stars. *Astron. J. Lett.* **2019**, *873*, L5, doi:10.3847/2041-8213/ab0750.

proceedings

Proceedings

Building High-Quality Datasets for Information Retrieval Evaluation at a Reduced Cost [†]

David Otero * , **Daniel Valcarce** , **Javier Parapar** and **Álvaro Barreiro**

Information Retrieval Lab, Centro de Investigación en Tecnoloxías da Información e as Comunicacións (CITIC), Universidade da Coruña, 15071 A Coruña, Spain
* Correspondence: david.otero.freijeiro@udc.es; Tel.: +34-881-01-1276
† Presented at the 2nd XoveTIC Conference, A Coruna, Spain, 5–6 September 2019.

Published: 1 August 2019

Abstract: Information Retrieval is not any more exclusively about document ranking. Continuously new tasks are proposed on this and sibling fields. With this proliferation of tasks, it becomes crucial to have a cheap way of constructing test collections to evaluate the new developments. Building test collections is time and resource consuming: it requires time to obtain the documents, to define the user needs and it requires the assessors to judge a lot of documents. To reduce the latest, pooling strategies aim to decrease the assessment effort by presenting to the assessors a sample of documents in the corpus with the maximum number of relevant documents in it. In this paper, we propose the preliminary design of different techniques to easily and cheaply build high-quality test collections without the need of having participants systems.

Keywords: information retrieval; evaluation; datasets; cost

---

1. Introduction

In Information Retrieval, test collections are the most widespread technique to evaluate the effectiveness of new developments [1]. These collections are formed by the document set, the information needs (topics) and the human judgments [2]. They are complex to construct because the need of human work to obtain the judgments [3,4]. Datasets of general purpose like TREC (https://trec.nist.gov), NTCIR (http://research.nii.ac.jp/ntcir) and CLEF (http://www.clef-initiative.eu) are useful but sometimes research teams need to build their own collections within a specific task [5].

Pooling methods allow building larger datasets with less effort [6]. When using a pooling approach, only a subset—the pool—of the whole document set is assessed for relevance. The pool is built by taking the union of the top k documents retrieved by each participant system, the runs. In TREC competitions these pools are built using the runs sent by the competition participants, who execute their algorithms on the original dataset and send back their results [2]. Historically, TREC applied the most basic pooling approach (DocID) [2], but recent publications [7,8] have shown that is possible to reduce the assessor's work without harming the quality of the obtained dataset. In particular, in TREC Common Core Track [9] NIST applied these techniques for the first time. The drawback of these techniques is that they are tied to having participant systems, condition that is not always met.

In some cases it may be necessary to obtain collections prior to the competition. Therefore, in these cases, it is not possible to use approaches where the participants are needed, such as CLEF eRisk competition (http://erisk.irlab.org) [10–12], where training data is released.

We propose a method to build the pool before having participant systems. Here the role of the runs will be played by different query variants and out of the box retrieval strategies. The top k documents from the runs produced by multiple combinations of query variants and retrieval strategies are used to build the pool.

2. Experiments

We made a series of experiments to preliminary compare the effectiveness between different pooling approaches. In particular, we want to test if the use of query variants is adequate.

2.1. Systems and Query Variants

We use four different retrieval models: BM25, TF-IDF, LM Jelinek-Mercer and LM Dirichlet. We want to test the effectiveness of this approach having only a few different systems.

To combine with the described models, we build a series of query variants from the original query. With the model×query variant combinations, we can obtain larger pools, ideally having more relevant documents in them. To build a query variant we combine the original query with one of the five terms from the topic description with the highest IDF, i.e., the more specific terms.

Combining these variants along with the systems, we end obtaining a number of different runs equal to $no.\ systems(4) \times no.\ variants(5) = 20$.

2.2. Pooling Algorithms

To perform these experiments we use two pooling algorithms. The first one is the traditional pooling strategy used in TREC competitions [2], i.e., DocID. The second one, DocPoolFreq, is a simple adaptation of the former, where we order the documents by the number of times they appear in the pool and if they tie, by DocID. This is based on the intuition that if a document appears on more systems is it going to be more relevant than other that appears less in all the systems, which is part of many complex pooling algorithms [13].

3. Results

We performed these experiments using the TREC5 dataset (disks 2 & 4, topics 251-300). The results can be observed in Figure 1. When it comes to finding more relevant documents we can observe that the approaches that use the query variants outperform the other two. This is because when using the variants we have more systems, which results in having more relevant documents.

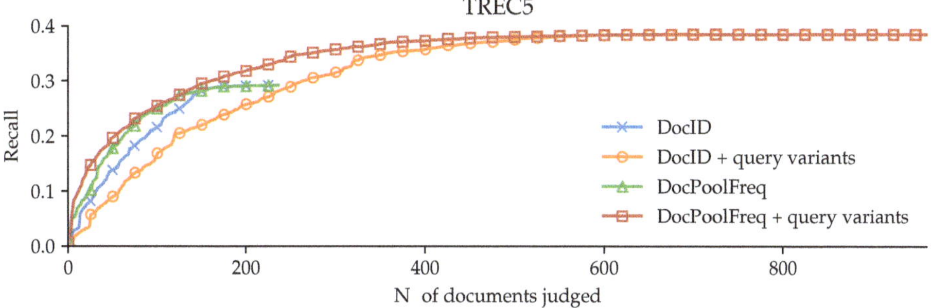

Figure 1. Comparison between pooling strategies.

We also can observe that DocPoolFreq outperforms DocID as it finds relevant documents earlier in the process. This confirms that with only four models and query variants it is possible to obtain the 40% of the relevant documents found in TREC 5 where 61 systems where used to build the pool.

4. Discussion

Results show that our research direction is promising. We also open a line of investigation which is to compare the quality of the datasets built with a participants-based approach with techniques that do not need the participant system, like the presented in this paper.

Funding: This work was supported by projects RTI2018-093336-B-C22 (MCIU & ERDF) and GPC ED431B 2019/03 (Xunta de Galicia & ERDF) and accreditation ED431G/01 (Xunta de Galicia & ERDF).

Conflicts of Interest: The authors declare no conflict of interest. The funders had no role in the design of the study; in the collection, analyses, or interpretation of data; in the writing of the manuscript, or in the decision to publish the results.

References

1. Sanderson, M. Test Collection Based Evaluation of Information Retrieval Systems. *Found. Trends® Inf. Retr.* **2010**, *4*, 247–375.
2. Voorhees, E.M.; Harman, D.K. *TREC: Experiment and Evaluation in Information Retrieval (Digital Libraries and Electronic Publishing)*; The MIT Press: Cambridge, MA, USA, 2005.
3. Kanoulas, E. Building Reliable Test and Training Collections in Information Retrieval. Ph.D. Thesis, Northeastern University, Boston, MA, USA, 2009.
4. Losada, D.E.; Parapar, J.; Barreiro, A. Cost-effective Construction of Information Retrieval Test Collections. In Proceedings of the 5th Spanish Conference on Information Retrieval, Zaragoza, Spain, 26–27 June 2018; ACM: New York, NY, USA, 2018; pp. 12:1–12:2.
5. Losada, D.E.; Crestani, F. A Test Collection for Research on Depression and Language Use. In *Experimental IR Meets Multilinguality, Multimodality, and Interaction: 7th International Conference of the CLEF Association, CLEF 2016, Évora, Portugal, 5–8 September 2016*; Springer: Berlin, Germany, 2016; pp. 28–39.
6. Kuriyama, K.; Kando, N.; Nozue, T.; Eguchi, K. Pooling for a Large-Scale Test Collection: An Analysis of the Search Results from the First NTCIR Workshop. *Inf. Retr.* **2002**, *5*, 41–59.
7. Losada, D.E.; Parapar, J.; Barreiro, Á. Feeling Lucky?: Multi-armed Bandits for Ordering Judgements in Pooling-based Evaluation. In Proceedings of the 31st Annual ACM Symposium on Applied Computing, Pisa, Italy, 4–8 April 2016; ACM: New York, NY, USA, 2016; pp. 1027–1034.
8. Losada, D.E.; Parapar, J.; Barreiro, A. Multi-armed bandits for adjudicating documents in pooling-based evaluation of information retrieval systems. *Inf. Process. Manag.* **2017**, *53*, 1005–1025.
9. Allan, J.; Harman, D.; Kanoulas, E.; Li, D.; Gysel, C.V.; Voorhees, E.M. TREC 2017 Common Core Track Overview. In Proceedings of The Twenty-Sixth Text REtrieval Conference, TREC 2017, Gaithersburg, MD, USA, 15–17 November 2017.
10. Losada, D.E.; Crestani, F.; Parapar, J. eRISK 2017: CLEF Lab on Early Risk Prediction on the Internet: Experimental Foundations. Proceedings of 18th Conference and Labs of the Evaluation Forum; Springer: Dublin, Ireland, 2017; CLEF '17, pp. 346–360.
11. Losada, D.E.; Crestani, F.; Parapar, J. Overview of eRisk: Early Risk Prediction on the Internet. Proceedings of 19th Conference and Labs of the Evaluation Forum; Springer: Avignon, France, 2018; CLEF '18, pp. 343–361.
12. Losada, D.E.; Crestani, F.; Parapar, J. Early Detection of Risks on the Internet: An Exploratory Campaign. In Proceedings of the 41st European Conference on Information Retrieval, Cologne, Germany, 14–18 April 2019; pp. 259–266.
13. Losada, D.E.; Parapar, J.; Barreiro, A. A rank fusion approach based on score distributions for prioritizing relevance assessments in information retrieval evaluation. *Inf. Fusion* **2018**, *39*, 56–71.

Proceedings

Intraretinal Fluid Detection by Means of a Densely Connected Convolutional Neural Network Using Optical Coherence Tomography Images [†]

Plácido L. Vidal [1,2,*], **Joaquim de Moura [1,2]**, **Jorge Novo [1,2]** and **Marcos Ortega [1,2]**

1   Department of Computer Science, University of A Coruña, 15071 A Coruña, Spain
2   CITIC-Research Center of Information and Communication Technologies, University of A Coruña, 15071 A Coruña, Spain
*   Correspondence: placido.francisco.lizancos.vidal@udc.es; Tel.: +34-981-16-70-00 (ext. 1330)
†   Presented at the 2nd XoveTIC Conference, A Coruña, Spain, 5–6 September 2019.

Published: 1 August 2019

Abstract: Hereby we present a methodology with the objective of detecting retinal fluid accumulations in between the retinal layers. The methodology uses a robust Densely Connected Neural Network to classify thousands of subsamples, extracted from a given Optical Coherence Tomography image. Posteriorly, using the detected regions, it satisfactorily generates a coherent and intuitive confidence map by means of a voting strategy.

Keywords: Computer-Aided Diagnosis; retinal imaging; Optical Coherence Tomography; deep learning; DenseNet; intraretinal cystoid region characterization

1. Introduction

A macular edema consists in a swelling of the macula caused by the accumulation of pathological fluid in between the retinal tissues. This disease corresponds to one of the main causes of blindness in developed countries, as its main triggers are related to an increasing lifespan and the lifestyle of the afflicted. To study, diagnose and treat these fluid accumulations, clinicians typically use Optical Coherence Tomography (OCT) images. This non-invasive medical imaging technique allows to generate a representation of the retina with a resolution of microns.

To date, this diagnostic is mostly done by means of a visual inspection by the expert ophthalmologist, prone to subjective factors. Thus, and given the relevance of the aforementioned pathologies, an automated methodology to facilitate the inspection is desirable.

2. Methodology

To solve this issue, we merged a regional analysis strategy that has proven to be resilient in the identification of fluid regions [1], a visualization technique specially designed to offer satisfactory results even when facing the most challenging conditions [2] and an artificial neural network architecture specially designed to overcome overfitting thanks to its densely connected layers, adding capabilities of self-supervision [3]. Thus, to generate the pathological confidence maps, the images are thoroughly sampled, extracting thousands of samples from them. Afterwards, using a previously trained DenseNet, these samples are classified and used as ballots to determine the confidence of the different regions in the image.

3. Results

The network was trained using a base dataset of 3247 samples from two different representative OCT capture devices, increased by means of data augmentation. Additionally, the training of the network was done by using an automated control of the learning rate depending on the validation results, and stopped by means of an early-stopping criteria that detects when the training quality has stagnated. To further study the capabilities of our system, the training process was repeated 50 times, randomly distributing the training and validation datasets and recalculating the data augmentation procedure. After all the repetitions, the system attained a satisfactory mean test accuracy of 97.45% ± 0.7611 and a mean area under the ROC curve (AUC) of 0.9961 ± 0.0029. Regarding maps, as shown in Figures 1 and 2, the DenseNet architecture is able to successfully represent both pathological and healthy regions in different representative devices of the domain.

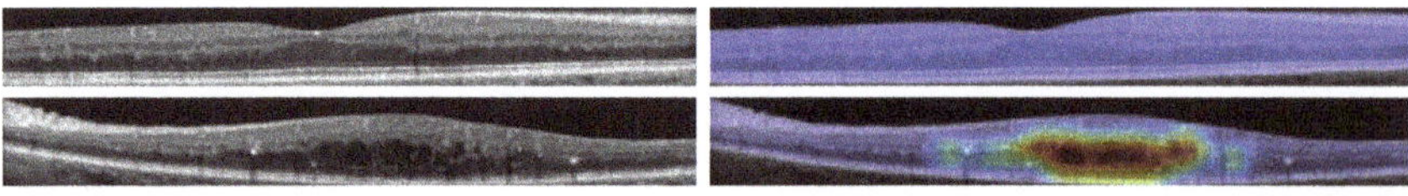

Figure 1. Results from a Spectralis OCT device from Heidelberg Engineering, including a healthy and a pathological example.

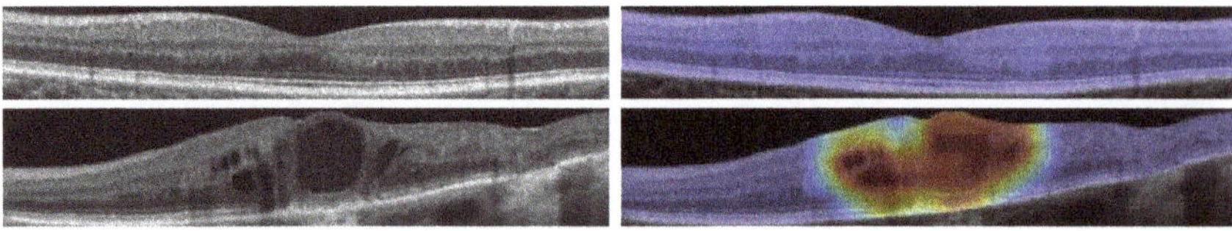

Figure 2. Results from a Cirrus HD-OCT OCT device from Carl Zeiss Meditec, including a healthy and a pathological example.

Author Contributions: P.L.V. and J.d.M. designed and performed the experiments. J.N. and M.O. contributed with their domain knowledge. All the authors helped with the analysis of the results and revision of the manuscript, written by P.L.V.

Funding: This research was funded by Instituto de Salud Carlos III grant number DTS18/00136, Ministerio de Economía y Competitividad grant number DPI 2015-69948-R, Xunta de Galicia through the accreditation of Centro Singular de Investigación 2016–2019, Ref. ED431G/01, Xunta de Galicia through Grupos de Referencia Competitiva, Ref. ED431C 2016-047 and Xunta de Galicia predoctoral grant contract ref. ED481A-2019/196.

Conflicts of Interest: The authors declare no conflict of interest.

References

1. de Moura, J.; Vidal, P.L.; Novo, J.; Rouco, J.; Ortega, M. Feature Definition, Analysis and Selection for Cystoid Region Characterization in Optical Coherence Tomography. In *Knowledge-Based and Intelligent Information & Engineering Systems, Proceedings of the 21st International Conference KES-2017, Marseille, France, 6–8 September 2017*; Elsevier: Amsterdam, The Netherlands, 2017; pp. 1369–1377. Available online: https://www.sciencedirect.com/science/article/pii/S1877050917313844 (accessed on 31 July 2019)
2. Vidal, P.L.; de Moura, J.; Novo, J.; Penedo, M.G.; Ortega, M. Intraretinal fluid identification via enhanced maps using optical coherence tomography images. *Biomed. Opt. Express* **2018**, *9*, pp. 4730–4754.
3. Vidal, P.L.; de Moura, J.; Novo, J.; Rouco, J.; Ortega, M. Cystoid Fluid Color Map Generation in Optical Coherence Tomography Images Using a Densely Connected Convolutional Neural Network. In Proceedings of the 2019 International Joint Conference on Neural Networks, Budapest, Hungary, 14–19 July 2019.

Proceedings

Proceedings

Solving Self-Interference Issues in a Full-Duplex Radio Transceiver †

Miguel Franco-Martínez *, **Francisco-Javier Martínez-Alonso and Roberto López-Valcarce**

Signal Processing in Communications Group, University of Vigo, 36310 Vigo, Spain
* Correspondence: mfranco@gts.uvigo.es, Tel.: +34-986812672
† Presented at the 2nd XoveTIC Conference, A Coruña, Spain, 5–6 September 2019.

Published: 1 August 2019

Abstract: Most wireless devices transmit and receive at different spectrum frequency bands. This approach is no longer optimal due to increasing electromagnetic exhaustion. Besides, interference among all present and future working services should be negligible. A full-duplex scheme using the same band for simultaneous uplink and downlink is a huge step towards solving this issue. However, sharing the same frequency band involves a large interference of transmitted signal over received signal. To fix this problem, we propose the usage of a hybrid multistage cancellation system, consisting of an analog cancellation setup at RF frequencies and a baseband digital cancellation stage.

Keywords: self-interference; full-duplex; Software Defined Radio; wireless communications

1. Introduction

Traditional communication systems are based on a half-duplex scheme, in which a transmitting node sends information to a receiver node through a specific channel. Using this scheme, it is necessary to use some sort of multiplexing, either in time domain or in frequency domain, to allow transmission and reception when it is needed that both tasks are performed simultaneously. These schemes are no longer valid in an environment where an increasing number of applications are demanding bandwidth from a limited electromagnetic spectrum. In-band full-duplex almost doubles spectral efficiency comparing to traditional multiplexed schemes, as shown in Figure 1.

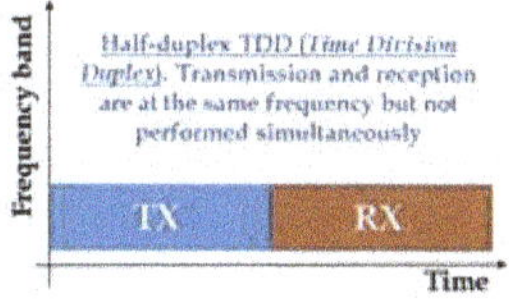

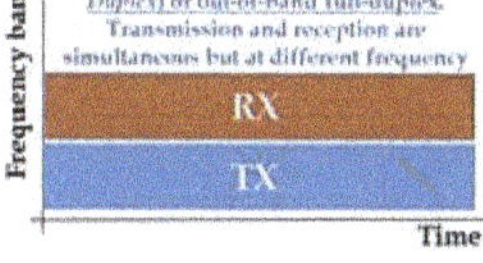

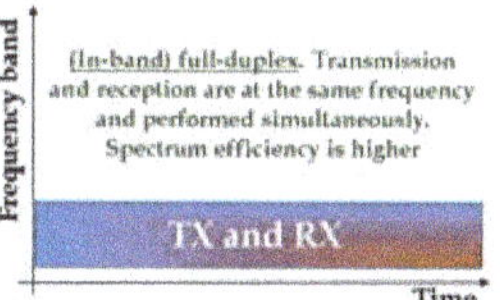

(**a**) Time-muxed half-duplex   (**b**) Freq.-muxed half-duplex   (**c**) Full-duplex scheme

Figure 1. Communication schemes.

In [1], a wide variety of topologies of in-band full-duplex are presented. However, the common challenge involving full-duplex development is self-interference. According to results shown in literature [1,2], self-interference power level should be below the noise floor or, alternatively, more than 70 dB of self-interference cancellation are needed to be able to recover information from a far transmitter troublelessly. In addition to that, self-interference signal has enough power to strongly saturate both RF front-end and converters at the receiver side. Thus, recovering information signal becomes an impossible task, and potential stress due to overpower may even damage electronic components.

2. Design

In order to solve self-interference issues, we propose the usage of a hybrid multi-stage cancellation system, consisting of an analog cancellation setup at RF frequencies following the so-called Stanford architecture, and a base-band digital cancellation stage.

The aim of building an analog cancellation setup is performing a first power reduction of self-interference signal so that receiver analog front-end interface will not be saturated or damaged. A real-hardware full-duplex setup may suffer from two main sources of self-interference, as shown in Figure 2a: internal coupling (α_i, signal power fraction that leaks between transmission and reception interfaces of most radio platforms), and external coupling (α_e, fraction of RF transmitted signal that leaks into the receiver chain through the antenna interface). For attenuating interference, a parallel branch (α_c) is introduced. The ideal value for this branch is the counterphase replica of the sum of the internal and external coupling signals, that is, $\alpha_c = -(\alpha_i + \alpha_e)$. With this value, self-interference would disappear. The parallel branch is based on a small network consisting of a set of voltage-variable attenuators and phase shifters, controlled from a PC through an embedded-system-based design, as shown in Figure 2b. Values of attenuation and phase to be generated by the RF devices network are calculated iteratively. These values are then transposed into codes by the embedded system and sent to the DACs (Digital-to-Analog Converters), so that the network can perform a real-time adaptation to changes in coupling.

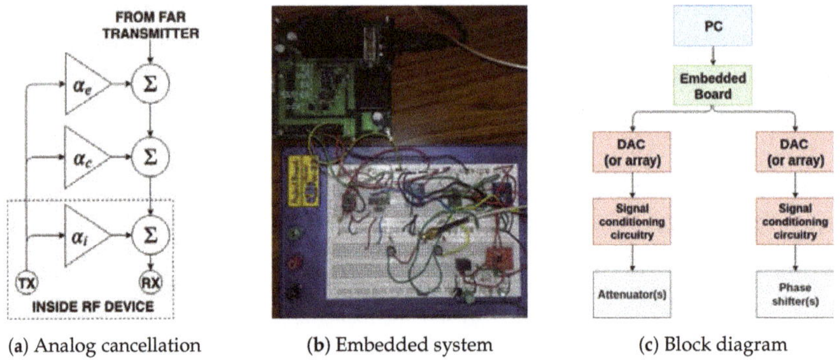

(a) Analog cancellation   (b) Embedded system   (c) Block diagram

Figure 2. Embedded system for controlling parallel cancellation branch.

Finally, digital cancellation performs the main interference removal task. The objective of digital cancellation is reducing the self-interference power to below the noise floor. Both LMS (Least Mean Squares) [3] and APA (Affine Projection Algorithm) [4] methods have been implemented to compare the cancellation ratio in both cases.

3. Implementation

This cancellation system has been implemented and tested in two Software Defined Radio platforms (USRP N210) using a custom made application over UHD API driver. RF parallel branch is built using off-the-shelf attenuators, phase shifters and RF splitters. RF gains higher than 30 dB were generated including a pair of LNAs (*Low Noise Amplifiers*, fixed 34 dB). Transmitted symbols have been generated using a QPSK constellation, then modulated using OFDM (Orthogonal Frequency-Division Multiplexing) with N = 512 subcarriers. Cyclic prefix length is 32 symbols, bandwidth used is 5 MHz, and sampling frequency is 12.5 MHz. Resulting stream is then upconverted to 900 MHz band.

4. Results

The base transmission signal, without any RF gain, has a power level of -48 dBm for these experiments. On the one hand, for results shown in Figure 3a, a RF gain of 50 dB is applied. Lines are Welch periodograms: yellow line, of the noise floor; green line, of the transmitted self-interference signal; black line, of the raw self-interference received signal; and red and blue lines, of the same received signal after analog cancellation and analog plus digital cancellation respectively. It can be seen that cancellations can lower self-interference signal power about 80 dB. LMS and APA algorithms perform similarly in terms of cancellation. On the other hand, for results shown in Figure 3b, a self-interference RF gain sweep has been performed. It can be seen that cancellation ratio grows in a linear proportional way with interference gain, so self-interference power level is below noise floor with lower values of RF interference gain. These results show that measured performance is enough to recover signal from a far transmitter. Besides, performance in terms of MER measured using this full-duplex scheme is comparable to the one measured using a traditional half-duplex scheme.

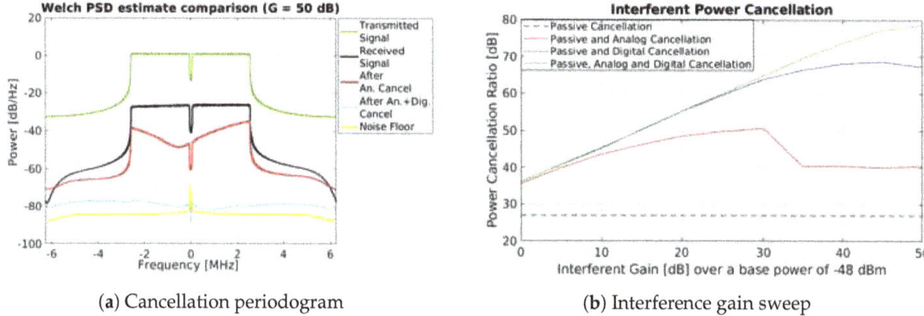

(a) Cancellation periodogram   (b) Interference gain sweep

Figure 3. Cancellation measurements.

5. Conclusions

Up to 80 dB of power interference cancellation can be achieved with a full-duplex OFDM scheme. The results show that is possible to perform a frequency-efficient full-duplex communication using mostly off-the-shelf components. This system can recover the original message with a MER level that is comparable to the one achieved with traditional half-duplex schemes. Some applications getting benefit from this new full-duplex approach are cognitive radio systems, MIMO, WiFi, 5G, and high-demanding Internet of Things applications and satellite communications.

Funding: Supported by Agencia Estatal de Investigación (Spain) and the European Regional Development Fund (ERDF) under project WINTER (TEC2016-76409-C2-2-R, BES-2017-080305), and by Xunta de Galicia (Agrupación Estratéxica Consolidada de Galicia accreditation 2016-2019; Red Temática RedTEIC 2017-2018).

References

1. Duarte, M.; Guillaud, M. Engineering Wireless Full-Duplex Nodes and Networks. EUSIPCO 2015. Available online: http://www.eusipco2015.org/content/tutorials/#tut8 (accessed on 27 May 2019).
2. Prasad, G.; Lampe, L.; Shekhar, S. Analog interference cancellation for full-duplex broadband power line communications. In Proceedings of the 2017 IEEE International Symposium on Power Line Communications and its Applications (ISPLC), Madrid, Spain, 3–5 April 2017; pp. 1–6, doi:10.1109/ISPLC.2017.7897108.
3. Wang, J.; Zhao, H.; Tang, Y. A RF adaptive least mean square algorithm for self-interference cancellation in co-frequency co-time full duplex systems. In Proceedings of the 2014 IEEE International Conference on Communications (ICC), Sydney, Australia, 10–14 June 2014; pp. 5622–5627, doi:10.1109/ICC.2014.6884217.
4. Ozeki, K. *Theory of Affine Projection Algorithms for Adaptive Filtering*; Springer: Japan, Tokyo, 2016; pp. 1–223, doi:10.1007/978-4-431-55738-8.

 *proceedings* 

Proceedings

Automatic Tool for the Detection, Characterization and Intuitive Visualization of Macular Edema Regions in OCT Images [†]

Iago Otero [1,*], Plácido L. Vidal [1,2], Joaquim de Moura [1,2], Jorge Novo [1,2] and Marcos Ortega [1,2]

[1] Department of Computer Science, University of A Coruña, 15071 A Coruña, Spain
[2] CITIC-Research Center of Information and Communication Technologies, University of A Coruña, 15071 A Coruña, Spain
* Correspondence: iago.oteroc@udc.es; Tel.: +34-981-16-70-00 (ext. 1330)
† Presented at the 2nd XoveTIC Conference, A Coruna, Spain, 5–6 September 2019.

Published: 1 August 2019

Abstract: The methodology presented in this paper aims to detect pathological regions affected by one or more of the three clinically defined types of Diabetic Macular Edema (DME). Using representative samples extracted from Optical Coherence Tomography (OCT) images, three representative classifiers are trained to analyze new input images and create an intuitive visualization of the detection results. The trained models provided a satisfactory performance for all three defined types of DME, and the visual feedback can effectively assists clinical experts in the diagnosis of this representative and extended disease.

Keywords: computer-aided diagnosis; retinal imaging; optical coherence tomography; macular edema

1. Introduction

In ophthalmology, Optical Coherence Tomography (OCT) imaging devices provide a non-invasive way to obtain the cross-sectional representation of the tissues that compose the retina. This imaging modality is used in many medical diagnostic procedures to identify a broad range of eye fundus-related diseases, both eye-specific and systemic to the body.

Diabetic Macular Edema (DME) is considered one of the main ocular pathologies related to the vision loss. It consists of abnormal fluid regions located in the macular area. Based on the OCT imaging modality, three types of structural patterns were clinically established for this pathology: Diffuse Retinal Thickening (DRT), Cystoid Macular Edema (CME) and Serous Retinal Detachment (SRD). Currently, the diagnostic process is carried out manually by clinical experts in a complex and tedious process that is conditioned by subjective factors. Thus, a methodology that automatically performs the analysis of OCT images is of great interest in the ophthalmological field.

2. Methodology

The developed system automatically identifies and characterizes the three associated pathological types of DME, generating color maps that facilitate the visual inspection of the specialist [1]. To achieve this, the system firstly identifies the layers of the retina that make up the boundaries of the region of interest. Within this region, representative samples were extracted and, after being selected the most relevant features by means of a feature selection strategy, used to train specific models for each type of DME [2]. Finally, the models are used to create intuitive color maps [3] representing the three DME types, thus facilitating the clinical work.

3. Results

The proposed system was validated using 96 OCT images that were labeled by an expert. With this ground truth, we have selected representative samples to create the training and test sets for each pathological type. In total, we extracted 1.811 representative samples. The CME dataset contains 968 samples, the DRT dataset 559 samples and the SRD dataset 284 samples; all of them including both pathological and healthy patterns.

The feature selection process resulted in the most relevant being *Gabor filters*, *Histogram of Oriented Gradients* and *Local Binary Patterns*. Regarding the trained models, the *Linear Discriminant Classifier* reached the best test accuracy of 90.49% with the CME dataset. On the other hand, the *k Nearest Neighbors* with $k = 5$ was the chosen model for the DRT dataset with an 93.23% of test accuracy. Finally, the *Parzen* classifier is the model that achieved the best accuracy for the SRD dataset with an 88.87% of test accuracy. Using these models, we can generate a color map for each of the different pathological detections and effectively assists clinical experts with a merged intuitive visualization (Figure 1).

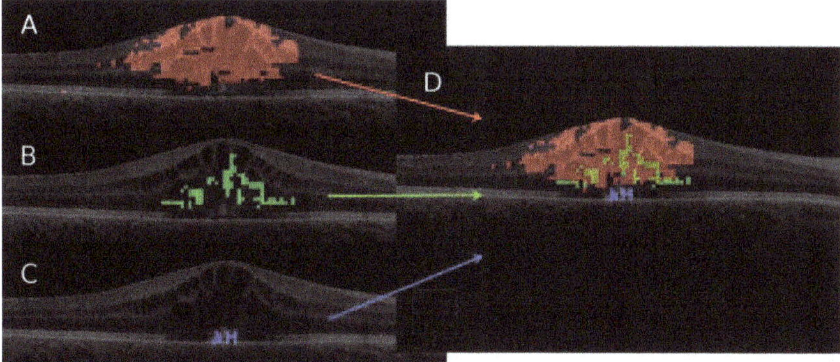

Figure 1. The three individual DME detections and the final merged pathological map. (**A**) CME in red. (**B**) DRT in green. (**D**) SRD in blue. (**D**) Global color map.

Author Contributions: Conceptualization, J.N. and M.O.; methodology, I.O., P.L.V. and J.d.M.; software, I.O. and P.L.V.; validation, I.O., P.L.V. and J.d.M.; formal analysis, I.O. and P.L.V.; investigation, I.O., P.L.V. and J.d.M.; resources, J.N. and M.O.; data curation, I.O.; writing–original draft preparation, I.O.; writing–review and editing, P.L.V. and J.N.; visualization, I.O.; supervision, P.L.V. and J.N.; project administration, J.N. and M.O.; funding acquisition, J.N. and M.O.

Funding: This research was funded by Instituto de Salud Carlos III grant number DTS18/00136, Ministerio de Ciencia, Innovación y Universidades grant numbers DPI 2015-69948-R and RTI2018-095894-B-I00, Xunta de Galicia through the accreditation of Centro Singular de Investigación 2016–2019, Ref. ED431G/01, Xunta de Galicia through Grupos de Referencia Competitiva, Ref. ED431C 2016-047 and Ministerio de Educación y Formación Profesional grant number 18CO1/006199.

Conflicts of Interest: The authors declare no conflict of interest.

References

1. Otero, I.; Vidal, P.L.; Moura, J.; Novo, J.; Rouco, J.; Ortega, M. Computerized tool for identification and enhanced visualization of Macular Edema regions using OCT scans. In Proceedings of the European Symposium on Artificial Neural Networks, Computational Intelligence and Machine Learning, Bruges, Belgium, 24–26 April 2019; pp. 565–570.

2. de Moura, J.; Vidal, P.L.; Novo, J.; Rouco, J.; Ortega, M. Feature definition, analysis and selection for cystoid region characterization in Optical Coherence Tomography. In *Knowledge-Based and Intelligent Information & Engineering Systems, Proceedings of the 21st International Conference KES-2017, Marseille, France, 6–8 September 2017*; Elsevier 2017; pp. 1369–1377. Available online: https://www.sciencedirect.com/science/article/pii/S1877050917313844 (accessed on 31 July 2019)
3. Vidal, P.L.; de Moura, J.; Novo, J.; Penedo, M.G.; Ortega, M. Intraretinal fluid identification via enhanced maps using optical coherence tomography images. *Biomed. Opt. Express* **2018**, *9*, 4730–4754.

 *proceedings*

Proceedings

Building a New Sentiment Analysis Dataset for Uzbek Language and Creating Baseline Models [†]

Elmurod Kuriyozov [1,*] and **Sanatbek Matlatipov [2]**

[1] CITIC, Grupo LYS, Departamento de Computación. Facultade de Informática, Campus de Elviña, Universidade da Coruña, 15071 A Coruña, Spain
[2] Applied Mathematics and Computer Analysis Department, National University of Uzbekistan, University Str. 4, Tashkent 100174, Uzbekistan
[*] Correspondence: e.kuriyozov@udc.es; Tel.: +34-698-374-159
[†] Presented at the 2nd XoveTIC Congress, A Coruña, Spain, 5–6 September 2019.

Published: 2 August 2019

Abstract: Making natural language processing technologies available for low-resource languages is an important goal to improve the access to technology in their communities of speakers. In this paper, we provide the first annotated corpora for polarity classification for Uzbek language. Our methodology considers collecting a medium-size manually annotated dataset and a larger-size dataset automatically translated from existing resources. Then, we use these datasets to train sentiment analysis models on the Uzbek language, using both traditional machine learning techniques and recent deep learning models.

Keywords: sentiment analysis dataset; Uzbek language; sentiment classification; Natural Language Processing; deep learning

---

1. Introduction

The advancement of technologies in the field of Natural Language Processing (NLP) over the past few years has led to achieve very high accuracy results, allowing the creation of useful applications that play an important role in many areas now. In particular, the adoption of deep learning models has boosted accuracy figures across a wide range of NLP tasks. As a part of this trend, sentiment classification, a prominent example of the applications of NLP, has seen substantial gains in performance by using deep learning approaches compared to its predecessor approaches [1]. However, low-resource languages still lack access to those performance improvements due to the requirements of significant amounts of annotated training data to work well. The language we focus on in this paper is Uzbek, which is spoken by more than 33 million native speakers in Uzbekistan as well as neighbouring countries. Uzbek is a Turkic language that is the first official and only declared national language of Uzbekistan. Uzbek is a null-subject, highly agglutinative language [2].

The main contribution of this paper is the annotated dataset for sentiment analysis in Uzbek language, obtained from Google Play Store reviews and a larger dataset by automatically translating an existing English dataset. Furthermore, we define the baselines for sentiment analyses in Uzbek by considering both traditional machine learning methods as well as recent deep learning techniques fed with fastText pre-trained word embeddings [3]. Although all the tested models are relatively accurate and differences between models are small, the neural network models tested do not manage to substantially outperform traditional models.

2. Experiments & Results

For data collection, the list of top 100 applications from Google Play App Store used in Uzbekistan have been selected, retrieving their review texts and related star rating using Google Play Store API.

Collected text has been cleaned (Removing names, brands, tags, links and emojis) and the reviews in Cyrillic alphabet have been converted to Latin. For the annotation process, the main task was binary classification: to label the them as positive or negative, so two authors manually labeled the reviews. A third score was obtained from the star rating of the review itself: positive if a certain review has more than 3 stars, otherwise negative (Majority of 3-starred reviews had negative sentiment). Finally, the review was given a polarity according to the majority label. This process resulted into 2500 reviews annotated as positive and 1800 as negative, 4300 in total.

In order to further extend the resources to support sentiment analysis, another larger dataset was obtained through machine translation. An available English dataset of positive and negative reviews of Android apps, containing 10,000 reviews of each class, was automatically translated using MTRANSLATE, an unofficial Google Translate API from English to Uzbek. We manually went through the translation results quickly and examined a random subset of the reviews, large enough to make a reasonable decision on overall accuracy. Although the translation was not clear enough to use for daily purposes, the meaning of the sentences was preserved, and in particular, the sentiment polarity was kept (except for very few exceptional cases). As a result, we have obtained almost 20,000 translated reviews, balances between polarity classes. Both obtained datasets have been split into a training and a test set with a 90:10 ratio, for the experiments.

To introduce the baseline models for Uzbek sentiment analysis, we chose various classifiers from different families, including different methods of Logistic Regression (LR), Support Vector Machines (SVM), and recent Deep Learning methods, such as Recurrent Neural Networks (RNN) and Convolutional Neural Networks (CNN). The standard parameters as well as the performance metric were chosen for all methods [4]. We implemented LR and SVM models by means of the Scikit-Learn [5] machine learning library in Python with default configuration parameters. In the case of Deep Learning models, we used Keras [6] on top of TensorFlow [7].

Table 1 shows the classification accuracy obtained in three different configurations: a first one working on the manually annotated dataset (ManualTT), a second one on the translated dataset (TransTT) and a third one in which training was performed on translated dataset while testing was performed on the manually annotated dataset.

Table 1. Accuracy results with different training and test sets. **ManualTT**—Manually annotated Training and Test sets. **TransTT**—Translated Training and Test sets. **TTMT**—Translated dataset for Training, Annotated dataset for Test set.

Methods Used	ManualTT	TransTT	TTMT
Support-vector Machines based on linear kernel model	0.8002	0.8588	0.7756
Logistic Regression model based on word ngrams	0.8547	0.8810	0.7720
Recurrent + Convolutional neural network	0.8653	0.8864	0.7850
Recurrent Neural Network with fastText pre-trained word embeddings	0.8782	0.8832	0.7996
Logistic Regression model based on word and character ngram	0.8846	**0.8956**	**0.8145**
Recurrent Neural Network without pre-trained embeddings	0.8868	0.8832	0.8052
Logistic Regression model based on character ngrams	0.8868	0.8945	0.8021
Convolutional Neural Network (Multichannel)	**0.8888**	0.8832	0.8120

We achieved our best accuracy (89.56%) on the translated dataset using a logistic regression model using word and character n-grams. The modern deep learning approaches have shown very similar results, without substantially outperforming classic ones in accuracy as they tend to do when used for resource-rich languages.

Although the results obtained have been good in general terms, those obtained for deep learning models have not clearly surpassed the results obtained by traditional classifiers. This is mainly due to the highly agglutinative aspect of Uzbek language, which it harder to rely on word embeddings.

Funding: This work has received funding from the ANSWER-ASAP project (TIN2017-85160-C2-1-R) from MINECO, and from Xunta de Galicia (ED431B 2017/01 and Oportunius program). Elmurod Kuriyozov receives funding for his PhD from El-Yurt-Umidi Foundation under the Cabinet of Ministers of the Republic of Uzbekistan.

Conflicts of Interest: The authors declare no conflict of interest. The founding sponsors had no role in the design of the study; in the collection, analyses, or interpretation of data; in the writing of the manuscript, and in the decision to publish the results.

References

1. Barnes, J.; Klinger, R.; Walde, S.S.I. Assessing State-of-the-Art Sentiment Models on State-of-the-Art Sentiment Datasets. *arXiv* **2017**, arXiv:1709.04219.
2. Matlatipov, G.; Vetulani, Z. Representation of Uzbek Morphology in Prolog. In *Aspects of Natural Language Processing*; Lecture Notes in Computer Science; Springer: Berlin/Heidelberg, Germany, 2009; Volume 5070.
3. Grave, E.; Bojanowski, P.; Gupta, P.; Joulin, A.; Mikolov, T. Learning Word Vectors for 157 Languages. In Proceedings of the International Conference on Language Resources and Evaluation (LREC 2018), Miyazaki, Japan, 7–12 May 2018.
4. Kuriyozov, E.; Matlatipov, S.; Alonso, M.A.; Gómez-Rodrıguez, C. Deep Learning vs. Classic Models on a New Uzbek Sentiment Analysis Dataset. In Proceedings of the Human Language Technologies as a Challenge for Computer Science and Linguistics—2019, Roznan, Poland, 6–8 November 2009; pp. 258–262.
5. Pedregosa, F.; Varoquaux, G.; Gramfort, A.; Michel, V.; Thirion, B.; Grisel, O.; Blondel, M.; Prettenhofer, P.; Weiss, R.; Dubourg, V.; et al. Scikit-learn: Machine Learning in Python. *J. Mach. Learn. Res.* **2011**, *12*, 2825–2830.
6. Chollet, F. Keras. 2015. Available online: https://github.com/fchollet/keras (accessed on 5 September 2019).
7. Abadi, M.; Agarwal, A.; Barham, P.; Brevdo, E.; Chen, Z.; Citro, C.; Corrado, G.S.; Davis, A.; Dean, J.; Devin, M.; et al. TensorFlow: Large-Scale Machine Learning on Heterogeneous Systems. 2015. Available online: tensorflow.org. (accessed on 5 September 2019).

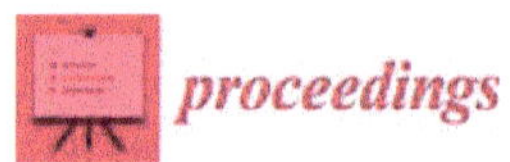 

Proceedings

Integration of Asterisk IP-PBX with ESP32 Embedded System for Remote Code Execution [†]

Juan Pablo Berrío López [1],[*] and Yury Montoya Pérez [2]

[1] Facultad de Ingeniería, Diseño e Innovación (FIDI), Institución Universitaria Politécnico Grancolombiano, 050034 Medellín, Colombia
[2] Facultad de Ciencias Básicas e Ingeniería, Corporación Universitaria Remington, 050012 Medellín, Colombia
[*] Correspondence: jberriol@poligran.edu.co; Tel.: +57-304-439-7353
[†] Presented at the 2nd XoveTIC Congress, A Coruña, Spain, 5–6 September 2019.

Published: 5 August 2019

Abstract: This paper explains the design and construction of a platform that implements the ESP32 embedded system and connects it to a telephone asterisk plant, to exchange data on both sides, commands sent from a telephone to the esp32 and make calls from an order of sending from a digital input of esp32. It is a low-cost device that can be implemented through the use of Wi-Fi, and as a use in the industry, it has a role in analogue communication in buildings, for example.

Keywords: sensors; wireless fidelity; internet of things; microcontrollers; ESP32; embedded systems

1. Introduction

Internet of Things is a concept based on the connection of electronic devices with each other or through the Internet, which has been generating expectation for years as it is expected to be a great driver of digital transformation in homes and cities, as well as in companies. IP telephony has taken a central role in the information highway so that the network can interconnect each home and each business through a packet switching network [1,2].

In this work, the Asterisk pbx was used based on the Issabel Linux distribution, which allowed to create dial plans to receive calls from the users and through an IVR to make a POST request to the ESP32 platform, which within its code has established methods that for investigation, allowed to move a servo motor and turn on led lights. Since the communication was bidirectional, from the side of the ESP32, push buttons were connected, which when pushed, sent commands to the code execution esp32, within this code a POST is made to a site ready to listen to POST requests in the Apache server that runs ISSABEL, this web service, performs an internal code execution through Asterisk and allows to raise telephone calls using Festival as a voice dictation service [3].

The connectivity technology used was Wi-Fi, the possibilities that this work opens up for a real application are several, among them the use of esp32 technology to connect with IP-PBX inside buildings, an additional infrastructure different from the IP will not be necessary.

2. Materials and Methods

1.   Operating System Linux Issabel [4].
2.   Dev Kit ESP32 by expressif
3.   Softphone IP PhonerLite
4.   Oracle VM VirtualBox [5].

3. Experimental Work and Results

A Wi-Fi connection was configured that was common to the three components of the work, the SERVER IP-PBX, the SOFTPHONE client and the ESP32 see Figure 1a, the SERVER IP-PBX works as a bridge in the communication between the ESP32 and the users that use a softphone, although it can be a hardphone too, said server receives POST requests through a web form Figure 1b.

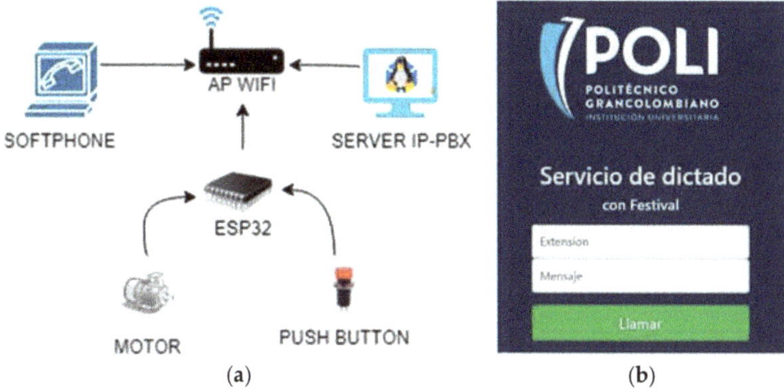

(a)   (b)

Figure 1. (**a**) Device topology; (**b**) web form.

The received web requests are interpreted in bash language and make a PORT request through curl in Linux, to send the POST request again to ESP32 and this perform an action like opening a garage, which can be seen implemented in Figure 2.

Also in Figure 2, you can see two buttons, which allow interacting from the esp32 to the SERVER-PBX, making automatic calls, which use the voice dictation of the service included in Issabel called Festival, which is a Text To Speech, and was given a use for example to warn if someone is pressing the P or G button.

Figure 2. Implementation of ESP32 with servo motor.

The implementation of the work allows the use of this connection architecture in a real case such as analogue cytophony, which can be replaced in its common point by an esp32 and in the end users by ip telephony, allowing to obtain greater benefits such as interacting with actions to be executed remotely and not only the voice.

Author Contributions: All work was done by J.P.B.L.

Conflicts of Interest: The author declares no conflict of interests.

References

1. Herranz, A.B. Desarrollo de Aplicaciones Para IoT con el Modulo ESP32. Universidad de Alcalá, Spain. 2019. Available online: https://ebuah.uah.es/dspace/handle/10017/35420 (accessed on 20 May 2019).
2. Gomez, J.; Gil, F. Lógica de marcado de dialplan. In *VoIP y Asterisk*, 2nd ed.; Grupo Editorial Ra-Ma: Madrid, Spain, 2014; Volume 1, Chapter 4, pp. 99–125.
3. Cusco, V.A. Implementación de una Central Telefónica Voip Interactiva, Utilizando Agi-Php y un Motor de Base de Datos, Para Consulta de Información de Estudiantes en el ditic de la u.t.a. Universidad Técnico de Ambato, Ecuador. 2016. Available online: http://repositorio.uta.edu.ec/jspui/handle/123456789/24022 (accessed on 20 May 2019).
4. Oracle VM Virtualbox. Available online: https://www.virtualbox.org/ (accessed on 15 May 2019).
5. Issabel Project—Unified Communications and More. Available online: https://www.issabel.org/ (accessed on 15 May 2019).

Proceedings

Time-Aware Detection Systems †

Manuel López-Vizcaíno *, **Laura Vigoya**, **Fidel Cacheda** and **Francisco J. Novoa**

CITIC, Universidade da Coruña, A Coruña 15071, Spain
* Correspondence: manuel.fernandezl@udc.es
† Presented at the 2nd XoveTIC Conference, A Coruna, Spain, 5–6 September 2019.

Published: 5 August 2019

Abstract: Communication network data has been growing in the last decades and with the generalisation of the Internet of Things (IoT) its growth has increased. The number of attacks to this kind of infrastructures have also increased due to the relevance they are gaining. As a result, it is vital to guarantee an adequate level of security and to detect threats as soon as possible. Classical methods emphasise in detection but not taking into account the number of records needed to successfully identify an attack. To achieve this, time-aware techniques both for detection and measure may be used. In this work, well-known machine learning methods will be explored to detect attacks based on public datasets. In order to obtain the performance, classic metrics will be used but also the number of elements processed will be taken into account in order to determine a time-aware performance of the method.

Keywords: IDS; early-detection; communication networks; time-aware metrics

---

1. Introduction

The systems dedicated to detect intrusions in communication networks are called Network Intrusion Detection Systems (NIDS) and have attracted a lot of attention due to the growth of networks and the importance of their correct behaviour to ensure business continuation [1]. As it was defined by Lockheed & Martin in 2011 [2] the time elapsed since the begin of an attack will affect directly to the possible damage caused. To avoid further risks, intruders and attackers should be detected as soon as possible in order to minimise the damage.

As part of this systems there are multiple works that explore the use of machine learning in order to detect anomalies in communication networks as it can be seen in [3–5]. This techniques are usually evaluated through the use of classical metrics as Precision, Recall [6] or F1 as a combination of both [7] which take into account the number of elements correctly and incorrectly classified.

In this article, results from the measurements with classical metrics and number of packets used to take the decision will be presented. Kitsune IoT dataset for OS Scan attack [8] will be used to perform experiments with several machine learning methods [5].

2. Methods

To perform this analysis, OS Scan from Kitsune dataset is used [8]. As the objective is to determine if a sequence of elements belongs to one class and to measure how the system performs, individual packets have been grouped into flows. Using the definition of flow [9] which are a set of packets with same source IP, destination IP, source port, destination port and protocol in a period of time, bidirectional flows have been created [10].

The dataset is divided randomly into 75% and 25% sets for training and testing. Then, each one has been splitted into 10 chunks containing 10% of the packets belonging to the flows. This is done in order to study the performance of the methods in different time points.

To conclude, several machine learning methods are then applied to all the chunks obtaining the predicted value for the classification or a delay if no decision is taken. This could happen if there are no packets in the flow yet or if there is not a majority in the flow, as individual packets are evaluated.

3. Results

Results are shown in Table 1 where chunks 1, 2 and chunks from 5 to 9 have been grouped together because there are no variation in the metric values. This, alongside with the 0.0 values for 1 and 2 chunks can be explained due to the dataset characteristics. As it represents an OS Scan, there are a high number of two packet size, scan and reset, flows which will not affect the results in any chunk but on chunks 4 and 10.

An increase in F1 values can be seen for the presented methods, as the number of packets evaluated increase. This rise is shown by the mean and the maximum number of packets. Also an increase in standard deviation can be seen as there is a big difference between two packet sized flows and the rest of the normal traffic.

Table 1. Performance for state-of-the-art machine learning models.

	Metrics	Chunks				
		1–2	3	4	5–9	10
RF	Precision	0.0	1.0	0.875	0.8452	0.8454
	Recall	0.0	0.0001	0.0004	0.8505	0.8519
	F1	0.0	0.0002	0.0009	0.8478	0.8487
J48	Precision	0.0	1.0	0.875	0.8452	0.8454
	Recall	0.0	0.0001	0.0004	0.8505	0.8519
	F1	0.0	0.0002	0.0009	0.8478	0.8487
JRip	Precision	0.0	1.0	0.8571	0.8451	0.8454
	Recall	0.0	0.0001	0.0004	0.8504	0.8518
	F1	0.0	0.0001	0.0007	0.8477	0.8486
Number of Packets	Max	45	68	91	206	229
	Avg	4.0203	6.0442	8.0848	19.1218	22.0911
	STD	11.4049	17.1423	22.9199	51.4238	57.0210

4. Conclusions

As it can be seen in Table 1 even if classical metrics show a good performance for the machine learning methods, it should be taken into account that more packets need to be processed. More packets imply longer times and an increase in the risk created by this particular threat. This is the reason why this metrics should be penalised depending on how much records have been processed to obtain this result.

Also, it must be said that even if an IoT environment could benefit from an early detection system, these techniques could also be applied to other fields where early detection is relevant to reach a good system performance.

Author Contributions: All authors have equally contributed to this article.

Funding: This research was supported by the Ministry of Economy and Competitiveness of Spain (Project TIN2015-70648-P) by the Xunta de Galicia (Centro singular de investigación de Galicia accreditation ED431G/01 2016-2019) and the European Union (European Regional Development Fund—ERDF).

Conflicts of Interest: The authors declare no conflict of interest. The founding sponsors had no role in the design of the study; in the collection, analyses, or interpretation of data; in the writing of the manuscript, or in the decision to publish the results.

References

1. Ashoor, A.S.; Gore, S. Importance of intrusion detection system (IDS). *Int. J. Sci. Eng. Res.* **2011**, *2*, 1–4.
2. Hutchins, E.M.; Cloppert, M.J.; Amin, R.M. Intelligence-Driven Computer Network Defense Informed by Analysis of Adversary Campaigns and Intrusion Kill Chains. *Lead. Issues Inf. Warf. Secur. Res.* **2011**, *1*, 80.
3. Kaur, H.; Singh, G.; Minhas, J. A review of machine learning based anomaly detection techniques. *arXiv* **2013**, arXiv:1307.7286.
4. Buczak, A.L.; Guven, E. A survey of data mining and machine learning methods for cyber security intrusion detection. *IEEE Commun. Surv. Tutor.* **2015**, *18*, 1153–1176.
5. Chawathe, S.S. Monitoring IoT Networks for Botnet Activity. In Proceedings of the 2018 IEEE 17th International Symposium on Network Computing and Applications (NCA), Cambridge, MA, USA, 1–3 November 2018; pp. 1–8.
6. Metz, C.E. Basic principles of ROC analysis. *Semin. Nucl. Med.* **1978**, *8*, 283–298, doi:10.1016/S0001-2998(78)80014-2.
7. Chinchor, N.; Nancy. MUC-4 evaluation metrics. In Proceedings of the 4th Conference on Message Understanding—MUC4 '92, McLean, VA, USA, 16–18 June 1992 ; Association for Computational Linguistics: Morristown, NJ, USA, 1992; p. 22, doi:10.3115/1072064.1072067.
8. Mirsky, Y.; Doitshman, T.; Elovici, Y.; Shabtai, A. Kitsune: An Ensemble of Autoencoders for Online Network Intrusion Detection *arXiv* **2018**, arXiv:1802.09089.
9. Aitken, P.; Claise, B.; Trammell, B. *Specification of the IP Flow Information Export (IPFIX) Protocol for the Exchange of Flow Information*; RFC 7011; Internet Engineering Task Force: Fremont, CA, USA, 2013, doi:10.17487/RFC7011.
10. Trammell, B.; Boschi, E. *Bidirectional Flow Export Using IP Flow Information Export (IPFIX)*; Technical Report; Internet Engineering Task Force: Fremont, CA, USA, 2008.

Proceedings

A Comparative Study of Low Cost Open Source EEG Devices [†]

Francisco Laport *, Francisco J. Vazquez-Araujo, Daniel Iglesia, Paula M. Castro and Adriana Dapena

Centro de investigación CITIC, Campus de Elviña, Universidade da Coruña, 15071 A Coruña, Spain
* Correspondence: francisco.laport@udc.es
† Presented at the 2nd XoveTIC Conference, A Coruña, Spain, 5–6 September 2019.

Published: 5 August 2019

Abstract: A comparison of two open source electroencephalography devices designed to acquire signals associated to the brain activity is presented in this work. The experiments are developed considering the task of determining the user eye state i.e., open eyes or closed eyes, applying an algorithm based on computing the sliding Fourier Transform of the captured signals.

Keywords: Brain Computer Interface; Electroencephalography; Sliding Fourier Transform

---

1. Introduction

The recent development of low cost Electroencephalography (EEG) devices has promoted the creation of new Brain Computer Interfaces (BCI) applications to different areas, such as home automation control or stress and fatigue monitoring, among others. We have shown in [1,2] a self-designed EEG prototype for Internet of Things (IoT). This prototype allows us to classify eye states i.e., open eyes and closed eyes, using a simple criterion based on the power of alpha and beta bands. The frequency-domain components of these brain rhythms are computed using the Fourier Transform (FT) over non-overlapped windows. The main limitation of this approach is the significant delay time required to determine changes in eye states.

In this paper, we study the use of sliding FT applied to overlapped windows as a solution for minimising that delay. We will test the performance of this proposed method using a self-designed prototype [2] and the consumer-grade OpenBCI device [3].

2. Materials and Methods

In our study, two different EEG devices have been used to capture user brain activity (see Figure 1). The consumer-grade OpenBCI platform [3] has been configured using the Cyton board and the 8 channels headset Ultracortex Mark IV. An electrode located in the O2 position was used as input channel, while the reference and ground were located in A2 and A1 positions, respectively. A sampling frequency of 250 Hz has been used to capture the EEG signals. On the other hand, the self-designed prototype [2] employs a sampling frequency of 128 Hz, an input channel located in O2 and ground and reference electrodes in the positions corresponding to right mastoid and FP2, respectively.

The brain activity of 5 male subjects was recorded and analysed for each experiment. Their mean age was 25 years old and none of them suffered from any disease or pain during the recordings. All the experiments were conducted in a quiet room and with the subject seated in a comfortable chair.

Recordings were composed of two tasks: 20 s of open eyes (OE) and 20 s of closed eyes (CE) with 3 s of rest between both tasks. A total of 10 recordings were registered for each subject. During the OE tasks, the subjects were asked for looking at a cross projected in the centre of a monitor just in front of them.

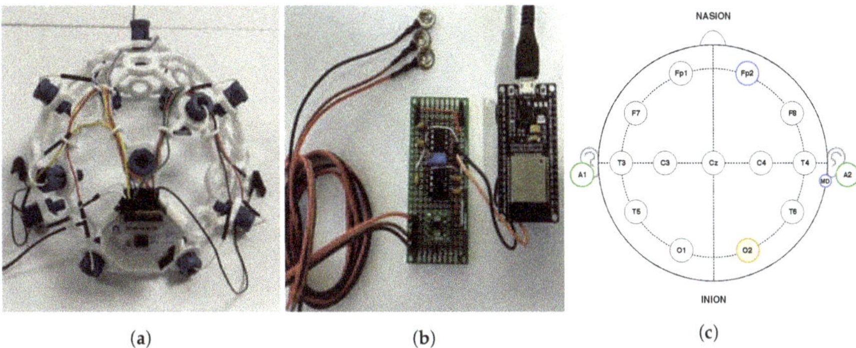

(a)   (b)   (c)

Figure 1. Both open source EEG devices employed in the experiment (Figure 1a,b). Figure 1c shows the electrode position used by the self-designed prototype (bordered by blue) and the OpenBCI hardware (bordered by green). The O2 electrode represents the common input channel used by both devices (bordered and filled in yellow). (**a**) OpenBCI device; (**b**) Self-designed prototype; (**c**) Electrode locations.

The acquired signals have been processed off-line using Matlab. Our algorithm computes the method already proposed in [2] using sliding FT. During the training step, the threshold parameter is calculated for each subject using 3 random recordings. This value will allow us to classify eye states for the remaining 7 test recordings, applying for this purpose the decision rule detailed in [2]. The best window size for each subject is also determined.

3. Experimental Results

The performance of both EEG devices is also analysed in a realistic scenario. For this purpose, the test recordings were concatenated composing eye tasks of different duration, thus simulating a continuous EEG recording with real eye state changes. The classification is performed for each subject taking into account the threshold parameters obtained from the training.

Tables 1 and 2 show the accuracy achieved for all the subjects considering four time frames of eye tasks, denoting by t that time size, and applying a 70% of overlapping for the sliding windows. The classification algorithm will apply the window size adequate to each subject as done in [2]. Therefore, the system delay suffered by all the subjects is not the same, as it is shown in Table 3 for both EEG devices.

Table 1. Accuracy obtained by the classification system for eye tasks of t duration and an overlap of 70% using OpenBCI hardware.

t	S1	S2	S3	S4	S5	Mean
19 s	69.92	68.05	83.83	75.56	85.71	76.61
38 s	79.82	87.19	88.16	79.82	91.67	85.33
57 s	87.28	93.86	87.72	85.53	97.37	90.35
76 s	94.08	99.34	94.08	88.16	100	95.13

Table 2. Accuracy obtained by the classification system for eye tasks of t duration and an overlap of 70% using the self-designed prototype.

t	S1	S2	S3	S4	S5	Mean
19 s	74.04	80.08	78.2	74.56	73.46	76.07
38 s	88.95	89.91	89.04	81.67	86.64	87.24
57 s	90.88	95.61	89.91	86.18	90.82	90.68
76 s	95.28	100	82.24	82.67	96.63	91.36

Table 3. Delay obtained by the classification system applying sliding windows with an overlap of 70%

EEG Device	S1	S2	S3	S4	S5
OpenBCI	3 s	4.2 s	3 s	3 s	3 s
Self-designed	3.9 s	3 s	3 s	4.8 s	4.2 s

4. Conclusions

The study presented in this paper shows that the sliding Fourier Transform allows us to reduce the delay between changes produced in eye states and their corresponding decision performed by the classifier. It can be noticed that the system performance is highly subject-dependent, but there are no significant deviations between average performances of both EEG devices. In addition, regardless of the hardware used to capture the brain signals, it can be seen that the classifier exhibits better accuracy for long-term eye tasks.

Author Contributions: F.L. has implemented the software used in this paper and wrote the paper; F.L. and D.I. have performed the experiments and the data analysis; F.J.V.-A. has developed the EEG hardware; P.M.C. and A.D. have designed the experiments and head the research.

Funding: This work has been funded by the Xunta de Galicia and the European Social Fund of the European Union (Francisco Laport, code ED481A-2018/156).

Conflicts of Interest: The authors declare no conflict of interest.

References

1. Laport, F.; Vazquez-Araujo, F.J.; Castro, P.M.; Dapena, A. Brain-Computer Interfaces for Internet of Things. *Proceedings* **2018**, *2*, 1179, doi:10.3390/proceedings2181179.
2. Laport, F.; Vazquez-Araujo, F.J.; Castro, P.M.; Dapena, A. Hardware and Software for Integrating Brain–Computer Interface with Internet of Things. In *International Work-Conference on the Interplay Between Natural and Artificial Computation*; Springer: Cham, Switzerland, 2019; pp. 22–31.
3. OpenBCI. Available online: http://openbci.com/ (accesed on 14 July 2019).

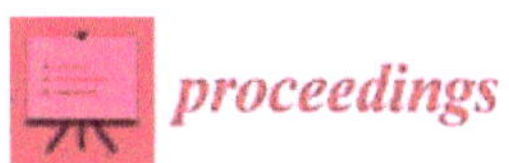 *proceedings*

Proceedings

Educational STEM Project Based on Programming [†]

Elena Segade [1,*], Jose Balsa [2] and Carmen Balsa [3]

[1] Faculty of Education, Universidade da Coruña (University of A Coruña), 15071 Elviña, Spain
[2] CITIC, Universidade da Coruña (University of A Coruña), 15071 Elviña, Spain
[3] IES As Mariñas, 15300 Betanzos, Spain
* Correspondence: elena.segade.pampin@udc.es
† Presented at the Presented at the XoveTIC Congress, A Coruña, 5–6 September 2019.

Published: 5 August 2019

Abstract: We propose a sequence of activities to be programmed to improve the learning of Science, Technology, Engineering and Mathematics in Secondary Education. This proposal consists on generate and transform images and figures programming in Octave. This enables the students to use basic and iterative instructions to construct a complex program, understand and structure problems, logic reformulation of problems, design of systematic processes for the resolution, generalization and comparison of solutions. Initial analyses of the implementation of the activities will be presented.

Keywords: STEM; educational innovation; modular programming

1. Introduction

The continuous development of a technological society makes teaching practices adapt to this changing reality. In this sense, the education should try to reflect the interconnection between subjects through a globalized curriculum [1]. So that, interdisciplinary teaching plays a fundamental role in the integral formation of people and improve the teaching and learning processes [2].

The students have the initial approach to the programming at the first courses of the Spanish Secondary Education. This teaching proposal is aimed to the students who start programming. We wanted to create learning resources using free software open to all.

The proposal consists in the elaboration of a set of modules based on the free software. Octave oriented to solve specific problems for the STEM area of the second year of Spanish Secondary Education in the subjects of Mathematics, Physics and Chemistry, Technology and Programming.

Our interdisciplinary teaching proposal uses basic instructions to model a mathematical problem and to explore the different rigid movements of the plane [3]. Besides, it has a positive impact in the learning of Physics and Chemistry through programming instructions to decompose an image in primary colours to knowing the decomposition of light in the visible spectrum. In this way, are solving technological problems in a programming environment that is the aim of the subject of Technology.

2. Proposed Activities

The main motivation of the project is to provide a programming learning tool. The platform is composed of modules that can be used in the STEM area. This proposal is free and open software created to provide resources to teachers. In addition, students can learn the importance of planning a project using the tools at their disposal for:

- Plan requirements using existing tools or modifying them.
- Simplify the programming language that use variables not previously defined.
- Execute, verify output and detect errors.

This proposal consists on programming using "GNU Octave" to transform images and figures. The algorithms have been programmed in sets of blocks or functions. The type of functions implemented are: load or generate an image or polygon, movements in the plane, color decomposition in primary colors, mosaics and friezes.

3. Results and Conclusions

The evaluation of activities consists of an initial and a final evaluation. The initial evaluation will help us to know the initial competences of the students. The comparison of both evaluations allows us to check their knowledge before and after the activities. The analysis of the evaluation results has been descriptive.

In the activity of measure the perimeter and area of a random polygon generate with a module (Figure 1), we observed that it is easier for them to calculate the area and the calculations of area and perimeter improved with respect to the initial results.

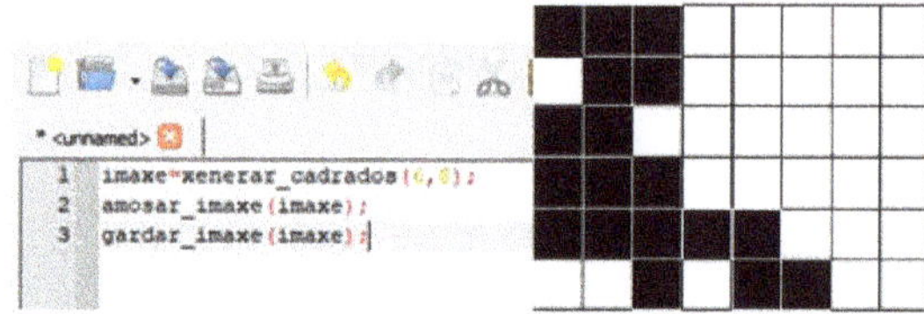

Figure 1. Example of code and output to generate random polygon over a grid.

In the activity of symmetry (Figure 2), we detected that through the programming its visualization improved, and they describe and verify better the properties that define it. As in the mosaics and friezes activity, students can easily explore direct and inverse movements in the plane.

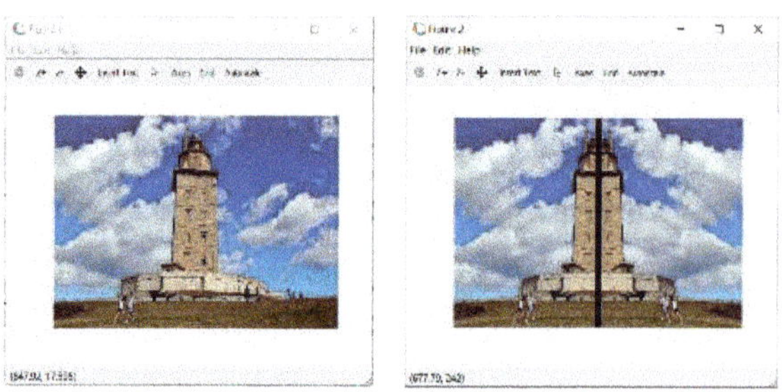

Figure 2. Example of two symmetries.

So that, it is an innovative teaching proposal oriented to use new technologies that can significantly improve the learning of Science, Technology, Engineering and Mathematics (STEM). In particular, the block programming improves the logical and mathematical reasoning, problem solving, structuring of ideas and graphic and spatial visualization. This could hardly be possible to make it work using traditional teaching methods (blackboard, paper and pencils).

References

1. Torres, J.; *Globalización e Interdisciplinariedad: El Currículum Integrado*; Morata: Madrid, Spain, 2012. Available online: http://www.terras.edu.ar/biblioteca/1/CRRM_Torres_Unidad_2.pdf (accessed on 31 July 2019).
2. Quesada, J.F.; Videojuegos matemáticos con Scratch. 2015. Available online: https://blogsaverroes. juntadeandalucia.es/viiencuentro-matematicas-sevilla/files/2017/10/T8.pdf (accessed on 31 July 2019).
3. Gutiérrez, A.; Jaime, A. Reflexiones sobre la enseñanza de la geometría en primaria y secundaria. *Tecné, Episteme y Didaxis: TED* **2012**, *32*, 55–70.

 *proceedings*

Proceedings

Bandwidth Selection for Prediction in Regression [†]

Inés Barbeito [1],*, Ricardo Cao [1] and Stefan Sperlich [2]

[1] Research Group MODES, Department of Mathematics, CITIC, Universidade da Coruña, Campus de Elviña, 15071 A Coruña, Spain

[2] Geneva School of Economics and Management, Université de Genève, Bd du Pont d'Arve 40, CH-1211 Genève, Switzerland

* Correspondence: ines.barbeito@udc.es; Tel.: +34-881011301

† Presented at the 2nd XoveTIC Conference, A Coruña, Spain, 5–6 September 2019.

Published: 5 August 2019

Abstract: There exist many different methods to choose the bandwidth in kernel regression. If, however, the target is regression based prediction for samples or populations with potentially different distributions, then the existing methods can easily be suboptimal. This situation occurs for example in impact evaluation, data matching, or scenario simulations. We propose a bootstrap method to select a global bandwidth for nonparametric out-of-sample prediction. The asymptotic theory is developed, and simulation studies show the successful operation of our method. The method is used to predict nonparametrically the salary of Spanish women if they were paid along the same wage equation as men, given their own characteristics.

Keywords: bandwidth selection; nonparametric prediction; smooth bootstrap

---

1. Introduction

While there exist a considerable literature on bandwidth selection for kernel based nonparametric density and regression estimation, the problem of nonparametric prediction has largely been ignored. To our knowledge, such selection method does not exist albeit the relevance and frequency of such prediction problems in practise. They include for example any situation for which you want to predict counterfactuals like in impact evaluation (also known as treatment effect estimation). Other examples are statistical matching or data matching (see [1–3], and references therein), the imputation of missings (see e.g., [4–6], and references therein), or the simulation of scenarios. Note that we are not thinking of extrapolation far outside of the support of the observed covariates, a problem that would go beyond the here described ones, see [7]. We do not refer to bandwidth selection in stationary time series. In this context, various bandwidth and other model selection methods have been developed, see e.g. the review of Antoniadis, [8] or [9].

In all these situations have the following three features in common: you can think of a regression model with Y being the left-hand, and X the observed right-hand variables. You have one sample, denoted as 'source', in which both are given such that you can conduct a nonparametric regression. At the same time you have or simulate another sample or population, denoted as 'target', for which the same (as for 'source') potential response Y is not obtained. The basic assumption is that the dependence structure between, or in our case the conditional expectation of Y given X, $m(x) := E[Y|X = x]$ is the same in both populations. In data matching, and similarly when imputing missings, the Y were not sampled for the target sample; in scenarios the X of the target refer to an artificial, maybe future population, for which we just cannot observe any Y; in counterfactual exercises you typically have Y observed for the target sample, but under a different situation, called 'treatment'. Then you use the source sample to impute the potential Y of the target group for the situation 'without treatment'. The difference between the observed Y (under treatment) and the imputed (without treatment) gives the so-called 'treatment effect for the treated'.

Our proposal relies on the so-called smooth bootstrap approach, see [10]. That is, you aim to draw bootstrap samples from a nonparametric pre-estimate of the joint distribution of (X, Y). For the original source sample, and for each bootstrap sample you estimate $m(x)$. These allow us to approximate the mean squared error of $\hat{m}(x)$ for any x inside the support of X. Finally you average these over the x_i observed in the target sample. We said 'you aim' because it can be shown that there exists a closed analytical form for the resulting MASE estimate. This simplifies the procedure drastically making it quite attractive in practise. One may argue that the exactness of this MASE approximation hinges a lot upon the pre-estimate. Yet, for finding the optimal bandwidth (or model) it suffices that our MASE approximations take their minimum at the same bandwidth as the true but unknown MASE. Our simulation studies show that this is actually the case. This work is collected in [11].

2. The Bandwidth Selection Method

Suppose we are provided with a complete sample $\{(x_i^0, y_i^0)\}_{i=1}^{n^0}$ from the source population with $X^0 \sim f^0$ and $m(x) := E_0[Y^0 | X^0 = x]$. For the target population we only are provided with observations $\{x_i^1\}_{i=1}^{n_1}$ from density f^1 which is potentially different from f^0. We are interested in predicting the expected $\{y_i^1\}_{i=1}^{n_1}$ assuming that $m(x) = E_1[Y^1 | X^1 = x]$, or to estimate $\mathbb{E}[Y^1] = \mathbb{E}[m(X^1)]$. Moreover, if some 'outcomes' y_i are observed for the target population, their conditional expectation is supposed to differ from $m(\cdot)$; recall our example of outcome under treatment vs without, or see our application were $m(x)$ is the expected wage given x if you were a man.

For the prediction we have to estimate $m(\cdot)$ by a Nadaraya-Watson estimator $\hat{m}_h^{NW}$ with bandwidth h. Let us suppress for a moment the hyper-indices thinking for now always in the source sample with Y observed. The challenge is to find a bandwidth h which is MASE optimal for our predicting problem. The point-wise MSE, and afterwards the MASE are approximated by their bootstrap versions obtained as follows: Imagine $(X_1^*, Y_1^*), \ldots, (X_n^*, Y_n^*)$ are bootstrap samples drawn from the kernel density $\hat{f}_g(x, y) = n^{-1} \sum_{i=1}^{n} K_g(x - X_i) K_g(y - Y_i)$ with bandwidth g. Then, for $\tilde{m}_h^{NW*}(x) f(x) = \hat{f}_h(x) \hat{m}_h^{NW}(x)$ we get

$$\tilde{m}_h^{NW*}(x) - \hat{m}_g^{NW}(x) \;=\; \frac{1}{n \hat{f}_g(x)} \sum_{i=1}^{n} K_h(x - X_i^*)(Y_i^* - \hat{m}_g^{NW}(x)), \tag{1}$$

where X^* has bootstrap marginal density $\hat{f}_g$, and $\mathbb{E}[Y^* | X^* = x] = \hat{m}_g^{NW}(x)$. Clearly, this is the bootstrap analogue to

$$\tilde{m}_h^{NW}(x) - m(x) \;=\; \frac{1}{n f(x)} \sum_{i=1}^{n} K_h(x - X_i)(Y_i - m(x)). \tag{2}$$

In order to compute the MASE we need to carefully distinguish between source and target sample, and have therefore to use the hyper-indices again. For finding a globally optimal bandwidth h we would like to minimise

$$MASE_{\tilde{m}_h^{NW}, X^1}(h) \;=\; \frac{1}{n_1} \sum_{j=1}^{n_1} \left[\mathbb{E}_0 \left[\left(\tilde{m}_h^{NW}(X_j^1) - m(X_j^1) \right)^2 \right] \right], \tag{3}$$

where $\mathbb{E}_0$ refers to the expectation in the source population. We have in the bootstrap world

$$MASE_{\tilde{m}_h^{NW}, X^1}^*(h) \;=\; \frac{1}{n_1} \sum_{j=1}^{n_1} \frac{1}{\hat{f}_g^0(X_j^1)^2} \left[\left(1 - \frac{1}{n_0} \right) \cdot \left(\left[K_h * \hat{q}_{X_j^1, g}^0 \right](X_j^1) \right)^2 \right.$$
$$\left. + \frac{1}{n_0} \left[(K_h)^2 * \hat{p}_{X_j^1, g}^0 \right](X_j^1) + \frac{g^2 d_K}{n_0^2} \sum_{i=1}^{n_0} \left[(K_h)^2 * K_g \right](X_j^1 - X_i^0) \right]. \tag{4}$$

A bootstrap bandwidth selector for prediction is defined as

$$h_{BOOT}^{NW} \;=\; h_{MASE^*_{\hat{m}_h^{NW},X^1}} \;=\; \arg\min_{h>0} MASE^*_{\hat{m}_h^{NW},X^1}(h).$$

Note that the computation of h_{BOOT}^{NW} does not require the use of Monte Carlo approximation nor the nonparametric estimation of the density f^1 of the target population.

References

1. De Waal, T.; Pannekoek, J.; Scholtus, S. *Handbook of Statistical Data Editing and Imputation*; John Wiley: New York, NY, USA, 2011.
2. Rässler, S. Data Fusion: Identification Problems, Validity, and Multiple Imputation. *Aust. J. Stat.* **2004**, *33*, 153–171.
3. Eurostat. *Statistical Matching: A Model Based Approach for Data Integration*; Methodologies and Working Papers; Eurostat: Luxembourg, 2013.
4. Horton, N.J.; Lipsitz, S.R. Multiple Imputation in Practice: Comparison of Software Packages for Regression Models With Missing Variables. *Am. Stat.* **2001**, *55*, 244–254.
5. Rubin, D.B. *Multiple Imputation for Nonresponse in Surveys*; John Wiley: New York, NY, USA, 2004.
6. Su, Y.-S.; Gelman, A.; Hill, J.; Yajima, M. Multiple imputation with diagnostics (mi) in R: Opening windows into the black box. *J. Stat. Softw.* **2010**, *45*, 1–31.
7. Li, X.; Heckman, N.E. Local linear extrapolation. *J. Nonparametr. Stat.* **2003**, *15*, 565–578.
8. Antoniadis, A.; Paparoditis, E.; Sapatinas, T. Bandwidth selection for functional time series prediction. *Stat. Probab. Lett.* **2009**, *79*, 733–740.
9. Tschernig, R.; Yang, L. Nonparametric lag selection for time series. *J. Time Ser. Anal.* **2000**, *21*, 457–487.
10. Cao-Abad, R.; González-Manteiga, W. Bootstrap methods in regression smoothing. *J. Nonparametr. Stat.* **1993**, *2*, 379–388.
11. Barbeito, I.; Cao, R.; Sperlich, S. Bandwidth Selection for Nonparametric Kernel Prediction. Unpublished work, 2019.

 *proceedings*

Proceedings

Design of Mutation Operators for Testing Geographic Information Systems †

Suilen H. Alvarado 

Laboratorio de Bases de Datos Campus de Elviña, Centro de investigación CITIC, Universidade da Coruña, 15071 A Coruña, Spain; s.hernandez@udc.es

† Presented at the 2nd XoveTIC Congress, A Coruña, Spain, 5–6 September 2019.

Published: 6 August 2019

Abstract: In this article, we propose the definition of specific mutation operators for testing Geographic Information Systems. We describe the process for applying the operators and generating mutants, and present a case study where these mutation operators are applied to two real-world applications.

Keywords: mutation operators; geographic information systems; mutation testing

---

1. Introduction

Mutation-based testing [1] is a test technique that involves artificially introducing errors into a System Under Test (SUT). A *mutant* is a copy of the system in which a change has been done that, in most cases, will lead to a behaviour different than expected. The different mutants are generated automatically by the application of mutation operators.

In the state of the art, we have found mutation operators, both general purpose and specific to different technologies, languages and paradigms [2–9]. However, these operators are not adequate when trying to test software features associated with specific domains.

In this article, we propose mutation operators specific to the domain of Geographic Information Systems (GIS) applications. These operators reproduce programming errors that are litely to occur during the development of this type of applications. In addition, we present the implementation of these operators and as proof of concept we apply these operators to two real-world GIS applications and we generate the mutants.

2. Mutation Operators for GIS

As a previous step to designing the mutation operators, we analyzed the main technologies used specifically in the development of GIS, and we identified typical errors a programmer can introduce during the development. These errors were formalized into mutation operators. In order to apply these operators to a SUT, we rely on Java reflection and aspect-oriented programming. Reflection allows us to obtain the list of classes and methods of the SUT, so the user can decide the methods to wish the operators will be applied.

Later, we capture information about the methods of the SUT to be mutated, together with the information of the mutation operators that were already defined. From these data, we generate the mutation operator, in the form of on aspect, which will then be possible to interweave with the SUT which generates a mutant of the SUT.

Next, we describe the definition of two operators and two cases of application on real-world GIS applications.

ChangeCoordSys Operator (Listing 1): It exchanges the coordinate system of a geometry, so it does not match the coordinate system that is being used in the user interface. It simulates the error of not checking that the coordinate system is correct. The error is introduced by directly modifying the coordinate system of geometry when recovering the wrapping of the figure.

```
 1
 2      public String getCode(String code) {
 3    code="double temp = (double) args[0];
 4          args[0] = (double) args[1];
 5          args[1] = temp;
 6          ";
 7    return code;
 8    }
 9
10      public String[] getOperationsNames() {
11    return new String[] { "getFromLocation" };
12    }
13 }
```

Listing 1: A simplified definition of the ChangeCoordSys Operator.

This operator was applied to a mobile technology GIS application. This application allows registering places of interest for the user. These areas of interest are called *Geofences*. A Geofence is determined by a geographical location expressed in terms of latitude, longitude, and a radius around that location. By creating a Geofence with an erroneous location from its central location, the device will receive incorrect location notifications. As a result, the user will see in the application's map viewer the Geofences drawn in erroneous zones (Figure 1).

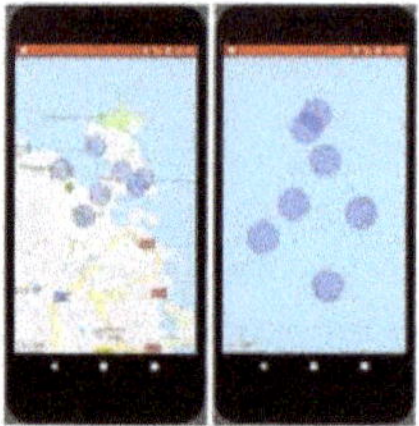

Figure 1. Original and mutant application.

BooleanPolygonConstraint Operator (Listing 2): It introduces errors in the processing of geometries, manipulating the result of the operations that carry out the verification of different topological restrictions between geometries, such as intersects, covers or overlap.

```
14
15      public String getCode(String code) {
16    code = "com.vividsolutions.jts.geom.Coordinate[]
17    coordinates = pGeometry1.getCoordinates();\n" +
18    "coordinates[0] = pGeometry1.getCentroid().getCoordinate();\n" +
19    "coordinates[coordinates.length-1] =
20     pGeometry1.getCentroid().getCoordinate();\n" +
21    "pGeometry1 = new com.vividsolutions.jts.geom.GeometryFactory()
22    .createPolygon(coordinates);\n" +
23    "args[0] = pGeometry1;";
24    return code;
25    }
26
27      protected String[] getOperationsNames() {
28    return new String[] {"contains", "coveredBy", "covers", "crosses",
29    "disjoint", "touches", "equalsTop", "intersects",
30    "overlaps", "within"};
31    }
32 }
```

Listing 2: A simplified definition of the BooleanPolygonConstraint Operator.

To test this operator it was applied to a land reparcelling system. The objective of the land reparcelling is to reunify the lands of an owner to facilitate their exploitation. In this application, the result of the operation between two polygons has been affected. This error causes the incorrect display of the resulting geometry that should be drawn in the user interface after the operation applied to the two initial geometries (Figure 2).

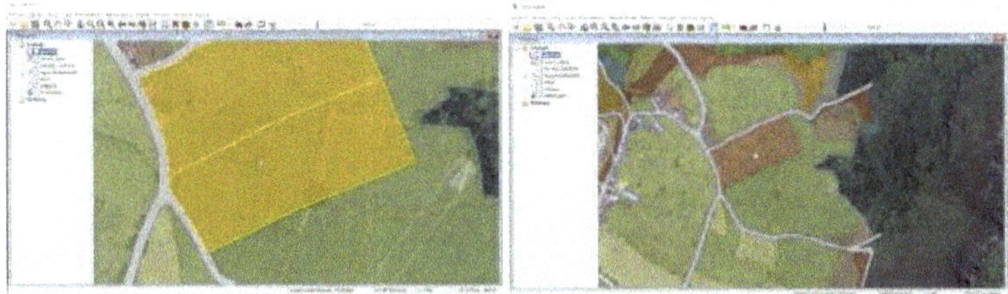

Figure 2. Original and mutant application.

3. Conclusions

In existing proposals, we can find both generic and specific mutation operators. However, these are not adequate to cover errors in particular domains. We have defined new operators specific to the GIS domain and a way to apply them to a SUT. In addition, we have tested the operators defined in two GIS applications. As future work, we intend to extend this approach to other domains, as well as to use the developed operators for the automatic improvement of sets of test cases.

Funding: Financed by: Xunta de Galicia / FEDER-UE CSI: ED431G/01 (Centros singulares de investigación de Galicia), Xunta de Galicia / FEDER-UE CSI: ED431C 2017/58 (Grupo de Referencia Competitiva), MINECO-AEI/FEDER-UE: Datos 4.0 (TIN2016-78011-c4-1-R) and BIZDEVOPS-GLOBAL (RTI2018-098309-B-C32), and EU H2020 MSCA RISE BIRDS: 690941 (S.H.A.).

References

1. Budd, T.A. Mutation Analysis of Program Test Data. Ph.D. Thesis, Yale University, New Haven, CT, USA, 1980.
2. Derezińska, A. Advanced mutation operators applicable in C# programs. In *Software Engineering Techniques: Design for Quality*; Springer: Berlin/Heidelberg, Germany, 2006; pp. 283–288.
3. Shahriar, H.; Zulkernine, M. Mutec: Mutation-based testing of cross site scripting. In Proceedings of the 2009 ICSE Workshop on Software Engineering for Secure Systems, Vancouver, BC, Canada, 19 May 2009; IEEE Computer Society: Washington, DC, USA, 2009; pp. 47–53.
4. Derezińska, A.; Hałas, K. Analysis of mutation operators for the python language. In Proceedings of the Ninth International Conference on Dependability and Complex Systems DepCoS-RELCOMEX, Brunów, Poland, 30 June–4 July 2014; Springer: Berlin/Heidelberg, Germany, 2014; pp. 155–164.
5. Delgado-Pérez, P.; Medina-Bulo, I.; Domínguez-Jiménez, J.J.; García-Domínguez, A.; Palomo-Lozano, F. Class mutation operators for C++ object-oriented systems. *Ann. Telecommun.-Ann. Télécommun.* **2015**, *70*, 137–148.
6. Ma, Y.S.; Offutt, J.; Kwon, Y.R. MuJava: An automated class mutation system. *Softw. Test. Verif. Reliab.* **2005**, *15*, 97–133.
7. Polo, M. Using aspect-oriented programming for mutation testing of third-party components. In Proceedings of the 17th Ibero-American Conference Software Engineering (CIBSE 2014), Pucón, Chile, 23–25 April 2014; pp. 247–260.

8. Usaola, M.P.; Rojas, G.; Rodríguez, I.; Hernández, S. An architecture for the development of mutation operators. In *2017 IEEE International Conference on Software Testing, Verification and Validation Workshops (ICSTW), Toyko, Japan, 13–17 March 2017*; IEEE: Piscataway, NJ, USA, 2017; pp. 143–148.

9. Rodríguez Trujillo, I.D.L.C.; Polo Usaola, M. Diseño de Operadores de Mutación para Características de Sensibilidad al Contexto en Aplicaciones Móviles. In Proceedings of the Actas de XXIII JISBD, Jornadas de Ingeniería de Software y Bases de Datos, Universidad de Sevilla, Sevilla, Spain, 17–19 September 2018.

 *proceedings*

Proceedings

Quasi-Regression Monte-Carlo Method for Semi-Linear PDEs and BSDEs [†]

Emmanuel Gobet [1], José Germán López Salas [2,*] and Carlos Vázquez [2]

[1] Centre de Mathématiques Appliquées, École Polytechnique and CNRS, route de Saclay,
   91128 Palaiseau CEDEX, France
[2] Department of Mathematics, Faculty of Informatics, Universidade da Coruña, Campus de Elviña s/n,
   15071 A Coruña, Spain
* Correspondence: jose.lsalas@udc.es
† Presented at the 2nd XoveTIC Conference, A Coruña, Spain, 5–6 September 2019.

Published: 6 August 2019

Abstract: In this work we design a novel and efficient quasi-regression Monte Carlo algorithm in order to approximate the solution of discrete time backward stochastic differential equations (BSDEs), and we analyze the convergence of the proposed method. With the challenge of tackling problems in high dimensions we propose suitable projections of the solution and efficient parallelizations of the algorithm taking advantage of powerful many core processors such as graphics processing units (GPUs).

Keywords: BSDEs; semi-linear PDEs; parallel computing; GPUs; CUDA

---

1. Introduction

In this work we are interested in numerically approximating the solution (X, Y, Z) of a decoupled forward-backward stochastic differential equation

$$Y_t = g(X_T) + \int_t^T f(s, X_s, Y_s)\mathrm{d}s - \int_t^T Z_s \mathrm{d}W_s, \tag{1}$$

$$X_t = x + \int_0^t b(s, X_s)\mathrm{d}s + \int_0^t \sigma(s, X_s)\mathrm{d}W_s. \tag{2}$$

The terminal time $T > 0$ is fixed. These equations are considered in a filtered probability space $(\Omega, \mathcal{F}, \mathbb{P}, (\mathcal{F}_t)_{0 \leq t \leq T})$ supporting a $q \geq 1$ dimensional Brownian motion W. In this representation, X is a d-dimensional adapted continuous process (called the forward component), Y is a scalar adapted continuous process and Z is a q-dimensional progressively measurable process. Regarding terminology, $g(X_T)$ is called *terminal condition* and f the *driver*.

2. Results

Our aim is to solve

$$Y_i = \mathbb{E}\left[g(X_N) + \sum_{j=i}^{N-1} f_j(X_j, Y_{j+1})\Delta \mid \mathcal{F}_{t_i}\right] \quad \text{for } i \in \{N-1, \dots, 0\}, \tag{3}$$

where $f_j(x,y) := f(t_j, x, y)$, f being the driver in (1). In other words, our subsequent scheme will approximate the solutions to

$$X_t = x + \int_0^t b(s, X_s)\mathrm{d}s + \int_0^t \sigma(s, X_s)\mathrm{d}W_s, \quad Y_t = \mathbb{E}\left[g(X_T) + \int_t^T f(s, X_s, Y_s)\mathrm{d}s \mid \mathcal{F}_t\right], \tag{4}$$

and

$$\partial_t u(t,x) + \mathcal{A}u(t,x) + f(t,x,u(t,x)) = 0 \ \text{ for } t < T \text{ and } u(T,.) = g(.). \tag{5}$$

One important observation is that, due to the Markov property of the Euler scheme, for every i, there exist measurable deterministic functions $y_i : \mathbb{R}^d \to \mathbb{R}$, such that $Y_i = y_i(X_i)$, almost surely. A second crucial observation is that the value functions $y_i(\cdot)$ are independent of how we initialize the forward component. Our subsequent algorithm takes advantage of this observation. For instance, let X_i^i be a random variable in $\mathbb{R}^d$ with some distribution ν and let X_j^i be the Euler scheme evolution of X_j starting from X_i; it writes

$$X_{j+1}^i = X_j^i + b(t_j, X_j^i)\Delta + \sigma(t_j, X_j^i)(W_{t_{j+1}} - W_{t_j}), \quad j \geq i. \tag{6}$$

This flexibility property w.r.t. the initialization then writes

$$y_i(X_i^i) := \mathbb{E}\left[g(X_N^i) + \sum_{j=i}^{N-1} f_j\left(X_j^i, y_{j+1}(X_{j+1}^i) \right) \Delta \mid X_i^i \right]. \tag{7}$$

Approximating the solution to (3) is actually achieved by approximating the functions $y_i(\cdot)$. In this way, we are directly approximating the solution to the semi-linear PDE (5). In order to control better the truncation error we define a weighted modification of y_i by $y_i^{(q)}(x) = \dfrac{y_i(x)}{(1+|x|^2)^{q/2}}$ for a damping exponent $q \geq 0$. For $q = 0$, $y_i^{(q)}$ and y_i coincide. The previous DPE (7) becomes

$$y_i^{(q)}(X_i^i) := \mathbb{E}\left[\frac{g(X_N^i)}{(1+|X_i^i|^2)^{q/2}} + \sum_{j=i}^{N-1} \frac{f_j\left(X_j^i, y_{j+1}^{(q)}(X_{j+1}^i)(1+|X_{j+1}^i|^2)^{q/2} \right)}{(1+|X_i^i|^2)^{q/2}} \Delta \mid X_i^i \right]. \tag{8}$$

The introduction of the polynomial factor $(1+|X_i^i|^2)^{q/2}$ gives higher flexibility in the error analysis, it ensures that $y_i^{(q)}$ decreases faster at infinity, which will provide nicer estimates on the approximation error when dealing with Fourier-basis.

Then we define some proper basis functions ϕ_k which satisfy orthogonality properties in $\mathbb{R}^d$ and which span some L^2 space. It turns out that the choice of measure for defining the L^2 space has to coincide with the sampling measure of $X_i^i \sim \nu$. Our strategy for defining such basis functions is to start from trigonometric basis on $[0,1]^d$ and then to apply appropriate changes of variable: later, this transform will allow to easily quantify the approximation error when truncating the basis. Using the notation

$$S_i^{(q)}(x_{i:N}^i) := \frac{g(x_N^i)}{(1+|x_i^i|^2)^{q/2}} + \sum_{j=i}^{N-1} \frac{f_j\left(x_j^i, y_{j+1}^{(q)}(x_{j+1}^i)(1+|x_{j+1}^i|^2)^{q/2} \right)}{(1+|x_i^i|^2)^{q/2}} \Delta,$$

we can rewrite the exact solution as $y_i^{(q)}(x) = \mathbb{E}\left[S_i^{(q)}(X_{i:N}^i) \mid X_i^i = x \right]$, $x \in \mathbb{R}^d$. Under mild conditions on f, g and ν, $S_i^{(q)}(X_{i:N}^i)$ is square-integrable, and therefore $y_i^{(q)}$ is in $L_\nu^2(\mathbb{R}^d)$, thus $y_i^{(q)}(x) = \sum_{k \in \mathbb{N}^d} \alpha_{i,k}^{(q)} \phi_k(x)$, for some coefficients $(\alpha_{i,k}^{(q)} : k \in \mathbb{N}^d)$. Using the orthonormality property of the basis functions ϕ_k's, $\alpha_{i,k}^{(q)} = (y_i^{(q)}, \phi_k)_{L_\nu^2(\mathbb{R}^d)} = \mathbb{E}\left[y_i^{(q)}(X_i^i)\phi_k(X_i^i) \right] = \mathbb{E}\left[\mathbb{E}\left[S_i^{(q)}(X_{i:N}^i) \mid X_i^i \right] \phi_k(X_i^i) \right] = \mathbb{E}\left[S_i^{(q)}(X_{i:N}^i) \phi_k(X_i^i) \right]$, thus allowing us to the use of Monte Carlo simulation in order to compute the Fourier coefficients. The resulting Algorithm 1 is shown below.

3. Discussion

A implementation on GPUs of the GQRMDP algorithm is proposed. It includes two kernels, one simulates the paths of the forward process and computes the associated responses, the other

---

Algorithm 1. Global Quasi-Regression Multistep-forward Dynamical Programming (GQRMDP) algorithm

---

Initialization. Set $\bar{y}_N^{(q,M)}(x_N) := \frac{g(x_N)}{(1+|x_N|^2)^{q/2}}$.

Backward iteration for $i = N-1$ **to** $i = 0$,

$$\bar{y}_i^{(q,M)}(\cdot) := \sum_{\mathbf{k}\in\Gamma} \bar{\alpha}_{i,\mathbf{k}}^{(q,M)} \phi_{\mathbf{k}}(\cdot), \tag{9}$$

where for all $\mathbf{k} \in \Gamma$,

$$\bar{\alpha}_{i,\mathbf{k}}^{(q,M)} := \frac{1}{M} \sum_{m=1}^{M} S_i^{(q,M)}(X_{i:N}^{i,m})\phi_{\mathbf{k}}(X_i^{i,m}), \tag{10}$$

and

$$S_i^{(q,M)}(x_{i:N}^i) := \frac{g(x_N^i)}{(1+|x_i^i|^2)^{q/2}} \sum_{j=i}^{N-1} \frac{f_j\left(x_j^i, \mathcal{T}_{L^*}\left(\bar{y}_{j+1}^{(q,M)}(x_{j+1}^i)(1+|x_{j+1}^i|^2)^{q/2}\right)\right)}{(1+|x_i^i|^2)^{q/2}} \Delta.$$

---

one computes the regression coefficients $(\alpha_{i,\mathbf{k}}^{(q)}, \mathbf{k} \in \Gamma)$. In the first kernel the initial value of each simulated path of the forward process is stored in a device vector in global memory, it will be read later in the second kernel. In order to minimize the number of memory transactions and therefore maximize performance, all accesses to global memory have been implemented in a coalesced way. The random numbers needed for the path generation of the forward process were generated on the fly (inline generation) taking advantage of the NVIDIA cuRAND library [1] and the generator MRG32k3a proposed by L'Ecuyer in [2]. Therefore, inside this kernel the random number generator is called as needed. Another approach would be the pre-generation of the random numbers in a separate previous kernel, storing them in GPU global memory and reading them back from this device memory in the next kernel. Both alternatives have advantages and drawbacks. In this work we have chosen inline generation having in mind that this option is faster and saves global memory. Besides, register swapping was not observed on the implementation and the quality of the obtained solutions is similar to the accuracy of pure sequential traditional CPU solutions achieved employing more complex random number generators. In the second kernel, in order to compute the regression coefficients, a parallelization not only over the multi-indices $\mathbf{k} \in \Gamma$ but also over the simulations $1 \leq m \leq M$ was proposed. Thus, blocks of threads parallelize the outer for loop $\forall \mathbf{k} \in \Gamma$, whilst the threads inside each block carry out in parallel the inner loop traversing the vectors of the responses and the simulations.

Conflicts of Interest: The authors declare no conflict of interest.

References

1. NVIDIA cuRAND Web Page. Available online: https://developer.nvidia.com/curand (accessed on 5 October 2018).
2. L'Ecuyer, P. Good parameters and implementations for combined multiple recursive random number generators. *Oper. Res.* **1999**, *47*, 159–164.

 *proceedings*

Proceedings

Paired and Unpaired Deep Generative Models on Multimodal Retinal Image Reconstruction [†]

Álvaro S. Hervella [1,2,]*, José Rouco [1,2], Jorge Novo [1,2] and Marcos Ortega [1,2]

1 CITIC-Research Center of Information and Communication Technologies, Universidade da Coruña, 15071 A Coruña, Spain
2 Department of Computer Science, Universidade da Coruña, 15071 A Coruña, Spain
* Correspondence: a.suarezh@udc.es; Tel.: +34-881011307
† Presented at 2nd XoveTIC Conference, A Coruña, Spain, 5–6 September 2019.

Published: 7 August 2019

Abstract: This work explores the use of paired and unpaired data for training deep neural networks in the multimodal reconstruction of retinal images. Particularly, we focus on the reconstruction of fluorescein angiography from retinography, which are two complementary representations of the eye fundus. The performed experiments allow to compare the paired and unpaired alternatives.

Keywords: deep learning; generative adversarial networks; eye fundus; multimodal

1. Introduction

Recently, deep learning algorithms have made possible to estimate the mapping between different image modalities. In that regard, different methods have been proposed to learn the multimodal transformation using paired [1] or unpaired data [2]. In medical imaging, the paired data can be easily gathered due to the common use of complementary image modalities in the clinical practice. Moreover, the paired data represents a rich and complementary source of information that facilitates the training of a neural network. However, to successfully exploit the available paired data, the multimodal images must be previously registered. This multimodal registration is a challenging task that may fail in the most complex scenarios.

In this work, we explore the use of paired and unpaired data for training neural networks in the multimodal reconstruction of retinal images. Specifically, we target the generation of fluorescein angiography, which represents an invasive capture technique, from color retinography.

2. Methodology

For the paired scenario, we use the methodology proposed by Hervella et al. [1]. This method requires the registration of different image pairs, which is performed following the approach in [3]. Then, a generative neural network is trained using the Structural Similarity (SSIM) between the target image and the network output as loss function. For the unpaired case, we use the methodology known as CycleGAN [2], which employs a generative adversarial setting. In particular, a discriminator network learns to distinguish between real and generated angiographies. At the same time, an additional generator network learns to reconstruct the original retinographies from the generated angiographies. This enforces the structural coherence between input and generated images.

In order to produce a fair comparison, we use the same network architectures for both approaches [4]. The neural networks are trained using the Adam algorithm and data augmentation [4]. For the training and evaluation, we used 59 image pairs from the Isfahan MISP database and 59 additional pairs obtained from the Complexo Hospitalario Universitario de Santiago (CHUS). Half of the data is used for training and the other half is hold out as test set.

3. Results and Conclusions

Examples of generated angiographies from the test set are depicted in Figure 1. Both approaches allow to estimate an adequate transformation from retinography to angiography. However, the images generated using the paired method are more realistic due to the use of the adversarial setting. Regarding the reconstruction error in the test set, both approaches achieveD similar results by means of MAE or MSE. However, the paired method achieved a lower error by means of SSIM. This evidences that the images generated using the unpaired method are structurally less accurate. However, the implications of this result depend on the specific target application.

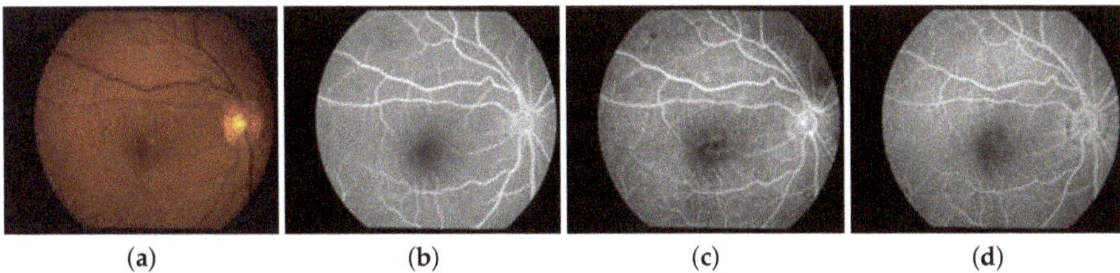

(a)   (b)   (c)   (d)

Figure 1. Examples of (**b**,**c**) generated angiographies together with (**a**) the original retinography and (**d**) the real angiography. (**b**) Generated using the paired approach. (**c**) Generated using the unpaired approach.

Author Contributions: Á.S.H., J.R. and J.N. contributed to the analysis and design of the computer methods and the experimental evaluation methods, whereas Á.S.H. also developed the software and performed the experiments. M.O. contributed with domain-specific knowledge, the collection of images, and part of the registration software. All the authors performed the result analysis. Á.S.H. was in charge of writing the manuscript, and all the authors participated in its critical revision and final approval.

Funding: This work is supported by Instituto de Salud Carlos III, Government of Spain, and the European Regional Development Fund (ERDF) of the European Union (EU) through the DTS18/00136 research project, and by Ministerio de Ciencia, Innovación y Universidades, Government of Spain, through the DPI2015-69948-R and RTI2018-095894-B-I00 research projects. The authors of this work also receive financial support from the ERDF and European Social Fund (ESF) of the EU, and Xunta de Galicia through Centro Singular de Investigación de Galicia, accreditation 2016-2019, ref. ED431G/01, Grupo de Referencia Competitiva, ref. ED431C 2016-047, and the predoctoral grant contract ref. ED481A-2017/328.

Conflicts of Interest: The authors declare no conflict of interest.

References

1. Hervella, A.S.; Rouco, J.; Novo, J.; Ortega, M. Retinal Image Understanding Emerges from Self-Supervised Multimodal Reconstruction. In Proceedings of the Medical Image Computing and Computer-Assisted Intervention (MICCAI), Granada, Spain, 16–20 September 2018.
2. Zhu, J.Y.; Park, T.; Isola, P.; Efros, A.A. Unpaired Image-to-Image Translation using Cycle-Consistent Adversarial Networks. In Proceedings of the 2017 IEEE International Conference on Computer Vision (ICCV), Venice, Italy, 22–29 October 2017.
3. Hervella, A.S.; Rouco, J.; Novo, J.; Ortega, M. Multimodal Registration of Retinal Images Using Domain-Specific Landmarks and Vessel Enhancement. In Proceedings of the International Conference on Knowledge-Based and Intelligent Information and Engineering Systems (KES), Belgrade, Serbia, 3–5 September 2018.
4. Hervella, A.S.; Rouco, J.; Novo, J.; Ortega, M. Deep Multimodal Reconstruction of Retinal Images Using Paired or Unpaired Data. In Proceedings of the International Joint Conference on Neural Networks (IJCNN), Budapest, Hungary, 14–19 July 2019.

 *proceedings*

Proceedings

Use of Multiple Astrocytic Configurations within an Artificial Neuro-Astrocytic Network [†]

Francisco Cedron *, **Sara Alvarez-Gonzalez**, **Alejandro Pazos** and **Ana B. Porto-Pazos**

Computer Science Department, Research Center on Information and Communication Technologies, University of A Coruña, 15071 A Coruña, Spain
* Correspondence: francisco.cedron@udc.es; Tel.: +34-881-01-2667
† Presented at the 2nd XoveTIC Conference, A Coruña, Spain, 5–6 September 2019.

Published: 7 August 2019

Abstract: The artificial neural networks used in a multitude of fields are achieving good results. However, these systems are inspired in the vision of classical neuroscience where neurons are the only elements that process information in the brain. Advances in neuroscience have shown that there is a type of glial cell called astrocytes that collaborate with neurons to process information. In this work, a connectionist system formed by neurons and artificial astrocytes is presented. The astrocytes can have different configurations to achieve a biologically more realistic behaviour. This work indicates that the use of different artificial astrocytes behaviours is beneficial.

Keywords: astrocyte; artificial neuron-astrocyte network; genetic algorithm; cooperative co-evolutionary genetic algorithm

---

1. Introduction

It has recently been shown that information processing in the brain is not carried out solely by neurons [1]. Astrocytes from glial system work together with the neurons, using a bidirectional communication called tripartite synapses [1].

From the perspective of artificial intelligence, this finding represents a new approach to connectionist systems (CS) [2]. Most of the CS that are used in tasks such as speech recognition prediction or medical diagnosis, only contain neurons [3]. The implementation of a CS with bidirectional communication between neurons and astrocytes supposes a more biologically realistic system (see Figure 1) that had improved the results obtained by artificial neural networks (ANN).

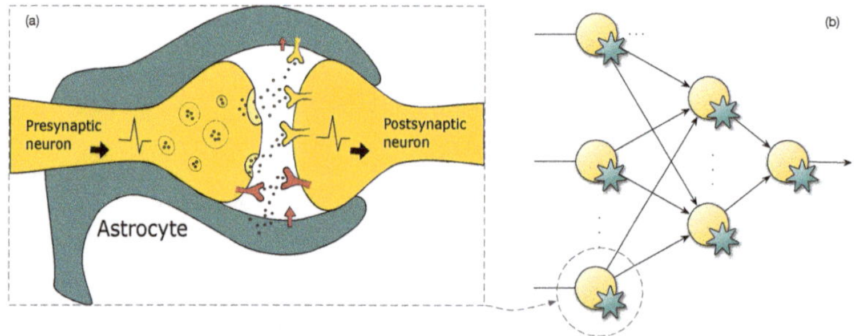

Figure 1. (**a**) Scheme of tripartite synapse in the brain. (**b**) ANAN structure, where artificial astrocytes and neurons are represented by green and yellow colors, respectively.

The simulation of astrocyte behaviour is based on biological observation. Unlike neurons that are electrically excitable and their communication is in milliseconds the astrocytes are slower, they communicate by means of calcium waves [4], taking seconds. To represent this behaviour, several algorithms have been implemented that can be seen in [5,6] biological astrocytes can boost or depress the exchange of neurotransmitters in the synaptic space [4]. These properties are collected in artificial astrocytes as hyperparameters [5]. The behaviour of the astrocytes on a different time scale than that of the neurons means that learning techniques based on the gradient cannot be used in the network because the elements of the network have non-smooth and discontinuous functions. This property is not a limitation because techniques such as genetic algorithms (GA) can be used for training because have no restrictions on functions.

The proposed method has been tested using different network architectures with a classification problem extracted from the UCI machine learning repository [7]. The results obtained by the ANAN are superior to those obtained with a classic ANN.

2. Cooperative Co-Evolutionary Genetic Algorithm to Train Networks

ANANs include elements that are non-smooth and discontinuous so gradient based techniques cannot be used to perform the training phase.

For the learning phase, it has been decided to use evolutionary learning techniques [8]. The use of canonical genetic algorithms has been ruled out because all the parameters of the ANAN (weights and parameters of the astrocytes) are too variable. It has been decided to use the cooperative co-evolutionary cooperative genetic algorithm (CCGA) because it allows the use of several species with different genotypes. The objective of the species is to work together to thrive.

The way to train ANAN with CCGA is by using two species: the weights of the net and the astrocytic parameters.

3. Proposal

This study aims to determine whether the use of different astrocytic behaviours improves the results obtained by the ANN and also those that can be obtained by an ANAN using a single astrocytic configuration across the entire network.

In order to train the ANAN with the two approaches, two different codings are used. For the approach using the same astrocytic configuration only the parameters of the astrocytes are stored once. The approach which using different astrocytic behaviours stores the astrocytic set-up for each layer.

4. Experiments and Results

The ANN and the ANAN have been compared under the same conditions. The only difference is that the ANN does not have astrocytes and a CCGA is not necessary since it only uses one species and a canonical GA is used instead.

The dataset used is breast cancer which analyzes the presence of cancer using 9 characteristics in 699 patients (9 inputs; a binary output) [9].

To secure independent results, 10cv cross validation was implemented [10]. Thus, 10 different sets were obtained where each of them include: 60% training patterns, 20% validations patterns and 20% test patterns. It was also used 10 different initial genetic populations. This means 100 runs to the cross validation set-up. Wilcoxon signed rank test was used to corroborate statistical significance [11].

As expected, ANAN obtains better results than ANN (see Table 1). ANAN with a different astrocytic configuration in each layer gets the best results when using networks with two and three hidden layers. This suggests that the use of astrocytes is more beneficial with larger networks and that different types of astrocytes are needed to complement each other.

Table 1. Comparative study of the classification accuracy (test values). The values described in the table refer to average performance (100 different runs) and the statistically significance (* $p < 0.05$, ** $p < 0.01$ and *** $p < 0.001$). The asterisks compare ANAN to ANN. The architecture shows the number of neurons used on each hidden layer.

Architecture	ANN	ANAN	
		Single Astrocityc Configuration	Astrocytic Configuration for Each Layer
1 hidden layer (7)	90.34% ± 2.34%	90.75% ± 3.63%	90.43% ± 3.40%
2 hidden layers (7,3)	90.50% ± 2.25%	91.25% ± 3.88% **	91.37% ± 2.96% ***
3 hidden layers (12,8,3)	90.78% ± 2.21%	91.28% ± 4.96% **	92.12% ± 4.09% ***

Funding: This work has received financial support from the Xunta de Galicia and the European Union (European Social Fund—ESF).

Acknowledgments: This project was also supported by the General Directorate of Culture, Education and University Management of Xunta de Galicia (Ref. ED431G/01, ED431D 2017/16), the "Galician Network for Colorectal Cancer Research" (Ref. ED431D 2017/23), and the Spanish Ministry of Economy and Competitiveness via funding of the unique installation BIOCAI (UNLC08-1E-002, UNLC13-13-3503) and the European Regional Development Funds (FEDER). All the experiments were supported by the computing resources at the Supercomputation Center of Galicia(CESGA), Spain.

References

1. Araque, A.; Parpura, V.; Sanzgiri, R.P.; Haydon, P.G. Tripartite synapses: Glia, the unacknowledged partner. *Trends Neurosci.* **1999**, *22.5*, 208–215.
2. Porto-Pazos, A.B. Modelos Computacionales para Optimizar el Aprendizaje y el Procesamiento de la Información en Sistemas Adaptativos, Redes Neurogliales Artificiales (RR.NG.AA). Ph.D. Thesis, University of A Coruña, A Coruña, Spain, 2004.
3. Goodfellow, I.; Bengio, Y.; Courville, A. *Deep Learning*; MIT Press: Cambridge, MA, USA, 2016.
4. Perea, G.; Sur, M.; Araque, A. Neuron-glia networks: integral gear of brain function. *Front. Cell. Neurosci.* **2014**, *8*, 378.
5. Alvarellos, A.; Pazos, A.; Porto-Pazos, A.B. Computational models of neuron-astrocyte interactions lead to improved efficacy in the performance of neural networks. *Comput. Math. Methods Med.* **2012**, *2012*, 476324.
6. Cedron, F.; Alvarez-Gonzalez, S.; Pazos, A.; Porto-Pazos, A.B. Modelling Astrocytic Behaviours to improve connectionist systems. In Proceedings of the 18th National Meeting of the Spanish Society of Neuroscience, Santiago De Compostela, Spain, 4–6 September 2019.
7. Dua, D.; Graff, C. *UCI Machine Learning Repository*; University of California, School of Information and Computer Science: Irvine, CA, USA, 2019. Available online: http://archive.ics.uci.edu/ml (accessed on 16 July 2019).
8. Holland, J. Adaptation in natural and artificial systems: An introductory analysis with application to biology. In *Control, and Artificial Intelligence*; U Michigan Press: Oxford, UK, 1975; pp. 17–18.
9. Tan, M.; Eshelman, L.J. Using Weighted Networks to Represent Classification Knowledge in Noisy Domains. In Proceedings of the Fifth International Conference on Machine Learning, Ann Arbor, MI, USA, 12–14 June 1988; p. 121.
10. Cantu-Paz, E.; Kamath, C. An empirical comparison of combinations of evolutionary algorithms and neural networks for classification problems. *IEEE Trans. Syst. Man Cybern. Part B Cybern.* **2005**, *35*, 915–927.
11. Wilcoxon, F. Individual Comparisons by Ranking Methods. *Biom. Bull.* **1945**, *1*, 80–83.

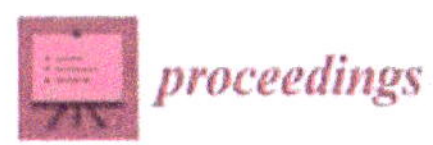 *proceedings*

Proceedings

A Machine Learning Solution for Distributed Environments and Edge Computing [†]

Javier Penas-Noce, Óscar Fontenla-Romero and Bertha Guijarro-Berdiñas *

Universidade da Coruña, CITIC, Campus de Elviña s/n, 15071 A Coruña, Spain
* Correspondence: berta.guijarro@udc.es
† Presented at the 2nd XoveTIC Conference, A Coruña, Spain, 5–6 September 2019.

Published: 9 August 2019

Abstract: In a society in which information is a cornerstone the exploding of data is crucial. Thinking of the Internet of Things, we need systems able to learn from massive data and, at the same time, being inexpensive and of reduced size. Moreover, they should operate in a distributed manner making use of edge computing capabilities while preserving local data privacy. The aim of this work is to provide a solution offering all these features by implementing the algorithm LANN-DSVD over a cluster of Raspberry Pi devices. In this system, every node first learns locally a one-layer neural network. Later on, they share the weights of these local networks to combine them into a global net that is finally used at every node. Results demonstrate the benefits of the proposed system.

Keywords: machine learning; distributed learning; artificial neural networks; Big Data; privacy-preserving; Internet of Things; edge computing; Raspberry; TensorFlow

---

1. Introduction

In 2009 Kevin Ashton revised the term "Internet of Things"(IoT), coined by him in 1999, and mentioned that "If we had computers that knew everything there was to know about things–using data they gathered without any help from us–we would be able to track and count everything, and greatly reduce waste, loss and cost" [1]. Nowadays, to be able to take advantage of data in such environments with hyperconnected devices, we need systems with the capacity of operating with massive quantities of data and, at the same time, being inexpensive and of reduced size. Moreover, it is desirable for such systems to operate in a distributed manner making use of their edge computing capabilities, reducing the information flow among devices and preserving at any time the privacy of the data being interchanged as, frequently, they contain sensitive information that can not or should not be shared. The main aim of this work is to provide a solution offering distributed and real time learning capabilities, with privacy-preserving, usable over Raspberry Pi devices of low cost and with limited computing power. Using this system we can built networks of geographically dispersed devices, where each node could learn individually and autonomously using the local data they capture. Later on, they will share their learnt knowledge (that is, the weights of their neural nets) with the other network's devices so that, between all of them, they can obtain global knowledge similar to that obtained by a centralized system that has been trained using the whole data.

2. Materials and Methods

Traditional training algorithms for neural networks are, in general, iterative, involve high computing times and require human intervention for fine-tuning. Very few of them allow real time (incremental) learning and, even less, allow privacy-preserving distributed learning. As a consequence, they do not adapt well to IoT with edge computing environments. The algorithm LANN-DSVD [2,3] (Linear Artificial Neural Network with Distributed Singular Values Decomposition), developed by the authors, provides all these desired properties and, for that reason, it will be the one employed in this work. We have implemented this algorithm using the TensorFlow platform and it has been deployed over Raspberry Pi devices. To demonstrate and illustrate the system performance and functioning we will use the MNIST dataset consisting of 28x28 pixels images representing of digits from 0 to 9 divided into a training set (60.000 images) and a test set (10.000 images).

3. Results

In this section, the proposed system is exemplified on a physical environment composed by three Raspberry Pi nodes. A management application allows an administrator, via a web service, to configure the cluster of devices, to activate/deactivate nodes, to force training or knowledge dissemination, among other things. To speed-up deployment and to allow the system scalability we have used Docker as the tool to optimize the launching of new nodes. Optionally, it is also possible to establish a higher power computer as a central node in order to derive the execution of those operations that requires more memory or CPU that the one available at the devices. In this illustrative example, we have use a portable PC as a fourth node but its functioning will we similar to the other devices. It has been included only to demonstrate the possibility of using an heterogeneous cluster. Initially, the MNIST training dataset has been divided in such a way that every node will train using only two or three of the 10 classes. Specifically, node 1 was trained using numbers 0 and 1, node 2 using numbers 3, 5 and 8, node 3 using numbers 2 and 6 and, finally, node 4 was trained with numbers 4, 7 and 9.

Once the nodes have been individually trained, results over the global test set show that, in each node, the sensibility obtained for the classes already included in their training set is always above 90%, while for the rest of classes is 0%, giving a global accuracy between 19.44% and 27.72%. After that, the central node sends a flooding petition to request the nodes for the weight matrices of the neural network every one has obtained using their local data. Later on, these matrices are combined following the LANN-DSVD algorithm and a generalized neural network is obtained that will be spread to every node. Using the same global test set and the generalized model, the new results show that the system is now able to solve the problem recognizing all digits with a global accuracy of 86.06% and a mean sensibility above 85.4% (74% for the worst case–number 5–and 97% for the best case–number 1).

4. Discussion and Conclusions

Distributed learning is an active line of research in order to deal with large and/or distributed data. In this paper, we have presented a physical functional system able to learn from distributed data while maintaining its privacy. It is fast and parameter free, a highly desirable characteristic for large-scale learning environments, where tuning a model can be a very time consuming task, or in situations where autonomous online learning from data streams is required. Although the learnt model is simple (one-layer neural net) it is accurate enough to solve many problems, and in return, it is low computational demanding. This makes the system very suitable for IoT environments. As a future line, we plan to apply the ideas of the LANN-SVD algorithm to deep neural nets.

Funding: This research was funded by the Spanish Secretaría de Estado de Universidades e I+D+i (Grant TIN2015-65069-C2-1-R), Xunta de Galicia (Grants ED431C2018/34, ED341D R2016/045) and FEDER funds.

References

1. Ashton, K. That "Internet of Things" Thing. *RFID J.* **2009**. Available online: http://www.rfidjournal.com/articles/view?4986 (accessed on 8 August 2019).
2. Fontenla-Romero, O.; Guijarro-Berdiñas, B.; Pérez-Sánchez, B. LANN-SVD: A Non-Iterative SVD-Based Learning Algorithm for One-Layer Neural Networks. *IEEE Trans. Neural Netw. Learn. Syst.* **2018**, *29*, 3900–3905.

3. Fontenla-Romero, O.; Guijarro-Berdiñas, B.; Pérez-Sánchez, B.; Gómez-Casal, M. LANN-DSVD: A privacy-preserving distributed algorithm for machine learning. In Proceedings of the 26th Eur Symp on Artificial Neural Networks, Computational Intelligence and Machine Learning, Bruges, Belgium, 25–27 April 2018.

 *proceedings*

Proceedings

Estimation of the Alcoholic Degree in Beers through Near Infrared Spectrometry Using Machine Learning [†]

Brais Galdo *, Daniel Rivero and Enrique Fernandez-Blanco

Faculty of Computer Science, CITIC, University of A Coruna, 15071 Galicia, Spain; daniel.rivero@udc.es (D.R.); enrique.fernandez@udc.es (E.F.-B.)

*   Correspondence: brais.cgaldo@udc.es

†   Presented at the 2nd XoveTIC Conference, A Coruña, Spain, 5–6 September 2019.

Published: 13 August 2019

Abstract: It is a fact that, non-destructive measurement technologies have gain a lot of attention over the years. Among those technologies, NIR technology is the one which allows the analysis of electromagnetic spectrum looking for carbon-link interactions. This technology analyzes the electromagnetic spectrum in the band between 700 nm and 2500 nm, a band very close to the visible spectrum. Traditionally, the devices used to measure are utterly expensive and enormously bulky. That is why this project was focused on a portable spectrophotometer to make measures. This device is smaller and cheaper than the common spectrophotometer, although at the cost of a lower resolution. In this work, that device in combination with the use of machine learning was used to detect if a beer contains alcohol or it can be labeled as non-alcoholic drink.

Keywords: NIR; Electromagnetic spectrum; Neural networks

1. Introduction

Spectroscopy is one of the main techniques when a non-destructive analysis on the composition of a sample is required, however those analysis usually has to be performed by expensive equipment host only on special laboratories. However recent advances allow the reduction of that expensive equipment into something portable. Those devices allow the analysis in field conditions of the samples, but what is now laking is the expertise to understand the collected spectra. There is where machine learning can help. The main aim of this work is to being able to classify "lagger" beers according to their alcohol level into "Non-alcohol" and "With alcohol". In order to accomplish this objective, a portable NIR scanner from Texas Instrument ([1]) was used. Because, the idea behind this development, was to perform the measurements with out destroying the sample. Therefore, the liquid has to be poured into an special container called cell to be scanned. The result of those scanner are a particular spectrogram of the beer which has to be processed in order to solve the problem. In this particular work, 36 beers of different brands were used, as well as different graduation levels. Following an strong methodology, the dataset was collected and subsequently analyzed by using ANNs. We must underline that the alcohol is situated by most of the works in the range of 1110 to 1300 nm [2] and there are some articles that use NIR technology with big spectrophotometer to treat problems like this [3–6].

2. Materials and Methods

The first task to be tackle in this study was to build the dataset, which requires:

- Spectrophotometry cells. These are the containers into which the sample will be poured.
- A glass container. Liquids would be poured into them to reduce the amount of gas as much as possible.

- Coffee filters. They were used to dramatically reduce the amount of gas in a short time period.

Once all the material was collected, the beers were leaved in a room for 3 days in order to ensure that the temperature of the beers was the same before performing the measurements. Those measurements were performed by a portable NIR scanner which operates in the range between 900 and 1700 nm and, therefore, contains the objective range of the alcohol. Attending to the spectrometer setup, an average of 30 measurements performed with the Hadamard's algorithm was chosen. This process was repeated 3 times for each beer.

Once the liquid was in the cells, the spectrometer was 2mm from the sample while the scan was performed. The resulting samples were labeled as "without alcohol" when the beer contains less than 1 degree, while the label "with alcohol" was reserved for the ones containing more than 1 degree.

3. Results

All ANNs develop in this work used TensorFlow as its development framework by following a K-fold Record-wise cross-validation schema. Therefore, all three measurements from the same beer were used only on train or on test. The developed ANNs are fully-connected forward networks with a single hidden layer. The optimizer was set to Adam and the loss function was the binary crossentropy. Table 1 shows the average of 50 repetitions of the training for each of the beers used in test. Additionally to the size of the hidden layer, the table shows the accuracies for train and test together with the corresponding standard deviation.

Table 1. Preliminary results.

Number of Neurons	Activation Function	Train		Train	
		Accuracy	STD	Accuracy	STD
32	Sigmoid	0.917	0.047	0.814	0.388
64	Relu	0.908	0.030	0.817	0.386
128	Relu	0.913	0.030	0.812	0.389

4. Discussion

First and foremost, we must emphasize that this are barely preliminary results although those have been encouraging. In this work a first dataset has been collected following a methodology pre-established by an expert in the field and it has proved that the machine learning technique can be of great utility in order to move the analysis from the laboratory to the field. As the measurements were collected, it has been possible to appreciate the difference between beers with alcohol of those without alcohol in the range between 1100 and 1300 nanometers, so it was to be expected that, making use of techniques of machine learning, it was possible to solve this problem. However, the high standard deviation observed on the test is something that requires additional study being the most probable reason the small size of the dataset and the use of a highly restricted technique as the K-fold Record-wise cross-validation. Consequently, the plan for the close future is to increase the size of the dataset and perform more test to solve it.

Author Contributions: Conceptualization, B.G.; methodology, B.G.; software, B.G.; validation, B.G.; formal analysis, B-G.; investigation, B-G.; resources, B.G., D.R., E.F.-B.; data curation, B.G.; writing—original draft preparation, B.G., D.R., E.F.-B.; writing—review and editing, B.G., D.R., E.F.-B.; visualization, B.G.; supervision, B.G., D.R., E.F.-B.; project administration, B.G.; funding acquisition, B.G., D.R., E.F.-B.

Funding: This work was partially funded by the Galician goverment and EFRD funds (ED431G/01).

Acknowledgments: The authors would like to thank the support from RNASA-IMEDIR group.

Conflicts of Interest: The authors declare no conflicts of interest.

Abbreviations

The following abbreviations are used in this manuscript:

NIR   Near Infrarred
ANN   Artificial Neural Network

References

1.   Texas Instruments. DLPNIRNANOEVM. Available online: http://www.ti.com/tool/DLPNIRNANOEVM (accessed on 15 July 2019).
2.   Wang, X.; Bao, Y.; Liu, G.; Li, G.; Lin, L. Study on the best analysis spectral section of NIR to detect alcohol concentration based on SiPLS. *Procedia Eng.* **2012**, *29*, 2285–2290.
3.   Castritius, S.; Kron, A.; Schafer, T.; Radle, M.; Harms, D. Determination of alcohol and extract concentration in beer samples using a combined method of near-infrared (NIR) spectroscopy and refractometry. *J. Agric. food Chem.* **2010**, *58*, 12634–12641.
4.   Iñón, F.A.; Garrigues, S.; de la Guardia, M. Combination of mid-and near-infrared spectroscopy for the determination of the quality properties of beers. *Anal. Chim. Acta* **2006**, *571*, 167–174.
5.   Dorado, M.P.; Pinzi, S.; De Haro, A.; Font, R.; Garcia-Olmo, J. Visible and nir spec- troscopy to assess biodiesel quality: Determination of alcohol and glycerol traces. *Fuel* **2011**, *90*, 2321–2325.
6.   Maudoux, M.; Yan, S.H.; Collin, S. Quantitative analysis of alcohol, real extract, original gravity, nitrogen and polyphenols in beers using nir spectroscopy. *J. Near Infrared Spectrosc.* **1998**, *6*, 363–366.

Proceedings

Sequence Tagging for Fast Dependency Parsing †

Michalina Strzyz *, David Vilares and Carlos Gómez-Rodríguez

CITIC, FASTPARSE Lab, Departamento de Computación, Campus de Elviña, Universidade da Coruña,
15071 A Coruña, Spain
*   Correspondence: michalina.strzyz@udc.es
†   Presented at XoveTIC Congress, A Coruña, Spain, 5–6 September 2019.

Published: 26 August 2019

Abstract: Dependency parsing has been built upon the idea of using parsing methods based on shift-reduce or graph-based algorithms in order to identify binary dependency relations between the words in a sentence. In this study we adopt a radically different approach and cast full dependency parsing as a pure sequence tagging task. In particular, we apply a linearization function to the tree that results in an output label for each token that conveys information about the word's dependency relations. We then follow a supervised strategy and train a bidirectional long short-term memory network to learn to predict such linearized trees. Contrary to the previous studies attempting this, the results show that this approach not only leads to accurate but also fast dependency parsing. Furthermore, we obtain even faster and more accurate parsers by recasting the problem as multitask learning, with a twofold objective: to reduce the output vocabulary and also to exploit hidden patterns coming from a second parsing paradigm (constituent grammars) when used as an auxiliary task.

Keywords: Natural Language Processing; Syntax; Parsing; Sequence Tagging, Multitask Learning

---

1. Introduction

One of the building blocks in Natural Language Processing (NLP) is parsing, that provides syntactic analyses of a text. A structure of a sentence is commonly represented as constituency [1] or dependency tree [2]. Constituency grammar introduces the notion of *constituents* where a sentence is decomposed into sub-phrases while in dependency, words are connected according to their *dependency relation* (every word in a sentence is *dependent* on another word that is defined as its *head*). An example of each tree structure is given in Figure 1. Various parsing algorithms have been developed for constituency and dependency parsing. For the latter, transition- and graph-based approaches have been most widely used. In transition-based (or shift-reduce) dependency parsing, the best transition (create an arc between two words, do a shift, reduce a word, ...) is predicted at each timestep given the state of the current configuration of the parser [3]. In contrast, a graph-based parser explores incrementally all possible parses of a tree through graph fragments and a tree with the highest score is chosen [4].

In this context, neural architectures have gained popularity in the field of NLP, where long short-term memory (LSTM) networks have been proven to be useful in many problems, because of their ability to decide which information to remember [5]. This is especially useful in dependency parsing, where we have to identify long-distance relationships between words. In addition, it has been shown that these architectures can benefit from learning various tasks jointly, the so-called *multitask learning* (MTL) [6]. In MTL setups, it can be also helpful to add an *auxiliary task*, whose result is not relevant but can be used to improve the performance on the main task. This is due to the ability of the network to exploit hidden patterns that are present in the main task and the ability of the shared representations to prevent overfitting.

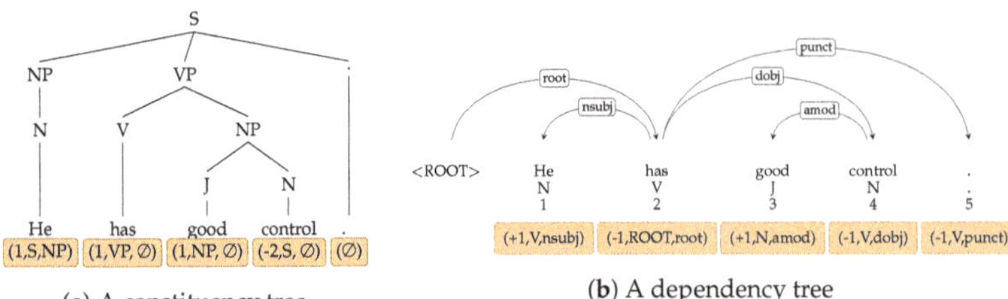

Figure 1. An example of syntactic trees for the same sentence represented under the constituency and dependency formalisms. Below, labels for each token encoding the trees.

2. Method

Recent research has shown that constituency parsing can be reduced to *sequence tagging*, a structured prediction problem where for each input token a single label output is generated [7]. To do so, the syntactic trees need to be linearized through an encoding method, as shown in Figure 1a.

In a similar fashion, we propose to apply sequence tagging models for dependency parsing [8], using NCRF++ [9] as our sequence tagging framework. We propose a part-of-speech tag-based (PoS) encoding where the information of token's head and dependency relation is encapsulated in a label of the form (p_i, h_i, r_i). The first element p_i of the tuple encodes the relative distance to the token's head in terms of words with a PoS tag h_i, and where r_i is the dependency relation between those two tokens. An example of an encoded dependency tree is shown in Figure 1b. For instance, the label for the token *"control"* is (-1,V,DOBJ) which means that the head is the first token to the left (-1) among those with the PoS tag V, and that the dependency relation is DOBJ.

Furthermore, it has been shown that constituency parsing can leverage from MTL setups [10]. Hence, our model attempts to learn dependency label as a 2-task setup where: one task consists of learning (p_i, h_i) since they are the most closely related among the elements in the tuple, and the second task consists in learning the dependency relation (r_i). Additionally, we also explore whether constituency parsing as auxiliary task can improve the performance of dependency parsing as the main task.

3. Results

We evaluate models on the English Penn Treebank [11]. We use the standard metrics: Unlabeled and Labeled Attachment Score (UAS/LAS). Table 1 shows that our single-task model provides a good trade-off between speed and accuracy in comparison with existing transition- and graph-based models. In Table 2 we show that our model achieves even better performance when applying MTL, where dependency parsing as tagging is better learned when treating it as 2-task (S-MTL). Finally, the best result for dependency parsing is achieved when adding constituency parsing as auxiliary task (D-MTL-AUX). More experiments on various languages and the reported speeds when including the MTL approach are presented in [12].

Table 1. Model's speed and accuracy compared with existing dependency parsers on the PTB test set. ⋄ speeds taken from the original papers.

Model	sent/s CPU	sent/s GPU	UAS	LAS
KG (transition-based) [13]	$76_{\pm1}$		93.90	91.90
KG (graph-based) [13]	$80_{\pm0}$		93.10	91.00
CM [14]	$654^{\diamond}$		91.80	89.60
DM [15]		$411^{\diamond}$	95.74	94.08
Stack-Pointer [16]		$10_{\pm0}$	95.87	94.19
Our model	$101_{\pm2}$	$648_{\pm20}$	**93.67**	**91.72**

Table 2. Unlabeled Attachment Score (UAS), Labeled Attachment Score (LAS) and speed on a single core CPU for the MTL models on the PTB test sets. S-S: single model, S-MTL: 2-task, D-MTL-AUX: with constituency parsing as auxiliary task.

| Model | Dependency Parsing | | Speed (CPU) |
	UAS	LAS	sent/sec
S-S	93.60	91.74	$117_{\pm 6}$
S-MTL	93.84	91.83	$133_{\pm 1}$
D-MTL-AUX	**94.05**	**92.01**	$133_{\pm 1}$

4. Discussion

We have obtained a fast and accurate dependency parsing method showing that the dependency parsing problem can be reduced to a conceptually simple sequence tagging task where dependency trees are encoded into labels. In this way, our research has put emphasis not only on the accuracy of dependency parsing, but also on improving the speed, to make it feasible to parse the big amounts of data available today.

Funding: This work has received funding from the European Research Council (ERC), under the European Union's Horizon 2020 research and innovation programme (FASTPARSE, grant agreement No 714150), from the ANSWER-ASAP project (TIN2017-85160-C2-1-R) from MINECO, and from Xunta de Galicia (ED431B 2017/01).

References

1. Chomsky, N. Three models for the description of language. *IRE Trans. Inf. Theory* **1956**, *2*, 113–124.
2. Mel'cuk, I.A. *Dependency Syntax: Theory and Practice*; State University of New York Press: Albany, NY, USA, 1988.
3. Nivre, J. An efficient algorithm for projective dependency parsing. In Proceedings of the Eighth International Conference on Parsing Technologies, Nancy, France, 23–25 April 2003; pp. 149–160.
4. McDonald, R.; Crammer, K.; Pereira, F. Online large-margin training of dependency parsers. In Proceedings of the 43rd Annual Meeting of the Association for Computational Linguistics (ACL'05), Ann Arbor, MI, USA, 25–30 June 2005; pp. 91–98.
5. Hochreiter, S.; Schmidhuber, J. Long short-term memory. *Neural Comput.* **1997**, *9*, 1735–1780.
6. Caruana, R. Multitask learning. *Mach. Learn.* **1997**, *28*, 41–75.
7. Gómez-Rodríguez, C.; Vilares, D. Constituent Parsing as Sequence Labeling. In Proceedings of the 2018 Conference on Empirical Methods in Natural Language Processing, Brussels, Belgium, 31 October–4 November 2018; pp. 1314–1324.
8. Strzyz, M.; Vilares, D.; Gómez-Rodríguez, C. Viable Dependency Parsing as Sequence Labeling. In Proceedings of the 2019 Conference of the North American Chapter of the Association for Computational Linguistics: Human Language Technologies, Minneapolis, USA, 2–7 June, 2019; pp. 717–723
9. Yang, J.; Zhang, Y. NCRF++: An Open-source Neural Sequence Labeling Toolkit. In Proceedings of ACL 2018, System Demonstrations, Melbourne, Australia, 15–20 July, 2018; pp. 74–79.
10. Vilares, D.; Abdou, M.; Søgaard, A. Better, Faster, Stronger Sequence Tagging Constituent Parsers. In Proceedings of the 2019 Conference of the North American Chapter of the Association for Computational Linguistics: Human Language Technologies, Minneapolis, USA, 2-7 June, 2019; pp. 3372–3383.
11. Marcus, M.P.; Marcinkiewicz, M.A.; Santorini, B. Building a large annotated corpus of English: The Penn Treebank. *Comput. Linguist.* **1993**, *19*, 313–330.
12. Strzyz, M.; Vilares, D.; Gómez-Rodríguez, C. Sequence Labeling Parsing by Learning Across Representation. In Proceedings of the 57th Annual Meeting of the Association for Computational Linguistics (ACL 2019), Florence, Italy, 28 July–2 August, 2019; pp. 5350–5357.
13. Kiperwasser, E.; Goldberg, Y. Simple and Accurate Dependency Parsing Using Bidirectional LSTM Feature Representations. *Trans. Assoc. Comput. Linguist.* **2016**, *4*, 313–327.

14. Chen, D.; Manning, C. A fast and accurate dependency parser using neural networks. In Proceedings of the 2014 Conference on Empirical Methods in Natural Language Processing (EMNLP), Doha, Qatar, 25–29 October, 2014; pp. 740–750.
15. Dozat, T.; Manning, C.D. Deep Biaffine Attention for Neural Dependency Parsing. In Proceedings of the 5th International Conference on Learning Representations, Toulon, France, 24–26 April 2017.
16. Ma, X.; Hu, Z.; Liu, J.; Peng, N.; Neubig, G.; Hovy, E. Stack-Pointer Networks for Dependency Parsing. In Proceedings of the 56th Annual Meeting of the Association for Computational Linguistics, Melbourne, Australia, 15–20 July, 2018; pp. 1403–1414.

MDPI

St. Alban-Anlage 66

4052 Basel

Switzerland

Tel. +41 61 683 77 34

Fax +41 61 302 89 18

www.mdpi.com

Proceedings Editorial Office

E-mail: proceedings@mdpi.com

www.mdpi.com/journal/proceedings